Minorities and Women:

A Guide to Reference Literature in the Social Sciences

By
Gail Ann Schlachter

With
Donna Belli

REFERENCE SERVICE PRESS

ii

lw
5-9-80

TABLE OF CONTENTS

INTRODUCTION

BACKGROUND

In recent years, the reference literature devoted to minorities and women has grown substantially. Yet—until now—no single guide has been available to provide quick and convenient access to these important reference publications. Consequently, librarians have had difficulty in identifying appropriate sources to add to their collections. Similarly, students and researchers interested in ethnic and women's studies have had difficulty in identifying appropriate reference sources to use in their search strategies.

In an effort to fill this bibliographic gap, the authors have spent the last seven years researching, reviewing, describing, and indexing the wealth of reference literature on women, Blacks, Spanish Americans, Asian Americans, American Indians, and other minority groups.

The result of their work is *Minorities and Women: A Guide to Reference Literature in the Social Sciences*. The bibliography has been prepared to assist students, faculty, librarians, researchers, and the general public interested in the social, educational, psychological, political, economic, anthropological, or historical aspects of minorities and women in America. Described are over 800 reference books which provide access to people, places, events, organizations, statistics, reports, court cases, treaties, laws, manuscripts, dissertations, books, articles, media, and other materials relating to ethnic groups and women.

SCOPE

The bibliography is intended to be selective. It is restricted to:

—*ETHNIC/WOMEN STUDIES SOURCES.* Only those reference materials focusing on minorities or women in America are included. Publications dealing primarily or exclusively with society in general are not covered (since such sources are described in depth in numerous other guides to the literature).

—*REFERENCE MATERIALS.* Studies, research reports, functional works, general histories, individual biographies, etc. are not included.

—*RECENTLY ISSUED PUBLICATIONS.* The publication cut-off date on listings in this bibliography is mid-1976. Generally, sources published in the late 1800s and early 1900s, which have not been reprinted, have been excluded unless they are standards or classics in the field.

—*ENGLISH LANGUAGE MATERIALS.* Reference materials written in foreign languages and/or emphasizing areas outside of the United States are usually not included.

—*CATALOGED MATERIALS.* Only sources which have been commercially available and would tend to be cataloged are included in this bibliography. Processed materials (such as holding lists of libraries) and pamphlet-like publications (60 pages or less) are generally excluded.

—*HIGH SCHOOL AND COLLEGE LEVEL MATERIALS.* Publications meeting the five criteria outlined above are included only if they are aimed at high school students, college students, or adults; reference works on minorities and women prepared for children are omitted.

ARRANGEMENT

The bibliography is arranged in two main sections: "Information Sources" and "Citation Sources."

Information sources are subdivided into chapters by form (fact books, biographies, documentary sources, directories, and statistical materials). Within each of these chapters, the entries are arranged by author under the groups covered: minorities, American Indians, Asian Americans, Black Americans, Spanish Americans, and women.

Citation sources (bibliographies, abstracts, indexes, catalogs, guides to the literature, etc.) are subdivided into chapters by group and listed alphabetically by title. In both sections, cross references are provided when there are title variations.

ANNOTATIONS

For each item in the bibliography, complete bibliographic information is provided: title, author, edition, place, publisher, date, number of pages, and series statement.

Full descriptive annotations are included for all publications cited. Each description details purpose, scope, arrangement, special features, publication history, etc.

INDEXES

The two main sections of the *Guide* are followed by a set of three indexes: author, title, and subject. All publications cited in the *Guide* (including those referred to in the annotations) are listed in the title and author indexes. Each reference source annotated in the bibliography is described by multiple descriptive terms in the subject index. Numerous cross references are provided in each index.

REFERENCES IN THE INDEXES ARE MADE TO
ITEMIZED ENTRY NUMBERS NOT TO PAGE NUMBERS

ON-GOING RESEARCH PROGRAM

As in any bibliography, a certain number of relevant citations—even after the most systematic and rigorous investigations—go undetected. Therefore, the authors of this *GUIDE* and Reference Service Press have established an on-going research program to identify any additional reference sources not covered in this first edition as well as any new materials issued since the publication of this volume.

Readers are urged to inform the authors of any additions or corrections to the listings included in this volume. These new citations will be incorporated into a future edition of the *GUIDE*.

ACKNOWLEDGMENTS

Several individuals deserve special recognition for their assistance in the preparation of this book: Julie Sorensen, who patiently and painstakingly typed the manuscript; Eddie Irwin (Publication Arts Service) and Lew Snow, who understand layout and lithography better than anyone; Dr. Alvin Renetzky, who served as a model in so many ways; Dr. David Weber, for all the hours he spent with us in library reference departments; and Charles Boorkman, Lloyd Kramer and Gail Cook, who, in their administrative capacities, not only understood the concept of professional development, but put it into practice for their librarians at California State University-Long Beach.

To
My Children, Sandy and Eric
and
My Parents, Helen and Lew Goldstein
from
Gail

To
My Mother, Helen
from
Donna

To
Librarians and
researchers everywhere
from
Both of Us

Chapter 1

FACT BOOKS

(Encyclopedias, Dictionaries, Almanacs,
Handbooks, Pictorial Works, etc.)

Minorities

1. *AMERICAN MAJORITIES AND MINORITIES: A SYLLABUS OF
    UNITED STATES HISTORY FOR SECONDARY SCHOOLS.* By
    Warren J. Halliburton and William Loren Katz. New
    York, Arno Press, 1970, 219p.
For annotation, see Entry No. 412.

2. *ANATOMY OF RACIAL INTOLERANCE.* Compiled by George
    B. de Huszar. New York, H.W. Wilson Co., 1946,
    283p. (The Reference Shelf, v. 18, no. 5).
Reprinted articles by outstanding journalists and experts on the topic of racial intolerance are grouped
into four sections: What Race Is; General Discussion;
Causes of Race Prejudice; Remedies for Race Prejudice.
An editorial introduction and a selective bibliography
complete the work. This compilation is issued as part
of *THE REFERENCE SHELF* series.

3. *THE CHRONOLOGICAL LIBRARY OF AMERICAN PEOPLES.*
    St. Clair Shores, Michigan, Scholarly Press,
    Inc., 1974- . To be published in 5 volumes.
Five volumes are planned for *THE CHRONOLOGICAL LIBRARY
OF AMERICAN PEOPLES* series: *CHRONOLOGY OF THE AMERICAN
INDIAN* (see Entry No. 25), *CHRONOLOGY OF BLACK AMERICA*
(see Entry No. 76), *CHRONOLOGY OF AMERICAN IMMIGRANTS*
(see Entry No. 4), *CHRONOLOGY OF WOMEN IN AMERICA* (see
Entry No. 113), and *CHRONOLOGY OF PROTEST IN AMERICA*.
Each chronology includes over 1,000 subject entries arranged by date, a general introductory essay overviewing
the subject, more than 200 illustrations, a bibliography
of sources used, and a detailed cross index.

4. *CHRONOLOGY OF AMERICAN IMMIGRANTS.* Edited by

Wayne Moquin.   St. Clair Shores, Michigan, Scholarly Press, Inc.   To be published.
Part of *THE CHRONOLOGICAL LIBRARY OF AMERICAN PEOPLES*
(see Entry No. 3), this publication will trace the immigration of the Irish, the Italians, the Germans, the
Poles, the Central European peoples, the Greeks, the
Scots, the Portuguese, the Swedes, the Puerto Ricans,
the Mexicans, and others into the United States.   Over
a thousand entries will make up the chronology.   Also
included will be hundreds of pictures, a general introductory essay, a bibliography of pertinent sources and
an index.

5.   *CIVIL RIGHTS*.   Edited by Grant S. McClellan.   New
     York, H.W. Wilson Co., 1964, 192p.   (The Reference
     Shelf, v. 36, no. 6).
For annotation, see Entry No. 77.

6.   *CIVIL RIGHTS: A CURRENT GUIDE TO THE PEOPLE, OR-
     GANIZATIONS AND EVENTS*.   By Joan M. Burke.   2nd
     ed.   New York, Bowker, 1974, 266p.   (A CBS News
     Reference Book).
For annotation, see Entry No. 132.

7.   *THE CIVIL RIGHTS ACT OF 1964*.   Prepared by the
     staff of the Bureau of National Affairs.   Wash-
     ington, D.C., B.N.A., 1964, 424p.
This operations manual provides the text, analysis and
legislative history of three titles of the Civil Rights
Act of 1964: Title VII (dealing with employment), Title
II (public accommodations) and Title VI (Federal assistance).   The manual consists of five parts: The Fair
Employment Practice Act; Public Accommodations/Federal
Assistance; Legislative history, including the entire
text of the Civil Rights Law of 1964; State anti-dis-
crimination laws; and Federal government contracts.   A
subject index is included.

8.   *CIVIL RIGHTS, 1960-68*.   Edited by Lester A. Sobel.
     New York, Facts on File, 1967-1972, 2v.   (Interim

History Series).
For annotation, see Entry No. 78.

9. *DICTIONARY OF RACES OF PEOPLES*. Prepared by the
   U.S. Immigration Commission. Washington, D.C.,
   G.P.O., 1911 (Its Reports, v. 5). Reprinted,
   Gale, 1969, 150p.
"While this 'dictionary' treats of more than 600 subjects covering all of the important and many of the
obscure branches of the human family, it is intended
primarily as a discussion of the various races and
peoples indigenous to the countries furnishing the
present immigration movement to the United States or
which may become sources of future immigration." There
are short articles on each of the 600 groups. A general bibliography, several maps, and cross-references
are included. The *DICTIONARY* was originally issued as
Senate Document no. 662, 61st Congress, 3rd Session.

10. *EQUAL EMPLOYMENT OPPORTUNITY FOR MINORITY GROUP
    COLLEGE GRADUATES: LOCATING, RECRUITING, EMPLOY-
    ING*. By Robert Calvert, Jr. Garrett Park, Mary-
    land, Garrett Park Press, 1972, 248p.
Intended as a guide to the recruitment of Black, Spanish-speaking, American Indian and Asian American college
graduates, this publication contains the following chapters: a background for recruiting, sources dealing with
recruiting,evaluation techniques, equal employment laws,
etc. In addition, several special sections are provided:
enrollment figures for Black students in colleges and
universities, lists of predominantly Black 2- and 4-year
colleges and universities, books for background reading
on minorities, state commissions involved in equal
employment opportunities, minority banks in the United
States, and an extensive bibliography of publications
dealing with minority group employment.

11. *ETHNIC CHRONOLOGY SERIES: CHRONOLOGY AND FACT
    BOOKS*. Dobbs Ferry, New York, Oceana Publica-
    tions, 1971- . 16v.
Each volume in this series focuses on a different ethnic

group (Blacks, American Indians, Spanish Americans, German Americans, etc.) The same basic format characterizes each volume: a chronological section of significant events; a documentary section (public documents, private letters, diaries, newspaper accounts, etc.), and a selective bibliography. For annotations to publications in the series which cover Blacks, American Indians, Spanish-surnamed, and Asian Americans, see Entry Nos. 20, 54, 57-8, 72, 109, 111.

12. *RACE RELATIONS IN THE USA, 1954-68*. Compiled by Keesing's Contemporary Archives. New York, Scribner, 1970, 280p. (Keesing's Research Report, 4).
For annotation, see Entry No. 97.

13. *SEGREGATION AND THE FOURTEENTH AMENDMENT IN THE STATES: A SURVEY OF STATE SEGREGATION LAWS 1865-1953; PREPARED FOR UNITED STATES SUPREME COURT IN RE: BROWN VS. BOARD OF EDUCATION OF TOPEKA.* Edited by Bernard D. Reams, Jr. and Paul E. Wilson. Buffalo, New York, William S. Hein and Co. Inc., 1975, 761p.
For annotation, see Entry No. 100.

14. *TEACHING ETHNIC STUDIES: CONCEPTS AND STRATEGIES.* Edited by James A. Banks. Washington, D.C., National Council for the Social Studies, 1973, 299p. (43rd Yearbook of the National Council for the Social Studies).
Included in this work are information on racism, cultural pluralism, and social justice and teaching strategies for incorporating into American history the roles of Asian Americans, Blacks, Chicanos, Native Americans, Puerto Ricans, white ethnic groups and women. Extensive footnotes and annotated bibliographies accompany the discussion of these topics.

15. *YEARBOOK OF EQUAL EDUCATIONAL OPPORTUNITY, 1975-76.* Chicago, Marquis Academic Media/Marquis Who's

Who, 1975, 479p.
All types of factual and statistical information on
equal educational opportunity in the United States is
presented in this yearbook. The source is arranged in
seven sections. Part One contains general information
on educational trends in the United States and how the
Office for Civil Rights assures equal educational opportunity. Parts Two through Six contain information
on the educational and job-related opportunities and
attainments of Blacks, Spanish-surnamed, American Indians, Japanese, Chinese- and Filipino-descended Americans, and women. Each section gives population, social
and economic statistics, school enrollment and legislation. Part Seven provides information on employment,
recruitment, organizations, professional examinations,
and activities of the U.S. Regional Manpower Administration. There is a comprehensive index.

American Indians

16.   *AMERICAN HERITAGE BOOK OF INDIANS*. By the edi-
      tors of American Heritage. Narrative by William
      Brandon. Introduction by John F. Kennedy. New
      York, American Heritage, 1961, 424p. Dist. by
      Simon and Schuster.
This pictorial history summarizes early Indian migra-
tions and prehistory in the Americas. The work focuses
on Indian relations with Europeans in the United States
and on the frontier. There are over 500 illustrations
(127 in color); they include early maps, portraits,
photographs and reproductions of Indian art and artifacts. There is a subject index.

17.   *THE AMERICAN INDIAN: A RISING ETHNIC FORCE*. Ed-
      ited by Herbert L. Marx, Jr. New York, Wilson,
      1973, 188p. (The Reference Shelf, v. 45, no. 5).
The purpose of this reference source is to reproduce
articles and chapters of books which "reflect changing

attitudes—both of and toward Indians...the material
presented here is a call to look at this force within
our society in the terms of the 1970s—the active, not
the passive Indian." The reprinted materials are arranged by topic (Red Power, Indians and the Federal
Government, The Indian in His Own Setting, The Urban
Indians, etc.); they are written by such well known
scholars as William Brandon, Wilcomb E. Washburn and
Vine Deloria, Jr. There is an 11 page bibliography of
books, articles, reports, etc. which indicates additional
sources of information.

18. *AMERICAN INDIAN ALMANAC*. By John Upton Terrell.
    New York, World Publishing Co., 1971, 494p.
This book is not an almanac, but a series of brief
articles on multivarious topics and tribes of prehistoric American Indians (two or three pages each) grouped
under 10 geographic regions (southwestern deserts and
mesa lands, gulf coasts and tribal swamps, southeastern
woodlands, northern great plains, etc.). Within each
section are maps, lists of important archaeological
sites, tribal locations, population estimates, place
names, important dates, descriptions of physical, cultural, institutional and migratory characteristics, etc.

19. *AMERICAN INDIAN CIVIL RIGHTS HANDBOOK*. By Michael
    R. Smith. Washington, D.C., G.P.O., 1972, 96p.
    (Clearinghouse Publication no. 33).
This guide explains the basic civil rights and liberties
of all Native Americans (American Indians and Alaskan
natives) living on or off reservations: freedoms of
speech, press, religion and assembly; due process of
law; equal protection under the law; etc. Information
is given on filing complaints. There is a list by state
of legal services and programs available to Native Americans.

20. *THE AMERICAN INDIAN 1492-1970: A CHRONOLOGY AND
    FACT BOOK*. Compiled and edited by Henry C. Dennis.
    Foreword by Robert L. Bennett. Dobbs Ferry, New
    York, Oceana Publications, 1971, 137p. (Ethnic

Chronology Series no. 1)
The main section of this volume consists of a chrono-
logy which presents an outline of important events in
American Indian history from 1000 B.C. to 1970. In
addition, biographical sketches are provided for 30
"Indians of the Past" and 50 contemporary Indians (e.g.,
Maria Tallchief, Buffy Sainte-Marie and Louis R. Bruce).
Several appendices provide information on Indian popu-
lation, tribal wars, museums, organizations, publica-
tions, audio-visual materials, monographic works, etc.
There is an index to Indian tribes and prominent leaders
mentioned in the text. This is the first volume in the
ETHNIC CHRONOLOGY SERIES (see Entry No. 11).

21. *AMERICAN INDIANS: A STUDY GUIDE AND SOURCE BOOK.*
    By Lynn P. Dunn. San Francisco, R & E Research
    Associates, 1975, 119p.
Intended as a beginning reference source for students
and teachers, this book concentrates on three themes:
the identity, conflict, and integration/nationalism of
the American Indian. Within each one of these topics,
there are two sections: a chronologically arranged
study outline and an accompanying list of publications
("Notes and Sources") which are appropriate study materials. In addition, there is a bibliography of materials on pages 105-119 and a four page glossary of terms
used in the text. This book is one of a four volume
series issued by R & E Research Associates on American
minorities; other volumes concentrate on Blacks (see
Entry No. 68), Chicanos (see Entry No. 104) and Asian
Americans (see Entry No. 53).

22. *THE BOOK OF AMERICAN INDIANS.* By Ralph B. Raphael.
    New York, Arco, 1973, 144p.
The life styles, languages and culture of American Indians are described and profusely illustrated (with
photographs and drawings) in Raphael's work. Treated
in separate chapters are great chiefs and their battles,
woodcarvers, statesmen, contemporary Indian life, etc.

23. *THE CALIFORNIA INDIANS: A SOURCE BOOK.* Compiled

and edited by Robert F. Heizer and M.A. Whipple.
2d ed. rev. and enl. Berkeley, University of
California Press, 1971, 619p.
"The present collection of essays is intended more for
a lay public than a professional audience and is a survey rather than an encyclopedia..." Essays about California Indians are arranged under such broad categories
as general surveys, archaeology, etc. The authors include such scholars as A.L. Kroeber, R.F. Heizer and
Franklin Fenenga.

24. *CALIFORNIA SPANISH AND INDIAN PLACE NAMES: THEIR
PRONUNCIATION, MEANING AND LOCATION*. By Laura
Kelly NcNary. Los Angeles, Wetzel Publishing
Co., 1931, 77p.
Spanish and Indian place names in California are arranged alphabetically, from Acampo (in San Joaquin
County) to Yuma (in Imperial County). Each name is
translated to indicate its English equivalent. County
locations are provided. In addition to the cities
identified in the main body of the work, there are
supplemental listings of missions (with historical
descriptions), forest reserves, and mountains (whether
or not their names are Spanish/Indian in origin) in
California.

25. *CHRONOLOGY OF THE AMERICAN INDIAN*. Edited by
Barbara A. Leitch. St. Clair Shores, Michigan,
Scholarly Press, Inc., 1975, 282p.
This chronology was prepared in conjunction with the
ENCYCLOPEDIA OF INDIANS OF THE AMERICAS (see Entry No.
30). Covering both the pre-Columbian and post-Columbian
periods, this source traces the story of the American
Indian from the cave-dwellings of the Southwest to the
eastern woodlands. Included in the chronology are over
a thousand entries, supplemented by hundreds of illustrations. The volume also contains a general introductory
essay, a bibliography of sources, and an index. This
publication is part of *THE CHRONOLOGICAL LIBRARY OF
AMERICAN PEOPLES* (see Entry No. 3).

26. *DICTIONARY OF INDIANS OF NORTH AMERICA.* Edited
    by Keith Irvine. St. Clair Shores, Michigan,
    Scholarly Press. To be published in 2v.
More than 2,000 articles on Indians north of Mexico
will be arranged alphabetically in this two volume
dictionary now in preparation. Information will be
provided on Indian tribes, treaties, reservations,
famous geographical sites, historic battles, customs,
lives of notable Indians, artifacts, environmental
practices, practical lore, etc. Hundreds of illustrations, charts, maps, photographs, and diagrams will
supplement the text.

27. *DICTIONARY OF PREHISTORIC INDIAN ARTIFACTS OF
    THE AMERICAN SOUTHWEST.* By Franklin Barnett.
    Flagstaff, Arizona, Northland Press, 1973, 130p.
The purpose of this dictionary is "to bring under one
cover illustrations, descriptions, and uses of the many
artifacts of the Indians of the prehistoric American
Southwest...Every effort is made to bring into focus
the varied nomenclature and certain other data concerned
with these artifacts." Only materials found in open
sites or caves in Southeastern Utah, Southwestern Colorado, Arizona and New Mexico are included. All artifacts (approximately 300) are listed in alphabetical
order. Cross references are included. Each definition
includes photographs or line drawings of the artifacts.
The dimensions and weights of the various materials are
frequently noted. A glossary of terms used in the dictionary and a list of references are found at the end of
the work.

28. *THE DICTIONARY OF THE AMERICAN INDIAN.* By John
    L. Stoutenburgh, Jr. New York, Philosophical
    Library, 1960, 462p.
Short definitions—one to two sentences—are provided in
this dictionary of Indian terms (e.g., Cutaantaqwapifsun),
people (e.g., Curly Head, a Mississippi Chipewa chief),
places (e.g., the Indian village of Cuscowilla) and
tribes (e.g., Chagindueftei). The entries are arranged
alphabetically and there are numerous cross references.

29. *A DICTIONARY OF THE TETON LAKOTA SIOUX LANGUAGE,
    LAKOTA-ENGLISH, ENGLISH-LAKOTA: WITH CONSIDERA-
    TIONS GIVEN TO YANKTON AND SANTEE.* By Rev.
    Eugene Buechel. Edited by Rev. Paul Manhart.
    Pine Ridge, South Dakota, Red Cloud Indian School,
    Inc., Holy Rosary Mission, published in coopera-
    tion with the Institute of Indian Studies, Univ-
    ersity of South Dakota, 1970, 852p.

The main section of the work contains a Lakota-English
dictionary (606p.), and an English-Lakota list (137p.).
Prefatory material includes a biography of Buechel, a
history of the Sioux by Leo P. Gilroy, a description of
Lakota pronunciation, and a condensed survey of Lakota
grammar prepared by the Rev. George Casey (based on
Buechel's *GRAMMAR OF LAKOTA* published in 1939). Appended are a supplemental list of words, data on the Oglala
Teton Society, and a table presenting the tribal and
linguistic order of the Sioux nation.

30. *ENCYCLOPEDIA OF INDIANS OF THE AMERICAS*. Edited
    by Keith Irvine. St. Clair Shores, Michigan,
    Scholarly Press, 1974-   . To be published in
    20 volumes.

The *ENCYCLOPEDIA OF INDIANS OF THE AMERICAS* emphasizes
North America, contains thousands of pictures, is up-
to-date as of 1974, and is prepared by hundreds of
authorities (e.g., Frederick Dockstader, Paul Gates,
Marion Gridley, Vine Deloria, Jr., and the Goodwills).
Volume 1 of the *ENCYCLOPEDIA* provides a conspectus
(13 articles surveying events in such areas as art,
science, religion, culture and image of the American
Indian) and a chronology of events from 25,000 B.C.
to 1974, followed by an index to the chronology. Volume
2 is planned to contain detailed information on more
than 1,000 Indians or others important in Indian affairs.
Volumes 3 through 18 will provide encyclopedic coverage
of topics relating to North American Indians. The
final two volumes will include a 25,000 reference bibliography and a detailed cross index to the entire set.
To date, only Volume 1 has been published.

31. *GREAT LAKES INDIANS: A PICTORIAL GUIDE*. By William

J. Kubiak. Grand Rapids, Michigan, Baker Book
     House, 1970, 255p.
The illustrations in this book (oils and drawings)
were done by the author and depict the prehistoric
origins of the Great Lakes Indians. For each of the
25 Algonquin, Iroquian or Siouan tribes discussed in
this book, there is a brief history given, a map identifying the regions inhabited, a listing of all synony-
mous names of the tribe and illustrations of the tribe's
dwellings, dress, ornaments, tools and weaponry. Thus,
this reference book is not only a pictorial guide, but
also an informative text.

32. *A GUIDE TO AMERICA'S INDIANS: CEREMONIES, RESER-
     VATIONS, AND MUSEUMS*. By Arnold Marquis. Norman,
     University of Oklahoma Press, 1974, 267p.
This reference guide contains general information about
Native American prehistory, languages, arts, and contemporary affairs. Although the Southwestern region of
the United States is emphasized, the Central, Northwes-
tern, Southeastern and Northeastern areas are also
covered. The tribes, population, reservations, camp-
ground facilities and Indian events occuring in these
areas are identified. Appendices list the names and
addresses of museums, organizations, and publications
concerned with Native Americans. In addition, there
are maps, black and white pictures, a bibliography and
an index in this source.

33. *A GUIDE TO THE INDIAN TRIBES OF OKLAHOMA*. By
     Muriel H. Wright. Norman, University of Okla-
     homa Press, 1951, 300p.
The purpose of this guide is "to present in compact
form authentic accounts of all the Indian tribes and
parts of tribes living in Oklahoma, which is the home
of one-third of the Indians of the United States."
Nearly 70 tribes, arranged in alphabetical order, are
described. Information is provided on: name, present
location, numbers, history, government and organization,
contemporary life and culture, ceremonial and public
dances, and suggested readings. There are some maps,
many illustrations (of Indian leaders, places, activi-

ties, events, etc.), a bibliography and index.

34. *HANDBOOK OF AMERICAN INDIANS: NORTH OF MEXICO*.
     Edited by Frederick W. Hodge. Washington, D.C.,
     G.P.O., 1907-10, 2v. (Bureau of American Eth-
     nology Bulletin no. 30).

Hodge's *HANDBOOK* "contains a descriptive list of the
stocks, confederacies, tribes, tribal divisions, and
settlements north of Mexico, accompanied with the various names by which these have been known, together
with biographies of Indians of note, sketches of their
histories, archaeology, manners, arts, customs, and
illustrations, and the aboriginal words incorporated
into the English language." Eskimos are included. For
each tribe, information is given on its history, locations, population, ethnic relations, etc. Many articles
have illustrations and photographs. Cross references to
the various forms and synonyms of names, arranged in
alphabetical order, are found in the second volume.
Also included in the second volume are over 40 pages
of citations to materials pertaining to the various
tribes. A reprint of this two volume set was issued in
1958 by Pageant Books and in 1968 by Scholarly Press.

35. *HANDBOOK OF FEDERAL INDIAN LAW WITH REFERENCE
     TABLES & INDEX*. Edited by Felix S. Cohen.
     Washington, D.C., G.P.O., 1942, 662p.

This handbook sorts and explains the vast array of
laws, treaties, judicial rulings, administrative acts,
etc. which govern relations between American Indians
and the Federal government. The Introduction states
that "If one who seeks to track down a point of federal
Indian law finds in this volume relevant background,
general perspective and useful leads to the authorities,
the handbook will have served the purpose for which it
was written." There is a very detailed index. In
1958, an abbreviated edition of the handbook was issued
(*FEDERAL INDIAN LAW*, 1958, 1106p. Reprinted by Oceana
Publications, 1966, 1125p.); it omits much of the valuable contents of the original 1942 edition. The 1942
edition was reprinted in 1971 by the University of New
Mexico Press.

36. *HANDBOOK OF INDIANS OF CALIFORNIA*. By A.L.
    Kroeber. Washington, D.C., G.P.O., 1925, 995p.
    (Bureau of American Ethnology Bulletin no. 76).
In encyclopedic fashion, this source devotes several
chapters to each tribe of California Indians. The
locale, history, civilization, origins, laws, customs,
religion, music, arts, etc. of each tribe is described.
The data were collected during short visits to the
tribes prior to 1918. There are numerous maps and illustrations. A subject and general index are included.
A reprint of this publication was issued in 1972 by
Scholarly Press.

37. *INDIAN NAMES OF PLACES, ETC. IN AND ON THE BORDERS
    OF CONNECTICUT: WITH INTERPRETATIONS OF SOME OF
    THEM*. By James H. Trumbull. Hamden, Connecticut,
    Linnet Books/Shoe String Press, 1974, 93p. (Fac-
    simile of 1881 edition).
Originally published in 1881, this is a listing of In-
dian place names in and on the borders of Connecticut.
The place names are listed alphabetically. Name deri-
vations are explained. Podunk, for example, is from
Potaecke, a brook or rivulet. Mistick, located between
Stonington and Groton, means a great tidal river. Many
entries contain citations to sources such as the *COLO-
NIAL RECORDS OF CONNECTICUT* and the *NEW HAVEN COLONIAL
RECORDS*. Cross references for variant spellings are
generally provided.

38. *THE INDIAN TRIBES OF NORTH AMERICA*. By John R.
    Swanton. Washington, D.C., G.P.O., 1952, 726p.
    (Bureau of American Ethnology Bulletin no. 145).
The purpose of this work is "to inform the general
reader what Indian tribes occupied the territory of his
state and to add enough data to indicate the place they
occupied among the tribal groups of the continent and
the part they played in the early period of our history
and the history of the States immediately to the north
and south of us." The emphasis is on Indian tribal
units within the United States, although some tribes in
Alaska, Canada, Greenland, Mexico, Central America and
the West Indies are also discussed. The tribal entries

are arranged by area of the world and, for the U.S., by
state. Information given for each tribe includes the
origin of tribal name, list of tribal synonyms, tribal
relations, linguistic stock, location, history, population, etc. A bibliography of important sources of information and an index of names and places complete the work.
A reprint of this publication was issued in 1968 by
Scholarly Press.

39. *INDIANS OF ARIZONA: A CONTEMPORARY PERSPECTIVE*.
     Edited by Thomas Weaver. Tucson, University of
     Arizona Press, 1974, 169p.
Various authorities have written chapters in this reference source on the legislation, city life, living conditions, employment, education, reservations, etc. of
Indians living historically and currently in Arizona.
The Cochise, Hohokim, Mongollon and Anasazi are discussed
in some detail. There are many photographs, tables and
some maps supplementing the text. The work is indexed.

40. *INDIANS OF THE AMERICAN SOUTHWEST*. By Bertha P.
     Dutton. Englewood Cliffs, New Jersey, Prentice-
     Hall, 1975, 298p.
A comprehensive survey of the history, traditions, cultural organization, and contemporary life of Indians
in the American Southwest is provided in this publication. The Indian tribes described include the Pueblo,
Ute, Hopi, Paiute, Rancherea, etc. For each tribe,
information is given on its historical background, social and religious customs and ceremonies, educational
and employment opportunities, etc. In addition to the
tribal descriptions, there are maps, photographs, a
calendar of annual Indian events, population figures
for 1970 and an extensive bibliography. The source was
written by the Director of the Museum of Navaho Ceremonial Art.

41. *INDIANS OF THE PLAINS*. By Robert H. Lowie. New
     York, published for the American Museum of Natur-
     al History by McGraw-Hill, 1954, 222p. (Anthropo-
     logical Handbook no. 1).

Indians who lived in the area between the Mississippi
and the Rocky Mountains are described in this reference
handbook. Separate chapters are devoted to the Indians'
social organization, recreation, art, history and acculturation, etc. The source also includes over 100 illustrations, a short bibliography and a general index.

42. *THE INDIANS OF THE SOUTHEASTERN UNITED STATES*. By
     John R. Swanton. Washington, D.C., G.P.O., 1946,
     1053p. (Bureau of American Ethnology Bulletin no.
     137).
The history, culture and daily life of the Creek Indians
and other Southeastern tribes are described in this handbook. Entries are arranged alphabetically by tribal
name. Separate sections deal with such topics as
clothing, housing, food, etc. The work is illustrated
with 13 maps and 107 plates. There is a 25 page bibliography and a general index. In 1968, the book was
reprinted under the same title by Scholarly Press.

43. *INDIANS: THE GREAT PHOTOGRAPHS THAT REVEAL NORTH
     AMERICAN INDIAN LIFE, 1847-1929; FROM THE UNIQUE
     COLLECTION OF THE SMITHSONIAN INSTITUTION*. By
     Joanna C. Scherer. New York, Crown Publishers,
     Inc., 1974, 188p.
The history of the North American Indian is presented
through reproductions of outstanding photographs and
daguerreotypes which are currently in the Smithsonian
Institution collection. These pictures were taken
between 1847 and 1929. Whenever possible, photographers
are identified. Historical essays provide background
information on the life, appearance, and customs of the
North American Indians. For a more extensive compilation of photographs, see the microfiche collection issued by the University of Chicago which is described in
Entry No. 48.

44. *LANGUAGE TERRITORIES AND NAMES OF CALIFORNIA
     INDIAN TRIBES*. By Robert F. Heizer. Berkeley,
     University of California Press, 1966, 62p.
Heizer's work provides an ethnographic sketch of Cali-

fornia Indians, including their tribal units and linguistic affiliations. The following information is
given: the identification and classification of California tribal groups, the history of language classification in California, and the nature of tribal territories and boundary lines in California. The appendix
includes a bibliography and five maps showing the location of California Indian tribes.

45. *MYTHOLOGY OF ALL RACES*. Edited by John A. Mac-
    Culloch, et. al. New York, Cooper Square Publi-
    cations, Inc., 1964, 13v. (Reprint of the 1932
    edition).
Volume 10 of this 13 volume set focuses on North America. Written by Hartley Burr Alexander, the volume
describes the mythology of tribes living in various
areas of North America (the forest, the plains, the
mountains, the desert, etc.) and contains numerous
color plates, maps, notes and bibliographies of sources
on which the text is based. There is no index in volume 10; volume 13 contains an index to the entire set.

46. *NATICK DICTIONARY*. By James Hammond Trumbull.
    Washington, D.C., G.P.O., 1903, 347p. (Bureau of
    American Ethnology Bulletin no. 25).
In the first section of the 25th *BULLETIN* of the Bureau
of American Ethnology, Natick words are translated into
English equivalents. In the second section, English words
are translated into Natick. In both sections, references
are made in the definitions to Eliot's Bible and to the
writings of American Indian linguistics. "Dr. Trumbull's
vocabularies constitute the most important contribution
to the scientific study of Eliot's Indian Bible which
has been made since that wonderful book was published."

47. *NATIVE AMERICANS OF CALIFORNIA AND NEVADA: A
    HANDBOOK*. By Jack D. Forbes. Berkeley, Calif-
    ornia, Far West Laboratory for Educational Re-
    search and Development, 1968, 181p.
This handbook is designed "to provide an introduction
to the evolution of Native American peoples in the Far

West (with strong emphasis upon California-Nevada), especially in relation to those historical-cultural experiences likely to have contributed to the present-day
conditions of native communities and individuals." Basic
concepts relating to Indian studies and Indian education
are covered in various chapters (e.g., The Evolution of
Native California and Nevada; The Conquest: Powerlessness
and Poverty; A Community Responsive; Multi-Cultural Approach to Indian Education). Maps, a linguistic classification of California and Nevada Indians, and a selected bibliography are presented in separate sections.
Forbes has written similar handbooks for Blacks (see
Entry No. 61) and Mexican-Americans (*MEXICAN-AMERICANS:
A HANDBOOK FOR EDUCATORS*. By Jack D. Forbes. Berkeley,
California, Far West Laboratory for Educational Research
and Development, 1967, 34p.).

48. *NORTH AMERICAN INDIANS; PHOTOGRAPHS FROM THE NA-
    TIONAL ANTHROPOLOGICAL ARCHIVES, SMITHSONIAN
    INSTITUTION*. Compiled by Herman Viola. Chicago,
    University of Chicago Press, 1974, 52 microfiche.
From the National Anthropological Archives of the Smithsonian Institution's collection of photographs, 5,000
pictures of North American Indians have been reproduced
here on 52 microfiche. The photographs in this set
were taken between 1860 and 1930 by such artists as
David F. Barry, Charles M. Bell, E. S. Curtis, R. Jay
Haynes, and William S. Soule. More than 128 tribes
are visually represented in these pictures. The photographs illustrate dwellings, costumes, domestic activities, the arts, tribal life, individual Indians, etc.
To provide easier access to the collection, many of the
tribes are cross-referenced in the index.

49. *A PICTORIAL HISTORY OF THE AMERICAN INDIAN*. By
    Oliver La Farge. Rev. ed. New York, Crown Publi-
    shers, Inc., 1974, 272p.
Many black and white photographs and paintings depicting
Indian life, artifacts, and culture accompany this
narrative history of the American Indian. Some of the
chapters included in the work are: They Discovered
America; The Western Farmers; Ghosts and Drugs; and

The Non-Vanishing Americans. There is a subject index.

50. *REFERENCE ENCYCLOPEDIA OF THE AMERICAN INDIAN*. By
     Barry T. Klein and Dan Icolari. 2nd ed. Rye, New
     York, Todd Publications, 1973-4, 2v.
More of a directory than an encyclopedia, this source
lists and describes in Volume 1 organizations (historical societies, foundations, local groups and associations working in Indian affairs), reservations and
tribal councils (arranged alphabetically-geographically),
newspapers, magazines and periodicals, government agencies on all levels, visual and instructional aids (films,
picture sets, songbooks, maps, charts, recordings, etc.)
arranged by type of aid, monuments, state parks, Indian
schools, urban Indian centers, museums, libraries, arts
and crafts shops, government publications, Indian
related course offerings, and 2,500 in-print books
dealing with American Indians. Volume 2 provides an
alphabetically arranged listing of American Indians
prominent in Indian affairs, business, the arts, and
professions, as well as non-Indians active in Indian
affairs, history, art, anthropology, archaeology, etc.
Selection and inclusion are based on achievement. Each
entry contains information on the biographee's education, affiliations, memberships, community activities,
interests, published works, etc. The first edition of
this work was published in one volume in 1967.

51. *SOUTHEASTERN INDIANS LIFE PORTRAITS: A CATALOGUE
     OF PICTURES, 1564-1860*. By Emma Lela Fundaburk.
     Metuchen, New Jersey, Scarecrow Press, 1969, 135p.
The *CATALOG* contains, in chronological order, 354 reproductions of drawings, paintings and engravings which
portray the personalities and life of Southeastern
Indians from 1564 to 1860. The Indians most frequently
portrayed include the Algonquin, Cherokee, Choctaw,
Creek, Seminole and Shawnee. The paintings are drawn
by such artists as Stanley, King, Du Pratz and Bry. There
are brief notes describing each portrait and artist. A
bibliography and an index complete the source. This is
a reprint of a 1958 edition.

52. *SPANISH AND INDIAN PLACE NAMES OF CALIFORNIA:
    THEIR MEANING AND THEIR ROMANCE.* By Nellie Van
    de Grift Sanchez. San Fransisco, A.M. Robertson,
    1914, 446p.
The purpose of this reference work is to serve "not
only as a source of entertainment to our own people,
but also as a useful handbook for the schools, and as
a sort of tourist's guide for those who visit the state
in such numbers, and who almost invariably exhibit a
lively interest in our Spanish and Indian place names."
The place names are arranged geographically (California,
San Diego, Los Angeles, Santa Clara Valley, etc.). The
origin and history of each of these locations are briefly discussed. Pronunciation is provided for the Spanish
names. There are several black and white illustrations.
A name index completes the work.

Asian Americans

53. *ASIAN AMERICANS: A STUDY GUIDE AND SOURCE BOOK.*
    By Lynn P. Dunn. San Francisco, R & E Research
    Associates, 1975, 111p.
One of a four volume set on American minority groups
(see also Entry Nos. 21, 68 and 104), this guide and
source book focuses on the identity, conflict, and inte-
gration/nationalism of Asian Americans. In each of
these sections, two types of material are presented: a
chronologically arranged study outline and an accompanying list of publications ("Notes and Sources") which
are appropriate study materials. Also included in the
publication are a glossary of terms used by and about
Asian Americans and a selected bibliography.

54. *THE CHINESE IN AMERICA 1820-1973: A CHRONOLOGY
    AND FACT BOOK.* By William L. Tung. Dobbs Ferry,
    New York, Oceana Publications, 1974, 150p. (Eth-
    nic Chronology Series no. 14).

This work divides the history of the Chinese in the
United States into three major sections. The first
section, "Chronology," is classified into four historical periods: free immigration (1820-1882), discrimina-
tory restrictions (1882-1904), absolute exclusion (1904-
1943), and gradual liberalization (1943 to the present).
Over 20 documents (representing laws, treaties and court
cases) are arranged chronologically in the second section. The final section is a selective, unannotated
bibliography of primary and secondary source materials
(government documents, books, pamphlets, articles, etc.)
arranged alphabetically. A list of Chinese organizations in major cities is included in the appendix. A
name index concludes the 14th volume in the *ETHNIC CHRO-
NOLOGY SERIES* (see Entry No. 11).

55. *CHINESE WORKING PEOPLE IN AMERICA: A PICTORIAL
     HISTORY*. By Wei Min Shè Labor Committee. San
     Francisco, California, United Front Press, 1974,
     71p.
The Wei Min Shè Labor Committee "compiled this pictorial
history of Chinese working people in America to dispel
the myths about our people." The photographs, drawings,
cartoons, etc. are arranged chronologically (e.g., Part
1: 1850-1900, Immigration, Building up the West, Exclusion; Part 2: 1900-1940, Participation in the American
Labor Movement; etc.) and supplemented with textual
comments. Wei Min Shè (Organization for the People)
is "an Asian American anti-imperialist organization
based in the San Francisco Bay Area" which is concerned
with "fighting for democratic rights in the community,
student organizing, building U.S.-China Friendship,
fighting against the oppression of women, building
working class struggles, and fighting against U.S.
aggression overseas."

56. *HANDBOOK OF CHINESE IN AMERICA*. By Yuchou Chen.
     New York, The Author, 1946, 213p.
This reference guide contains information on exclusion
laws, immigration laws, Chinese-American relations,
characteristics (demographic, economic, political) of
overseas Chinese throughout the world, history of

Chinese in America, etc. The text is written in both Chinese and English.

57. *THE JAPANESE IN AMERICA 1843-1973: A CHRONOLOGY AND FACT BOOK*. Compiled and edited by Masako Herman. Dobbs Ferry, New York, Oceana Publications, 1974, 152p. (Ethnic Chronology Series no. 15).

Basically, this source contains four separate sections. The first part is a chronology which identifies significant political, economic, social and historical events affecting Japanese Americans which occurred between 1843 and 1973. The second section includes major treaties, executive orders, laws, court cases, editorials, and letters (e.g., the 1908 Gentlemen's Agreement, Hirabayashi vs. United States in 1913, Truman's veto of the McCarran-Walter Immigration Act, etc.). The third section "Appendices," contains statistical data (Japanese in the United States 1940-1970, Immigrants by country, 1820-1957, etc.); directories of assemblies and relocation centers; battles fought and awards received by Japanese-Americans; Japanese-American newspapers; organizations and lists of Nisei scientists; Japanese scientists in the United States; and Japanese-Americans listed in biographical directories. The last section is a short, unannotated bibliography of pertinent books. There is a name index. This book is the 15th volume in the *ETHNIC CHRONOLOGY SERIES* (see Entry No. 11).

58. *THE KOREANS IN AMERICA 1882-1974: A CHRONOLOGY AND FACT BOOK*. Compiled and edited by Hyung-Chan Kim and Wayne Patterson. Dobbs Ferry, New York, Oceana Publications, 1974, 147p. (Ethnic Chronology Series no. 16).

The purpose of this 16th volume in the *ETHNIC CHRONOLOGY SERIES* (see Entry No. 11) is to "provide readers with information which will increase their basic understanding of the persons and events that have left a lasting influence upon the development of the history of Koreans in America." The source consists of three basic parts: chronology, documents, and selected bibliography. The

documents included in the publication are drawn basically from two different groups: people responsible for
the emigration of Koreans to America and Korean immigrants. There is a name index.

Black Americans

59. *AFRO-AMERICAN ENCYCLOPEDIA*. Compiled and edited
    by Mertin Rywell, Charles H. Wesley and others.
    North Miami, Florida, Educational Book Publishers,
    1974, 10v.
The purpose of this encyclopedia is to provide "objective facts and truthful declarations and descriptions
dealing with the aspects of Negro life and history in
Africa, the United States, the West Indies, and Canada,
as well as Latin America." Articles are alphabetically
arranged. They vary considerably in length. There is
a 10 page section on court cases focusing on Blacks from
1771 to 1972 and a 59 page general chronology covering
1492 to 1973. A general index is provided in the last
volume of the set.

60. *AFRO-AMERICAN ENCYCLOPEDIA, OR THE THOUGHTS, DOINGS,
    AND SAYINGS OF THE RACE*. By James T. Haley. Nash-
    ville, Tennessee, Haley and Florida, 1895, 639p.
Many essays, sermons, speeches, and surveys written on
all aspects of Black life by notable Black scholars make
up this 19th century encyclopedia. Photographs and
illustrations (of leaders, schools, houses, institutions, etc.) supplement the text. Black newspapers are
listed and statistics are given on the racial composition of each state and county. A great deal of biographical information is included.

61. *AFRO-AMERICANS IN THE FAR WEST: A HANDBOOK FOR
    EDUCATORS*. By Jack D. Forbes. Berkeley, Calif-

ornia, Far West Laboratory for Educational Research and Development, 1970, 106p.
This handbook represents an effort to acquaint school
personnel with data relevant to the Afro-American in
the western United States. Reference is made to national developments where pertinent and general background is summarized when important for the understanding of educators. The focus is on the West and, especially, California. Suggestions are given to teachers
and administrators to improve the teaching process in
a Black community. Citations are provided for readings
on Afro-Americans in the far West, Afro-American history,
contemporary issues, education of culturally different
and low-income groups, audio-visual sources, etc. Similar handbooks have been developed for American Indians
(see Entry No. 47) and Mexican-Americans (*MEXICAN-AMER-
ICANS: A HANDBOOK FOR EDUCATORS*. By Jack D. Forbes.
Berkeley, California, Far West Laboratory for Educational Research and Development, 1967, 34p.).

62. *AFRO-U.S.A., A REFERENCE WORK ON THE BLACK EXPER-
IENCE*. Edited by Harry Ploski and Ernest Kaiser.
New York, Bellwether, 1971, 1110p.
This is "a special deluxe presentation of the regular
edition of the prestigious new revised Negro Almanac."
For a complete annotation, see Entry No. 90.

63. *THE AMERICAN NEGRO REFERENCE BOOK*. Edited by
John P. Davis. Englewood Cliffs, New Jersey,
Prentice-Hall, 1966, 969p.
This single volume reference work covers the major aspects of Black life in America from colonial times to
the present. Langston Hughes and LeRoi Jones are
among the more than 20 specialists who have written
chapters covering such topics as Blacks in urban life,
history, education, civil rights, politics, sports,
religion, art, music, and the economy. A short bibliography follows each chapter. Many statistical tables
(138) cover population, employment, and the economic
conditions of American Blacks. An extensive index
(86p.) is provided. Appendices list Black organizations, colleges, financial institutions and insurance

companies. This same source is also being distributed
as part of Prentice-Hall's *NEGRO HERITAGE LIBRARY* (see
Entry No. 93). For an up-date, see *THE BLACK AMERICAN
REFERENCE BOOK* (Entry No. 66).

64. *ANTHOLOGY: QUOTATIONS AND SAYINGS OF PEOPLE OF
    COLOR*. By Walter B. Hoard. San Francisco, R & E
    Research Associates, 1974, 137p.

Hundreds of quotations and sayings of "people of color"
are included in this anthology. The arrangement is by
subject. There is an author index.

65. *THE BLACK ALMANAC*. By Alton Hornsby, Jr. Rev.
    ed. Woodbury, New York, Barron's Educational
    Service, 1975, 212p.

American Black history from 1619 to the 1970's is
described in 10 chronological sections (involuntary
servitude, 1619-1800; war and freedom, 1816-1876; the
attack on segregation, 1945-1954, etc.). Within these
sections, Hornsby (who is Chairman of the Department of
History at Morehouse College in Atlanta) identifies
chronologically the events, legislation, judicial decisions and people important in Afro-American history.
The book emphasizes current developments. Bibliographical aids, major repositories, general surveys, and books
and articles on each of the broad periods from 1619 to
the present are also identified and described. There
is an extensive name, title and subject index.

66. *THE BLACK AMERICAN REFERENCE BOOK*. Edited by
    Mabel M. Smythe. Englewood Cliffs, New Jersey,
    Prentice-Hall, 1976, 1026p.

Based on *THE AMERICAN NEGRO REFERENCE BOOK* (see Entry
No. 63), this one volume encyclopedia provides up-to-
date information on the American Black experience.
Through such topics as legal status, women, sports,
education, the arts, religion and politics, it tells
the story of 300 years of being Black in America. Each
of these subjects is covered in a separate chapter and
is written by a well known scholar or specialist in the
field. The material is extensively indexed.

67. *BLACK AMERICANS: A CHARTBOOK*. Washington, D.C.,
     G.P.O., 1971, 141p.
For annotation, see Entry No. 361.

68. *BLACK AMERICANS: A STUDY GUIDE AND SOURCE BOOK*.
     By Lynn P. Dunn. San Francisco, R & E Research
     Associates, 1975, 112p.
This study guide is one of a set of four volumes issued
by R & E Research Associates on American minority groups.
Other volumes cover Asian Americans (see Entry No. 53),
Chicanos (see Entry No. 104), and American Indians
(see Entry No. 21). In *BLACK AMERICANS*, three themes
are stressed: the identity, conflict, and integration/
nationalism of Black Americans. Each page is arranged
in two columns: one column presents a study outline and
the other lists publications to accompany the outline.
A glossary of terms used by and about Black Americans
is included.

69. *BLACK JARGON IN WHITE AMERICA*. By David Claer-
     baut. Grand Rapids, Michigan, Eerdmans, 1972,
     89p.
Although predominately an essay focusing on the importance of understanding the Black cultural experience,
one-third of Claerbaut's book is composed of a glossary
which lists words and phrases characterizing Black culture. Terms used to describe sexual activity are excluded. A bibliography of books and articles on Black
language is provided.

70. *BLACK NAMES IN AMERICA: A GUIDE TO THEIR HISTORY
     AND MEANING*. Collected by Newbell Niles Puckett.
     Edited by Murray Heller under the Newbell Niles
     Puckett Memorial Gift. Cleveland, John G. White
     Department, Cleveland Public Library, 1974, 700p.
Useful for developing an understanding of the social
values related to naming and the importance of naming
in the context of social change, this one volume work
lists over 340,000 Black names in America dating from
1619 to the mid-1940s. The material is divided chronologically; names of the 17th and 18th centuries can be

found in one chapter, the period 1800-1864 in succeeding chapters, and the Civil War to the 1940's in the last chapters. A description of the development of names and naming practices is included. There are also sections devoted to the names of college students and Black names of African origin (including their meaning, popularity, and usage). Other parts of the book present statistical information and graphs taken from local city directories, welfare roles, student enrollments, municipal and national censuses, etc.

71. *BLACK SLANG: A DICTIONARY OF AFRO-AMERICAN TALK.* By Clarence Major. London, Routledge and K. Paul, 1971, 127p.
For annotation, see Entry No. 79.

72. *BLACKS IN AMERICA 1492-1970: A CHRONOLOGY AND FACT BOOK.* Compiled by Irving J. Sloan. 3rd rev. ed. Dobbs Ferry, New York, Oceana Publications, 1971, 149p. (Ethnic Chronology Series no. 2).
This 3rd revised edition chronicles the achievements of American Blacks through 1970. The first half of the publication consists of brief chronological entries which provide an outline of events important in Black history between 1492 and 1970. The rest of the source is made up of a bibliography, excerpts from executive orders on civil rights, a discography, a list of Black colleges, organizations, museums, Black members in Congress and reprints of selected tables from the U.S. *STATISTICAL ABSTRACT.* There is a name index. This publication is part of the multivolume *ETHNIC CHRONOLOGY SERIES* (see Entry No. 11).

73. *CHANGING CHARACTERISTICS OF THE NEGRO POPULATION: CENSUS OF POPULATION. MONOGRAPH.* Daniel O. Price. Washington, D.C., U.S. Bureau of the Census, 1970, 263p.
For annotation, see Entry No. 363.

74. *CHICAGO NEGRO ALMANAC AND REFERENCE BOOK.* Com-

piled by Ernest R. Rather. Chicago, Chicago
Negro Almanac Publishing Co., 1972, 256p.
Current and historical information on Blacks in Chicago
is presented both descriptively and statistically in
this source. Biographical sketches, complete with photographs, make up a "who's who" of Chicago Blacks.
Another section of the publication chronologically
lists important events in Chicago's Black history.
There is a general index.

75. *THE CHRONOLOGICAL HISTORY OF THE NEGRO IN AMERICA.*
    Edited by Peter M. Bergman and Mort N. Bergman.
    New York, Harper and Row, 1969, 698p.
Starting with 1441, when the Portuguese began the African
slave trade, information about Blacks (particularly in
America) is presented chronologically through 1968. Each
yearly entry contains information on events, court decisions, legislation, literature, and personalities important in Black history. Primary sources of information
are not indicated. Personalities and publications are
emphasized. There is a 70 page index (which includes more
than 20,000 entries) and a bibliography of bibliographies.

76. *CHRONOLOGY OF BLACK AMERICA.* St. Clair Shores,
    Michigan, Scholarly Press, 1975, 312p. (Chrono-
    logical Library of American People).
CHRONOLOGY OF BLACK AMERICA is one volume of *THE CHRO-
NOLOGICAL LIBRARY OF AMERICAN PEOPLES* reference set
(see Entry No. 3). This handbook lists social and
political events in Black American history by date.
The volume contains over 1,000 subject entries listed
chronologically, a general introductory essay surveying
Black America, more than 200 illustrations, a bibliography of sources used, and a detailed cross index. Subject entries, such as the Deslandes Revolt in Louisiana
in 1811, the Executive Order establishing the Fair
Employment Practices Commission, and the 1963 March on
Washington for Jobs and Freedom, are chronicled.

77. *CIVIL RIGHTS.* Edited by Grant S. McClellan. New
    York, H.W. Wilson Co., 1964, 192p. (The Reference

Shelf, v. 36, no. 6).

This compilation "surveys the Negroes' demands for advances and recognition of their civil rights in American society. It also considers the recent advances made in the protection of traditional civil rights, the claims for the extension of rights into new areas, and the efforts toward achievement of human rights on a global basis." Reprints of articles by outstanding journalists and experts on the topic are grouped into four sections: The Mid-Century Civil Rights Movement; The Role of Law and Government; Protecting Traditional Rights; New Rights and Universal Rights. An introductory essay and a selective bibliography complete the source.

78. *CIVIL RIGHTS, 1960-68.* Edited by Lester A. Sobel. New York, Facts on File, 1967-1972, 2v. (Interim History Series).

This is a very detailed chronological description of people, places, events and legislation affecting the struggle for civil rights from 1960 through 1966. The history of the movement from the peaceful sit-ins of the 1960's to the "long hot summers" at the end of the decade is described in the two volume set. Volume 1 covers the non-violent period of the movement: the freedom rides, the Voting Rights Act of 1965, the move toward equal educational opportunities and the beginnings of the major race riots. Volume 2 chronicles such events as the riots in Detroit and Chicago and the assassination of Martin Luther King, Jr. A detailed table of contents and an analytical index provide access to the information.

79. *DICTIONARY OF AFRO-AMERICAN SLANG.* Edited by Clarence Major. New York, International Publishing Co., 1970, 127p.

Issued in England under the title *BLACK SLANG: A DICTIONARY OF AFRO-AMERICAN TALK*, this dictionary briefly defines words, phrases and nicknames used by Blacks (even if the terms did not originate with them). Urban jargon, rather than Black agricultural or industrial workers' terms, is emphasized. Many jazz and drug terms are included. Derivations are not traced, but vogue periods are identified.

80. *DICTIONARY OF BLACK CULTURE*. By Wade Baskin and
    Richard N. Runes. New York, Philosophical Library,
    1973, 493p.
Prepared by Dr. Wade Baskin, Chairperson, Classical
Languages Department, Southeastern State College, Dur-
rant, Oklahoma and Richard N. Runes, a public defender
with the Legal Aid Society, New York, this dictionary
contains alphabetically arranged descriptions of Black
organizations, leaders, court cases, laws, issues,
events, etc. Areas outside the United States are
unevenly covered. The entries describe a wide variety
of subjects, ranging from singing groups like the
Supremes to the Civil Rights Act of 1960 and Negro
colleges like Howard University. Biographical entries,
however, predominate.

81. *THE EBONY HANDBOOK*. Compiled by Ebony editors
    and Doris E. Saunders. Chicago, Johnson Publi-
    shing Co., 1974, 553p.
This is a revised edition of the 1966 publication, *THE
NEGRO HANDBOOK*. It is designed to document the current
status of Black Americans. Each of the 20 chapters
deals with a different subject: education, politics
and government, civil rights, crime, the professions,
the press, etc. One section provides an annotated bibliography of books by and about Blacks. In addition
to the text, there are 122 statistical tables. An
appendix lists Black organizations. A subject, title,
and name index completes the source.

82. *EBONY PICTORIAL HISTORY OF BLACK AMERICA*. Edited
    by *EBONY* editors and Lerone Bennett, Jr. Nash-
    ville, Tennessee, published for Johnson by
    Southwestern Co., 1971-1974, 4v.
This is a popularly written pictorial (primarily photographs) history of Afro-American events from the
17th century to the present. Over 1,000 pictures are
included. Volume 1 covers "African Past to the Civil
War;" volume 2 deals with "Reconstruction to Supreme

Court Decision 1954;" volume 3 outlines the "Civil
Rights Movement to Black Revolution;" volume 4 is
"The 1973 Yearbook" - a review of the major events
of 1971-72. Each volume is indexed separately, but
all four indexes are placed in the last volume.

83. *ENCYCLOPEDIA OF BLACK FOLKLORE AND HUMOR.*
     Edited by Henry D. Spalding. Illustrated by
     Rue Knapp. Middle Village, New York, Jonathan
     David Publishers, Inc., 1972, 589p.
Black folktales, jokes, songs, proverbs, stories,
poems, superstitions, and a few soul food recipes are
presented in chronological sequence (beginning with
the Black folksayer Aesop). Also included are tables
on Black history and biographical sketches of Black
inventors and scientists. The name index references
persons, songs, stories and books.

84. *ENCYCLOPEDIA OF THE NEGRO IN AFRICA AND AMERICA.*
     St. Clair Shores, Michigan, Scholarly Press,
     1974, 18v.
For annotation, see Entry No. 102.

85. *ENCYCLOPEDIA OF THE NEGRO, PREPARATORY VOLUME
     WITH REFERENCE LISTS AND REPORTS.* By W.E.B.
     DuBois, Guy B. Johnson and others. New York,
     The Phelps-Stokes Fund, 1945, 207p.
Modeled after the *ENCYCLOPEDIA OF THE SOCIAL SCIENCES*
(N.Y., Macmillan, 1930-35, 15v.), the *ENCYCLOPEDIA OF
THE NEGRO* was intended to be a four volume scholarly
discussion, listing of materials, and guide to repositories of materials dealing with Black life and culture.
Only one volume (1945) was ever published. It lists
proposed subject headings (to be covered in the other
volumes of the *ENCYCLOPEDIA*) and bibliographies for
each of these subjects. Lack of financial backing
precluded the publication of the remaining three
volumes in the set.

86. *FAMOUS FIRST FACTS ABOUT NEGROES.* By Romeo B.

Garrett. New York, Arno Press, 1972, 212p.
This publication lists and describes famous first
facts about American Blacks from their earliest
beginnings in Africa through 1970 alphabetically by
subject (e.g., Black power, civil rights, labor,
libraries, mayors, police, state legislators, etc.).
For example, the first incorporated town for Blacks,
the first Negro founder of a public library, the nation's first Black jurist, and the appearance of the
term "black is beautiful" are identified. There is an
index of names and specific subjects.

87. *A GUIDE TO NEGRO HISTORY IN AMERICA.* By Phillip
    T. Drotning. 2nd rev. ed. Garden City, New
    York, Doubleday, 1968, 247p.
Intended as a "chronicle of the most significant historical contributions--and of the Negroes who made
them...," this book consists of brief accounts of
Blacks who distinguished themselves in American history arranged alphabetically by the state and city with
which the account is associated. For example, under
"New York--Auburn" the Harriet Tubman Home is identified as a monument and Tubman's anti-slavery activities
are described. The index covers names, places, and
selected subjects.

88. *INTERNATIONAL LIBRARY OF NEGRO LIFE AND HISTORY.*
    New York, Publishers Co., under the auspices of
    the Association for the Study of Negro Life and
    History, 1967-69, 10v.
Each of the 10 volumes of the *INTERNATIONAL LIBRARY OF
NEGRO LIFE AND HISTORY* set is extensively illustrated,
contains bibliographic references and has individual
indexes. Each of the original volumes deals with a
different aspect of Black life or history:

*IN FREEDOM'S FOOTSTEPS, FROM THE AFRICAN BACKGROUND
TO THE CIVIL WAR.* By Charles H. Wesley, 1968, 307p.

*NEGRO AMERICANS IN THE CIVIL WAR: FROM SLAVERY TO
CITIZENSHIP.* By Charles H. Wesley and Patricia W.
Romero. 2nd rev. ed., 1969, 291p.

THE QUEST FOR EQUALITY: FROM CIVIL WAR TO CIVIL RIGHTS. By Charles H. Wesley, 1968, 307p.

NEGRO IN MUSIC AND ART. Compiled by Lindsay Patterson, 1967, 304p.

ANTHOLOGY OF THE AMERICAN NEGRO IN THE THEATRE: A CRITICAL APPROACH. 2nd ed., 1969, 306p.

AN INTRODUCTION TO BLACK LITERATURE IN AMERICA FROM 1746 TO THE PRESENT. Compiled by Lindsay Patterson, 1969, 302p.

THE BLACK ATHLETE: EMERGENCE AND ARRIVAL. By Edwin B. Henderson and the editors of *SPORT MAGAZINE.* Introduction by Jackie Robinson, 1969, 306p.

THE HISTORY OF THE NEGRO IN MEDICINE. By Herbert M. Morais. 3rd ed., 1969, 322p.

HISTORICAL NEGRO BIOGRAPHIES. By Wilhelmena S. Robinson. 2nd ed., 1968, 291p.

I TOO AM AMERICAN: DOCUMENTS FROM 1619 TO THE PRESENT. Compiled by Patricia W. Romero, 1968, 304p.

Two supplementary yearbooks have been published: *IN BLACK AMERICA -- 1968: THE YEAR OF AWAKENING* (edited by Patricia W. Romero) and *IN BLACK AMERICA* (1970).

89. *LIBRARY OF THE BLACK AMERICANS.* St. Clair Shores, Michigan, Scholarly Press Inc., 1975- . To be published in 5 volumes.

To be published in five volumes, the *LIBRARY OF THE BLACK AMERICANS* examines the contributions of Blacks to the culture of the Americas. The first volume, *BOTANY OF THE BLACK AMERICANS* (by William Ed Grime) was issued in 1975; it details the botanical contributions made by Black slaves and citizens. The other volumes planned for the series are *MEDICINE OF THE BLACK AMERICANS, LEGENDS OF THE BLACK AMERICANS, CLOTHING OF THE BLACK AMERICANS,* and *MUSIC OF THE BLACK AMERICANS.*

90. *THE NEGRO ALMANAC*. Compiled by Harry A. Ploski
    and Ernest Kaiser. 2nd ed. New York, Bellwether
    Co., 1971, 1110p.
Also issued as *AFRO-U.S.A.* (1971) and the *REFERENCE
LIBRARY OF BLACK AMERICA* (1971), this handbook presents
a picture of Black life and history through biographical,
bibliographical, statistical, survey and documentary
information. Various chapters cover important events
(chronologically listed), significant documents in
Black American history, civil rights organizations and
their leaders, growth and distribution of the Black
population, Black workers, Black families, the Black
press, Federal employment and government assistance
programs, etc. A detailed index provides an analytical
approach to the text.

91. *THE NEGRO HANDBOOK*. Compiled and edited by Flo-
    rence Murray. New York, W. Malliet and Company,
    1942-9. Biennial.
Issued four times, this handbook provides factual and
statistical information on financial, political, artistic, and religious developments in Black America between
1942 and 1949. "In short, The Handbook is meant to be a
sort of newspaper, without editorial comment." No attempt is made to evaluate or analyze the data in terms
of sociological or economic significance. Material is
organized into subject chapters: population, civil
rights, crime, labor and industry, housing, etc. There
are also separate chapters listing books (by and about
Negroes) and Black organizations. The emphasis is on
current information; little historical comparison is
made. Statistical and biographical information is
included. Each *HANDBOOK* has its own subject index.

92. *THE NEGRO HANDBOOK*. Compiled by the editors of
    EBONY. Chicago, Johnson, 1966, 535p.
For annotation, see Entry No. 81.

93. *THE NEGRO HERITAGE LIBRARY*. Yonkers, New York,
    Educational Heritage, 1964-66, 6v.
In this multivolume set, the publishers have assigned

themselves the task of providing "a truthful and ac-
curate recounting of the Negro's remarkable story."
Each volume contains numerous illustrations, "Notes"
which indicate the sources of information used, a bib-
liography, and an index; there is no overall index to
the set. Some of the volumes in the set are: *THE WINDING
ROAD TO FREEDOM: A DOCUMENTARY SURVEY OF NEGRO EXPER-
IENCES IN AMERICA* (1965), *EMERGING AFRICAN NATIONS AND
THEIR LEADERS* (1964), *NEGROES IN PUBLIC AFFAIRS AND
GOVERNMENT* (1966) and *PROFILES OF NEGRO WOMANHOOD* (1966).

94. *NEGRO YEAR BOOK: AN ANNUAL ENCYCLOPEDIA OF THE
     NEGRO.* By Monroe N. Work. Tuskegee, Alabama,
     Tuskegee Institute Department of Records and
     Research, 1912-52, 11v. Irregular.
Designed as a contemporary record of Blacks in America,
the *NEGRO YEAR BOOK* was issued irregularly between 1915
and 1952, when it ceased publication. Many statistical
tables and some photographs supplement the factual description of Negro life. Both the table of contents and
the index are detailed.

95. *A PICTORIAL HISTORY OF BLACK AMERICANS.* By
     Langston Hughes, Milton Meltzer and C. Eric
     Lincoln. 4th rev. ed. New York, Crown Pub-
     lishers, Inc., 1973, 377p.
The history of Blacks in America from slavery to the
present day is presented through numerous illustrations (old and contemporary photographs and facsimi-
les) and a brief narrative text which highlights
important events and figures. Emphasis is placed on
post-Civil War days. As with earlier editions (the
3rd edition, 1968, was entitled *A PICTORIAL HISTORY
OF THE NEGRO IN AMERICA*), this issue tries "to tell
who the Negro is, where he came from and to show what
he has contributed and how he has affected, and in turn
has been affected by, American life, as well as to
indicate where he is headed." The material is arranged
chronologically within broad topics, with an extensive
table of contents, bibliography, and index.

96. *A PICTORIAL HISTORY OF THE NEGRO IN AMERICA.* By
     Langston Hughes and Milton Meltzer. 3d rev. ed.
     New York, Crown Publishers, Inc., 1968, 380p.
For annotation, see Entry No. 95.

97. *RACE RELATIONS IN THE USA, 1954-68.* Compiled by
     Keesing's Contemporary Archives. New York,
     Scribners, 1970, 280p. (Keesing's Research
     Report, 4).
This is another in a series based on the extensive
research facilities of Keesing's Contemporary Archives
(Earlier numbers do not relate to ethnic studies; they
cover such topics as the Arab-Israeli conflict and the
cultural revolution in China). *RACE RELATIONS IN THE
USA* is an essay-like chronology of events occuring
between the historic 1954 Supreme Court decision and
the 1968 assassination of Martin Luther King, Jr.
Supplementing the textual comments are excerpts taken
from relevant speeches and legislation.

98. *REFERENCE LIBRARY OF BLACK AMERICA.* Compiled
     and edited by Harry A. Ploski, with Otto J.
     Lindenmeyer and Ernest Kaiser. New York, Bell-
     wether, 1971, 5v.
For annotation, see Entry No. 90.

99. *THE SCHOOL BUSING CONTROVERSY: 1970-75.* Edited
     by Judith F. Buncher. New York, Facts on File,
     1975, 267p. (Editorials on File Series).
This is a detailed month-by-month record of the court
decisions, local controversies, and political debates
over school busing which occurred between 1970 and mid-
1975. Included are more than 300 editorials on the
busing issue. In addition, there is a chronology of
key events and a descriptive index.

100. *SEGREGATION AND THE FOURTEENTH AMENDMENT IN THE
      STATES: A SURVEY OF STATE SEGREGATION LAWS 1865-
      1953; PREPARED FOR UNITED STATES SUPREME COURT IN
      RE: BROWN VS. BOARD OF EDUCATION OF TOPEKA.* Edited

by Bernard D. Reams, Jr. and Paul E. Aidson.
Buffalo, New York, William S. Hein and Co.,
Inc., 1975, 761p.

The school segregation cases (e.g., Brown v. Board
of Education of Topeka) were first argued in the U.S.
Supreme Court in 1952. After hearing early arguments,
the Court requested counsel to present briefs and oral
arguments which examined the Fourteenth Amendment and
its impact on racial segregation in public education
and other areas. This book represents the response to
the Court's request. Following a background discussion
is a state by state report of significant segregation
statutes, court cases, and primary legal sources which
relate to racial separation in the period following the
Civil War to 1954. Population tables, commentaries on
equal protection and race, a ratification history of
the Fourteenth Amendment, and a table of cases are
found in the appendices. There is a general index.

101.   *TEACHERS' GUIDE TO AMERICAN NEGRO HISTORY*.   By
        William Loren Katz.   Chicago, Quadrangle Books,
        1971, 192p.

For annotation, see Entry No. 625.

102.   *WORLD ENCYCLOPEDIA OF BLACK PEOPLES*.   St. Clair
        Shores, Michigan, Scholarly Press, 1974, 18v.

This publication was originally announced as the *EN-
CYCLOPEDIA OF THE NEGRO IN AFRICA AND AMERICA*, but it
was published under the title *WORLD ENCYCLOPEDIA OF
BLACK PEOPLES*. Arranged in alphabetical order, this
18 volume set covers contemporary and historical events
in Black culture, tradition and history. Numerous
illustrations, charts, figures, and photographs appear
throughout. One of the volumes is devoted entirely
to citations of materials dealing with Black studies.
There are both comprehensive index and conspectus
volumes.

Spanish Americans

103. *BARRIO LANGUAGE DICTIONARY: FIRST DICTIONARY OF
CALÓ*. By Dagoberto Fuentes and Jóse A. López.
La Puente, California, El Barrio Publications,
1974, 160p.
An attempt has been made on the part of the authors
"to include most of the words that are used univer-
sally by Chicanos. Generally they are words known and
used by a great number of the people in the Barrios of
the United States." Over 1,500 words and expressions
are listed and briefly defined.

104. *CHICANOS: A STUDY GUIDE AND SOURCE BOOK*. By Lynn
P. Dunn. San Francisco, R & E Research Associates, 1975, 122p.
This Chicano study guide is arranged around three themes:
identity, conflict, and integration/nationalism of Chicanos in the United States. Within each of these themes,
the organization is basically chronological. The outline
format is supplemented by citations to appropriate study
materials. A glossary of terms used by and about Chicanos and a bibliography are appended. Similar study
outlines have been prepared by Dunn for Asian Americans
(see Entry No. 53), Blacks (see Entry No. 68), and
American Indians (see Entry No. 21).

105. *COMEXAZ: NEWS MONITORING SERVICE*. Oakland, California, Comité de México y Aztlán, 1973- . Monthly.
To facilitate research on contemporary Chicano activities,
the Comité de México y Aztlán (a non-profit corporation
specializing in educational research about the contemporary Mexicano) clips relevant news articles in seven
American newspapers and reproduces them in *COMEXAZ : NEWS
MONITORING SERVICE*. The following newspapers are moni-

tored: *ARIZONA REPUBLIC, DENVER POST, LOS ANGELES TIMES, SAN ANTONIO EXPRESS, EL PASO TIMES, SAN FRANCISCO CHRONICLE,* and *ALBUQUERQUE JOURNAL.* The service offers comprehensive coverage in the generalized categories of political, educational, economic, and editorial news. Selective coverage is provided in the following areas: sports, archaeology and anthropology, natural disasters and accidents, travel, book reviews, obituaries, social and cultural events, letters to the editor, advertisements, and marriages. The reproduced clippings are indexed by bylines, geographic area, personal names and subject. There is a cumulative annual index.

106. *GUIDE FOR THE STUDY OF THE MEXICAN AMERICAN PEOPLE IN THE UNITED STATES.* By Feliciano Rivera. San Jose, California, Spartan Bookstore, 1969, 226p.
The historical background of Mexican Americans is traced in outline form and complemented by citations to suggested reading sources. Also included are varied documents, black and white photographs, drawings and maps.

107. *A MEXICAN AMERICAN SOURCE BOOK.* By Feliciano Rivera. Menlo Park, California, Educational Consulting Associates, 1970, 196p.
Several types of information are included in this source book. It begins with an outline of Chicano history. The second section is a short, partially annotated bibliography of Chicano newspapers, films and filmstrips. An excerpt from *MISSIONS OF CALIFORNIA* (San Francisco, PG&E, 1970) is reprinted in the next section. There is an extensive pictorial chapter which illustrates 400 years of Spanish culture in the Southwest. In another part of the work, there is an English-Spanish who's who of outstanding Mexican Americans. The Treaty of Guadalupe Hidalgo is reprinted in the last portion of the book.

108. *PUERTO RICAN EXPERIENCE: A SOCIOLOGICAL SOURCEBOOK.* By Francesco Cordasco and Eugene Bucchioni. Totowa, New Jersey, Littlefield Adams and Company, 1973, 397p.

The history of Puerto Ricans in the United States is
divided into three sections in this source: Part I:
The Island Background; Part II: The Migration; and
Part III: Life on the Mainland. Considerable material
is included which deals with educational programs in
general and bilingual education for Puerto Rican students in particular.

109. *THE PUERTO RICANS 1493-1973: A CHRONOLOGY AND FACT
      BOOK.* Compiled and edited by Francesco Cordasco.
      Dobbs Ferry, New York, Oceana Publications, 1973,
      137p. (Ethnic Chronology Series no. 11).
Cordasco's work is one of a series of information sources dealing with ethnic groups issued by Oceana Publications (see Entry No. 11). The first section of the
reference work presents a chronology of dates significant in the history of Puerto Rico and of Puerto Ricans
on the U.S. mainland. The second section of the source
includes documents (whole or excerpted) which concentrate on life among Puerto Ricans on the island or in
mainland cities along the Eastern seaboard. The final
section of the publication is a classified, annotated
bibliography of pertinent Spanish and English books and
articles.

110. *REGIONAL DICTIONARY OF CHICANO SLANG.* By Librado
      Ken Vasquez and Maria Enriqueta Vasquez. Austin,
      Texas, Jenkins Publishing Co., 1975, 111p.
This dictionary lists hundreds of words and their mean-
ings as employed in "Tex-Mex," "Calo," "Pachuquismo,"
"Cali-Mex," and other speech variants used by Spanish
speaking people in the Southwest (particularly in California and Texas). It traces the development of Chicano words, phrases and idiomatic expressions. Printed
in dictionary form, the book also includes tracings of
the probable origin of Chicano regional dialects, a
pronunciation guide, Chicano-Hispana Americano phrases,
sections on Chicano folk medicines and folk songs, a
bibliography, and in index.

111. *THE SPANISH IN AMERICA 1513-1974: A CHRONOLOGY*

AND FACTBOOK. Compiled and edited by Arthur A. Natella, Jr. Dobbs Ferry, New York, Oceana Publications, 1975, 139p. (Ethnic Chronology Series no. 12).

In the twelfth volume of the *ETHNIC CHRONOLOGY SERIES* (see Entry No. 11), Natella has outlined the history and contribution of the Spanish in America between 1513 and 1974, reprinted numerous pertinent documents (e.g., The Treaty of Tordesillas in 1494, the Articles of Agreement between the Viceroy and Don Juan de Oñate in 1595, Father Junipero Serra Reports on California Missions in 1773, the Treaty of Peace with Spain in 1898, etc.) and provided a bibliography of relevant books, articles, and doctoral dissertations in English and Spanish. The purpose of the publication is "to introduce to its readers the background and foundation for the Spanish motif that exists in art, music, movies ... etc., as well as to proudly identify the varied roles that people of Hispanic origin have played in the development of our country." A name index completes the source.

Women

112. *AMERICAN WOMEN AND AMERICAN STUDIES*. By Betty E. Chmaj. Pittsburgh, Know, Inc., 1971, 258p.
For annotation, see Entry No. 683.

113. *CHRONOLOGY OF WOMEN IN AMERICA*. Compiled by Carol Thompson. St. Clair Shores, Michigan, Scholarly Press, 1974, 368p. (The Chronological Library of American Peoples).
THE CHRONOLOGY OF WOMEN IN AMERICA, one volume of *THE CHRONOLOGICAL LIBRARY OF AMERICAN PEOPLES* reference set, concentrates on people and events important in the women's movement. The source contains over 1,000 chronologically arranged subject entries, a general introductory essay, more than 200 illustrations, a

bibliography of sources used, and a detailed cross index. Some of the questions which can be answered by referring to the *CHRONOLOGY* include: When was the first American woman granted a law degree? Who was the first American woman to win a Nobel Prize? When was *MS. MAGAZINE* founded?

114. *DISCRIMINATION AGAINST WOMEN; CONGRESSIONAL HEAR-*
     INGS ON EQUAL RIGHTS IN EDUCATION AND EMPLOYMENT.
     Edited by Catharine R. Stimpson. New York, Bow-
     ker, 1973, 558p.
This publication is an edited transcript of the 91st
Congress' hearings on discrimination against women.
Part 1 is the oral testimonies of 23 witnesses (such
as Shirley Chisholm, Frankie Freeman, Lucy Komisar and
others). Part 2 contains many substantiating documents,
including position papers, surveys, charts and tables.
These documents are arranged by subject areas: women
and work; women and the law; women and education; and
women and the professions; etc. There is an index of
persons and organizations.

115. *ENCYCLOPEDIA OF WOMEN.* Detroit, Encyclopedia
     Publishing Center, 1974- . To be published in
     18v.
Designed to provide comprehensive coverage of thousands
of topics relating to women, feminism and women's history, this multi-volume reference work will contain
over 9,000 articles written by women scholars and editorial advisers. Biographical profiles, organizational
descriptions, historical information, statistical data,
and illustrations (photographs, portraits, foldout maps,
etc.) will be included in the articles. The *ENCYCLOPE-*
DIA will also provide a complete chronology with over
1,400 events listed in order. An entire volume of the
set will be devoted to bibliographic references (21,500
citations to books, articles, and audio-visual materials)
for further reading. The citations, many of which
are annotated, will be arranged by Library of Congress
subject headings, and indexed by author, editor, title,
and series. A detailed index (comprising an entire
volume of the set) will provide access to the other 17

volumes. A pronunciation guide will also be included
in the index volume to help readers with difficult names
and terms. To complete the *ENCYCLOPEDIA*, a yearbook
will be published annually and contain a continuing
chronology, bibliography, and detailed index. In
addition, the publishers plan to issue 13 two-volume
sets (which can be purchased separately) made up of
articles relating to specific topics extracted from the
ENCYCLOPEDIA. The sub-sets will cover: *WOMEN IN SUF-
FRAGE, WOMEN IN ECONOMICS, WOMEN IN EDUCATION, WOMEN IN
MARRIAGE AND FAMILY, WOMEN IN ANTHROPOLOGY, WOMEN IN
PSYCHOLOGY, WOMEN IN LAW, WOMEN IN HISTORY*, etc. The
first of the two volumes in each of these sub-sets will
contain an introductory essay, a chronology, and approximately one-half of the articles; the second volume will
contain the other half of the articles, an annotated
bibliography, and a detailed index to the two volumes.

116. *A GENERAL GUIDE TO ABORTION*. By Bruce Sloane and
      Diana Frank Horvitz. Chicago, Nelson-Hall, 1973,
      265p.
"This book will provide some guidelines and facts about
therapeutic abortion." It covers such topics as relevant laws, moral and religious reactions, techniques,
costs, counseling agencies, etc. Bibliographies are
appended at the end of each chapter. There is a subject index.

117. *HANDBOOK OF WOMEN'S LIBERATION*. By Joan Robins.
      North Hollywood, California, Now Library Press,
      1970, 280p.
This handbook covers a variety of issues relating to
the women's movement: women and the law, women and the
work force, women and sex, media images, lesbianism,
etc. Separate chapters are devoted to each of these
topics. An appendix includes a bibliography of books
and a list of newspapers and journals. Several illustrations and photographs depicting the women's movement supplement the text.

118. *HANDBOOK ON WOMEN WORKERS*. Issued by the U.S.

Women's Bureau. Washington, D.C., G.P.O.,
     1948- . Biennial (Its Bulletin).
For annotation, see Entry No. 396.

119. *MEDIA REPORT TO WOMEN INDEX/DIRECTORY*. Edited
      by Martha Leslie Allen. Washington, D.C., Media
      Report to Women, 1975, 225p.
MEDIA REPORT TO WOMEN is a monthly journal which provides information relating to women in the media:
agreements between broadcasters, magazines, newspapers
and women on their staffs; FCC and court rulings; documentation on ownership and control of print/broadcast
media; responses to excessive sex and violence; steps
women are taking toward obtaining access to the public
through establishing their own newspapers; publishing
houses and recording companies; etc. This information
is indexed by subject, name, organization, and title
in the *MEDIA REPORT TO WOMEN INDEX/DIRECTORY*--a publication which also provides biographic information (address, telephone number, specialization) for media
women and directory information (address, phone, contact
person) for women's media groups (e.g., radio-TV, film,
music, bookstores, library collections, news services,
periodicals, etc.).

120. *THE NEW WOMAN'S SURVIVAL SOURCEBOOK*. Edited by
      Kirsten Grimstad and Susan Rennie. New York,
      Knopf, 1975, 245p.
Intended as a sequel to *THE NEW WOMAN'S SURVIVAL CAT-
ALOG* (see Entry No. 317), the sourcebook provides "an
inventory of the *ideas* of feminism." It is divided
into broad subject (e.g., law and politics, health,
work, etc.). Within these divisions, essays providing
the radical feminist view are followed by critical
bibliographies identifying sources of additional information (books, pamphlets, government documents, periodicals, organizations, resource people, films and other
media). The book uses a *WHOLE EARTH CATALOG* format and
is profusely illustrated. Selective indexing of names,
groups and subjects is provided.

121. *NORTH AMERICAN REFERENCE ENCYCLOPEDIA OF WOMEN'S*
      LIBERATION. Edited by William White, Jr. Phila-
      delphia, North American, 1972, 194p. (North Amer-
      ican Reference Library).
It is the purpose of this encyclopedia "...not only to
present thousands of citations and cross references,
but also to define all the terms generated and defined
by feminists in the context of their writings." Over
20 articles on women in politics, women and the law,
women in education, history, literature, occupations,
etc. are written by Shirley Chisholm, Bella Abzug,
Caroline Bird, Gloria Steinem and other movement leaders. Chapter 7, "Selected and Annotated Directory
and Bibliography of Women's Liberation" lists 3,500
books, articles, newsletters, films, tapes, and women's
organizations. The work is illustrated and includes an
index to references and articles. *REFERENCE ENCYCLOPE-*
DIA ON WOMEN'S LIBERATION is volume one of the *NORTH*
AMERICAN REFERENCE LIBRARY series; volumes two and
three cover drugs and ecology respectively.

122. *NOTABLE THOUGHTS ABOUT WOMEN: A LITERARY MOSAIC*.
      By Maturin Ballou. Boston, Houghton Mifflin,
      1882. Republished by Gryphon Books; distri-
      buted by Gale, 1971, 409p.
Nearly 3,500 quotations dealing with women (e.g., "All
women of the world crave excitement," "What a woman says
to her lover should be written on air or swift water,"
"Woman, the precious porcelain of human clay") are arranged randomly in this source. The author of each
quotation is identified, but no mention is made of the
source from which the statement is taken. An alphabetical list of authors and a subject index are supplied.

123. *RAPE: THE FIRST SOURCEBOOK FOR WOMEN*. Edited by
      Noreen Connell and Cassandra Wilson. New York,
      New American Library, 1974, 283p.
This book "is a direct result of discussions on rape in
New York Radical Feminists consciousness raising groups."
Guidelines for organizing consciousness raising and rape
action groups, the feminist analysis of rape as a form
of social control, medical needs of rape victims, legal

aspects, self-defense tactics and suggestions for feminist action against rape are discussed. A selected
bibliography on rape is appended.

124. *THE RIGHTS OF WOMEN: THE BASIC ACLU GUIDE TO A
WOMAN'S RIGHTS*. By Susan D. Ross. New York,
Sunrise/Dutton, 1973, 384p. (An American Civil
Liberties Union Handbook).
This book is one of an ACLU series on the rights of
various oppressed groups--prisoners, mental patients,
teachers, students, the poor, suspects, and women. It
is written by a woman who serves as a partner in a New
York law firm specializing in feminist litigation. A
question-and-answer format is used to provide information on the following subjects: employment discrimination, education, mass media, crimes and juvenile
delinquency, a woman's right to control her body,
divorce, names and name changes, and the legal system.
Employment discrimination is the most thoroughly covered
topic in the book. The Equal Pay Act, Title VII of the
1964 Civil Rights Act, and Executive Orders 11246 and
11467 are discussed and steps for filing discrimination
claims with governmental agencies are outlined. Four
appendices chart state laws affecting women, procedures
to be followed to change names, sources of legal aid,
and women's organizations. There is no index into the
publication, but there is a fairly detailed table of
contents.

125. *STATE BY STATE GUIDE TO WOMEN'S LEGAL RIGHTS*. By
Shana Alexander. Los Angeles, Willstonecraft,
Inc., 1975, 156p.
Prepared by Shana Alexander, columnist for *NEWSWEEK* magazine, this guide presents information on women's rights
in respect to marriage, divorce, children, work, abortion, rape, widowhood, etc. The material is arranged
state by state within each of these sections. Each chapter has an introduction which identifies differences in
state laws, new trends and developments, and areas in
need of reform. A glossary of terms completes the publication.

126. *WOMEN AND SOCIETY*. Edited by Diana Reische. New
      York, Wilson, 1972, 234p. (The Reference Shelf,
      v. 43, no. 6).
WOMEN AND SOCIETY is part of *THE REFERENCE SHELF* series;
other volumes include *AMERICAN INDIAN: A RISING ETHNIC
FORCE; CIVIL RIGHTS; CRIME: ITS PREVENTION; CRISIS IN
URBAN HOUSING; PARADOX OF POVERTY*. The publication is
comprised of articles reprinted from leading journals
and newspapers, or excerpts from books. Using these
materials, it details the history of women in the
United States as well as the growth of the women's
liberation movement. The work is arranged in four
sections: The Quest for Options, Women in the Market-
place, Some Perspectives--Social and Historical, and
Biology and the Social Role. An extensive bibliography of books, articles, and pamphlets is included.
Like other volumes in *THE REFERENCE SHELF* series, it is
edited objectively to present all points of view on the
topic of women in society.

127. *WOMEN IN TRANSITION: A FEMINIST HANDBOOK ON SEPA-
      RATION AND DIVORCE*. New York, Scribners, 1975,
      538p.
This handbook provides practical information on separation, divorce and related topics in first person narratives written by "women in transition" from marriage to
divorce. Chapters on the legality of common law marriages, legal services, financial resources, mental
health, beatings, rape, and self defense are presented.
A directory of women's centers, clinics, and rape crisis
groups is included. Appended is a bibliography of
relevant reading materials arranged by subject. There
is no index.

128. *WOMEN LAW REPORTER*. Washington, D.C., Women Law
      Reporter, Inc., 1974- . Bi-weekly.
This is a bi-weekly legal service covering judicial,
legislative, and administrative actions involving sex
discrimination. It reports on current developments,
duplicates decisions of relevant cases, provides texts
of legislation and reproduces documents signaling agencies' actions. There is a topic index, an index to

cases and book reviews, and a classified bibliography
of court cases covered in legal periodicals.

129. *WOMEN: THEIR CHANGING ROLES*. Edited by Elizabeth
      Janeway. New York, New York Times/Arno Press,
      1973, 556p. (The Great Contemporary Issues Ser-
      ies).
News items, essays, reports, and advertisements having
to do with women and published in the *NEW YORK TIMES*
from the 1880's through 1972 are included in this publication. Using the material presented, an in-depth
study can be made of women's changing role in every
facet of society--in the home, on the job, and in public
life. Some illustrations are included. The book is
divided into nine sections: Social Feminism, the Twen-
ties, the Thirties, Women and World War II, the Post-
war Period, Women in the Arts, Sexual Emancipation,
Radical Feminism, and Challenge and Change. Access
is provided through a 14 page subject index and a two
page by-line index. A summary of key legislation affecting women through the years and a 27 item supplementary reading list are appended. This book is Volume
IV in *THE GREAT CONTEMPORARY ISSUES* series; other
volumes cover drugs, the sexual revolution, crime and
justice, Black Africa, etc.

130. *WOMEN'S LEGAL HANDBOOK SERIES*. Edited by Lee
      Ellen Ford. Butler, Indiana, Ford Associates,
      Inc., 1975, 2v.
The *WOMEN'S LEGAL HANDBOOK SERIES* is an attempt to "take
the legal format of actual statutes and then translate
same into lay language so that the legal ramifications
are more readily understandable to the average reader
who might not have had opportunity to attend law
school." The first seven volumes cover job and sex
discrimination: the Civil Rights Act, Title VII and
cases, equal pay, Equal Rights Amendment, etc. The
next nine volumes focus on state government affirmative
action programs; in addition to state-by-state reproductions of affirmative action plans, Ford presents
guide-lines for establishing affirmative action plans,
statistics/tables used in affirmative action consider-

ations, and answers to questions frequently raised by
employers unacquainted with affirmative action law and
responsibility. The last five volumes of the set deal
with the right of privacy in public/private records;
privacy bills and statutes in the various states are
presented.

131. *WOMEN'S RIGHTS ALMANAC, 1974.* Edited by Nancy
      Gager. Bethesda, Maryland, Elizabeth Cady Stan-
      ton Publishing Co., 1974, 620p.
Oriented toward women's interests in general and the
national and international women's movement in particular, this classified reference tool provides a variety
of factual and statistical information in four sections.
The first section contains a state-by-state presentation
of statistics and data on organizations, women officials,
employment, demographic characteristics, sources of legal
assistance, etc. The second section provides information
on Federal legislation, women in Congress, and women's
organizations. The third part contains brief essays
on such current women's issues as abortion and lesbianism. The final section includes a chronology of important events, an essay on international feminism and a
list of feminist periodicals. Much of the statistical
information is taken from the U.S. census, but sex
breakdown of state and county officials is a unique
feature. The source also contains a bibliography of
bibliographies, a glossary of feminist terms, a directory for legal assistance and an index. The editor
plans to issue the *ALMANAC* annually.

Chapter 2

BIOGRAPHICAL SOURCES

Minorities

132. *CIVIL RIGHTS: A CURRENT GUIDE TO THE PEOPLE,*
ORGANIZATIONS, AND EVENTS. By Joan Martin Burke.
2nd ed. New York, Bowker, 1974, 266p. (A CBS
News Reference Book).
Originally prepared by the News Research Desk of
Columbia Broadcasting System for its news staff, the
first edition (1970) covered the civil rights movement from 1954 to the end of the 1960's. The second
edition reflects developments which have occurred
since then. It contains comprehensive biographies of
250 persons and groups active in the civil rights
movement since 1945. The sketches (of such leaders
as Angela Davis, Ralph Abernathy and Shirley Chisholm)
provide information on present position, civil rights
activities, publications, civil rights affiliations,
date, and place of birth. In addition, descriptions
of civil rights organizations (such as the Congressional Black Caucus, CORE, NAACP) are provided; each
entry identifies the founders, year of establishment,
history, aims and accomplishments, director, address,
and biographical sketches of the people who have been
prominent in the organization. Finally, information
is also included on the Congressional voting records
on civil rights measures between 1957 and 1970, civil
rights laws passed in various states, a listing of
major sources and collections of works on minority
rights, and a bibliography of civil rights books.

133. *CIVIL RIGHTS DIRECTORY, 1975.* Prepared by the
U.S. Commission on Civil Rights Clearinghouse.
Rev. ed. Washington, D.C., G.P.O., 1975, 224p.
(CHP no. 15).
This directory lists and describes officials of Federal
agencies responsible for enforcing equal opportunity

laws and policies, Federal agencies which administer
social and economic progress programs, private organizations with civil rights programs, and state/county/
municipal agencies with civil rights responsibilities.
The source consists of five sections. Section A lists
officials of Federal agencies who are responsible for
monitoring, administering, coordinating, and enforcing
various aspects of equal opportunity laws and policies.
A name index immediately follows this section. Section
B, "Federal officials with liaison responsibility for
programs of special interest to Mexican Americans"
includes agencies which administer programs "to assist
in furthering the social and economic progress of the
American people." Section C lists organizations which
are concerned almost exclusively with civil rights.
Section D lists official state agencies with civil
rights responsibilities. Section E covers county and
municipal agencies. The first edition was issued in
1968.

134.   *CONTEMPORARY PEOPLE SERIES*. Detroit, Michigan,
        Publishing Center, 1975- .
The *CONTEMPORARY PEOPLE* series is made up of a number
of different volumes: *CONTEMPORARY WOMEN* (See Entry
No. 183), *CONTEMPORARY FOREIGNERS*, *CONTEMPORARY POLITI-
CIANS AND GOVERNMENT OFFICIALS*, *CONTEMPORARY ATHLETES*,
CONTEMPORARY SOCIAL SCIENTISTS, *CONTEMPORARY PEOPLE IN
BUSINESS*, etc. Each volume contains hundreds of biographic profiles with pictures and bibliographies. The
following categories of information are provided in
each sketch: personal, education, career, awards and
honors, future ambitions, sidelights, avocational
interests, personal habits, quotations, and biographical sources. According to the publishers, over 75
percent of the people included in this series are
not covered in any other reference source. Future
volumes will be published periodically with additional
profiles, updating of previous profiles, and cumulating
subject indexes.

135.   *THE EMERGING MINORITIES IN AMERICA: A RESOURCE
        GUIDE FOR TEACHERS*. Edited by Santa Barbara

County Board of Education. Santa Barbara, California, ABC-Clio, 1973, 256p.
Prepared as a specific reference and resource guide for
teachers, this book "is designed to provide assistance
in curriculum development through incorporation into
the curriculum of the cultural and historical contributions of minority groups." The main section of the
source contains 500 biographical sketches of important
Afro-Americans, Asian Americans, Indian Americans, and
Mexican Americans. Each chapter contains a brief introduction to the group, a bibliography of sources used to
prepare the biographical sketches and a listing of
materials dealing with the group. There are two indexes:
a historical index of individuals by periods and an alphabetical index of individuals by subjects.

136. *PATHS TOWARD FREEDOM.* Edited by Frank Emory.
     Raleigh, North Carolina State University. To be
     published in 1976.
PATHS TOWARD FREEDOM provides a biographical history of
over 100 Blacks and Native Americans in North Carolina.
Both historical and contemporary figures are included.
Essays covering the contributions of these two groups
to the history of North Carolina are presented in the
first two sections. The source is indexed.

American Indians

137. *AMERICAN INDIAN PAINTERS: A BIOGRAPHICAL DIREC-
     TORY.* Compiled by Jeanne Snodgrass. New York,
     Museum of the American Indian, Heye Foundation,
     1968, 269p.
Compiled to provide information on American Indian
graphic artists, this directory includes more than
11,000 biographical sketches. It presents information
on the artists' lives and careers, identifying birth
date, marital status, educational background, career

activity, honors, exhibitions, awards, etc. Citations
include both Anglo and Indian names, if both are used.

138. *AMERICAN INDIAN WOMEN*. By Marion E. Gridley.
      New York, Hawthorn Books, 1974, 178p.
For annotation, see Entry No. 177.

139. *BIOGRAPHICAL AND HISTORICAL INDEX OF AMERICAN
      INDIANS AND PERSONS INVOLVED IN INDIAN AFFAIRS*.
      Prepared by the U.S. Department of the Interior.
      Boston, G.K. Hall, 1966, 8v.
For annotation, see Entry No. 468.

140. *BIOGRAPHICAL SKETCHES AND ANECDOTES OF NINETY-
      FIVE OF 120 PRINCIPAL CHIEFS FROM THE INDIAN
      TRIBES OF NORTH AMERICA*. By Thomas L. McKenney
      and James Hall for the U.S. Bureau of Indian
      Affairs. Washington, D.C., G.P.O., 1967, 452p.
Originally published in 1838 and then reprinted by the
Government Printing Office in 1967, this reference work
contains detailed biographical sketches, anecdotes,
and portraits of 95 principal chiefs from Indian tribes
in North America. Included in the set are such notables as Sequoyah (inventor of the Cherokee alphabet),
Young Mahaskan (Chief of the Iowans) and Thayendanegea
(Great Captain of the Six Nations). The data for many
of the biographical sketches were obtained during the
life time of the biographees. Another reprint of the
1838 publication was issued in 1975 by Scholarly Press
under the title *INDIAN TRIBES OF NORTH AMERICA WITH
BIOGRAPHICAL SKETCHES AND ANECDOTES OF THE PRINCIPAL
CHIEFS* (St. Clair Shores, Michigan, Scholarly Press,
1975, 3v).

141. *INDIAN CHIEFS OF SOUTHERN MINNESOTA*. By Thomas
      Hughes. Minneapolis, Ross and Haines, Inc., 1969,
      122p.
The purpose of these sketches is "to record and preserve
the careers and lives of those picturesque and prominent
chieftains of a race that has practically disappeared

from a Southern Minnesota which was once their home, and to make those of us who live there now better acquainted with them and their times." The focus of this source is on prominent chieftains of the Dakota and Winnebago tribes from 1825 to 1865. Newspaper articles, histories, government documents, diaries, narratives, and notebooks were used to write the biographical profiles. These sketches are arranged by chapters, with a general index. Numerous illustrations and portraits supplement the text.

142. *INDIAN TRIBES OF NORTH AMERICA WITH BIOGRAPHICAL SKETCHES AND ANECDOTES OF THE PRINCIPAL CHIEFS.* Edited by Frederick Webb Hodge. St. Clair Shores, Michigan, Scholarly Press, 1975, 3v.
For annotation, see Entry No. 140.

143. *INDIAN WOMEN OF NORTH AMERICA.* Edited by Keith Irvine. St. Clair Shores, Michigan, Scholarly Press, 1975, 382p. (American Indian Biography Series).
For annotation, see Entry No. 189.

144. *INDIANS OF TODAY.* By Marion E. Gridley. 4th ed. Chicago, Indian Council Fire, 1971, 494p.
This fourth edition of *INDIANS OF TODAY* "salutes the many outstanding American Indian leaders who have made, and continue to make, significant contributions to the lives of their people and to the Nation." The editorial thrust of the work is to present Indians in terms of personal accomplishments rather than in the perspective of national prominence. The biographical sketches are arranged randomly; access to the entries is through the name index. Each of the biographies contains factual information (birthplace, education, memberships, etc.) as well as an editorial assessment of the individual's contributions. There are portraits of each of the biographees and numerous illustrations throughout the work. The first edition of *INDIANS OF TODAY* was issued in 1936.

145. *PATHS TOWARD FREEDOM*. Edited by Frank Emory.
     Raleigh, North Carolina State University. To
     be published in 1976.
For annotation, see Entry No. 136.

146. *REFERENCE ENCYCLOPEDIA OF THE AMERICAN INDIAN*.
     Edited by Barry T. Klein and Dan Icolari. Rye,
     New York, Todd Publications, 1974, 2v.
Volume II is "an alphabetically arranged listing of
American Indians prominent in Indian affairs, business,
the arts and professions, as well as non-Indians active
in Indian affairs, history, art, anthropology, archaeology, etc." For a description of the entire set, see
Entry No. 50.

Asian Americans

147. *ASIAN WHO? IN AMERICA*. Compiled and edited by
     Samuel E. Lo. Roseland, New Jersey, published
     by East-West Who? Inc., in cooperation with Seton
     University Press, 1971, 329p.
Biographical sketches of Asians residing in the United
States are presented in this reference source. The
following types of people are included: occupants of
administrative positions in government agencies, educational institutions, businesses and industry; holders
of teaching or research professorships in institutions
of higher learning; recipients of doctoral degrees
from American or foreign universities; and persons with
unique contributions through publications, inventions,
discoveries, pioneering works, artistic or other perfor-
mances and exhibitions. Over 1,000 Asians born or
living in the United States in the early 1970s are
described; information is given on their education,
honors, personal situations, employment, publications,
memberships, etc.

148. *A BIOGRAPHICAL RECORD OF AMERICANS OF JAPANESE*
      ANCESTRY. Edited by Blanche L. Kort. Honolulu,
      Stawe & Associates, 1963, 106p.
"This particular volume is a chronicle of the contributions of Americans of Japanese ancestry to the cultural,
economic, and professional life of our progressive 50th
state. Though it contains the biographies of individuals,
it is, in a sense the collective biography of what has
long been the largest ethnic group in Hawaii -- the
Japanese." Over 200 short, descriptive biographies are
presented. The information given includes education,
professional jobs, marriage, children, hobbies and
interests.

Black Americans

149. *THE AFRO-AMERICAN PRESS AND ITS EDITORS.* By
      I. Garland Penn. New York, Arno, 1969, 565p.
      (American Negro--His History and Literature,
      Series No. 2).
For annotation, see Entry No. 297.

150. *BIOGRAPHIC ENCYCLOPEDIA OF BLACKS.* Chicago,
      World Biography Press, 1976, 10v.
In depth profiles of 7,750 Blacks--both living and
deceased--who have made significant contributions to
life and culture are included in this biographical
source. Each profile is between 500 and 3,500 words, was
written by a biographic expert with information supplied
by the biographee, and contains a comprehensive annotated bibliography. Many portraits are included. Updating and additional profiles will be issued periodically to keep the set current.

151. *A BIOGRAPHICAL HISTORY OF BLACKS IN AMERICA SINCE*
      1528. By Edgar A. Toppin. New York, McKay, 1971,

499p.
This book grew out of a series of articles published in
the *CHRISTIAN SCIENCE MONITOR* (1969) and an educational
TV course prepared by Toppin. It is arranged in two
sections. The first part consists of 15 chronologically
arranged essays (covering pre-history through 1971).
Suggestions for additional readings supplement this
section. The second part of the book consists of biographical sketches of 145 contemporary and historical
Black figures arranged alphabetically. The biographies
are also listed by vocation and historical time period.
There is a general index.

152. *BLACK DEFENDERS OF AMERICA: 1775--1973; A REFER-
ENCE AND PICTORIAL HISTORY.* By Robert Ewell Greene.
Chicago, Johnson Publishing Company, 1974, 416p.
"This partial account of Negro military personnel in
the armed forces from 1775 until 1973 is presented as
a reference and guide for those who want to learn the
truth about America's neglected black soldiers, sailors,
marines and airmen. Using pictures and documented biographies, an attempt has been made to illustrate the
black American's presence in the past and present wars."
The material is arranged chronologically in 10 chapters,
each dealing with the period of a particular war--from
the American Revolution to the Vietnam conflict. Each
chapter is introduced by a short statement which discusses the part played by Blacks in that war. Some
persons only indirectly connected with the armed services
are included (e.g., Crispus Attucks and Robert E. Lee's
body servant, Reverend William Mack Lee). Hundreds of
photographs accompany the biographical sketches. The
source of information for each sketch is identified.
References are provided in each chapter and there is
an extensive bibliography of books, articles, and government publications at the end of the book. Included
in the appendices are: 1) photographs of Black commissioned and noncommissioned officers; 2) a chronology of
important contributions Blacks have made to U.S. military; and 3) a collection of documents related to Black
involvement in military affairs. There is a name index.

153. *BLACK FACES IN HIGH PLACES: NEGROES IN GOVERNMENT*.
By Helen G. Edmonds. New York, Harcourt, Brace,
Jovanovich, 1971, 277p.
This is an illustrated directory of over 500 American
Blacks who have held political offices in local, state,
or Federal government through 1970. For each entry,
job descriptions and tests of accomplishments are provided. The source is arranged by branch of government
(legislative, judicial and executive). There is a name
index.

154. *BLACK HISTORIANS: A CRITIQUE OF BLACK HISTORIANS*.
By Earl E. Thorpe. Rev. ed. New York, Morrow,
1971, 260p.
This is a "study of the Black historian in the broadest
and most inclusive sense. Any Afro-American who wrote
history, as distinct from other literary forms such as
poetry, drama, fiction and autobiography, has been included." These historians are grouped into several
schools: The Beginning School (1800 - 1896), The Middle
Group (1896 - 1930), The Modern Laymen (1896 to the
present), and The New School (1930 - 1960). Also included is a section on writers of church history. Both
major and minor historians are covered. They are discussed in terms of quantity of their writings, literary
merits, training in historical methodology, philosophy
of history, breadth and soundness of their interpretations of historical events, objectivity, and impact
which their writings have had on people of their own
and subsequent periods. There is a 10 page selected
bibliography and a general index. An earlier edition
(*NEGRO HISTORIANS IN THE UNITED STATES*) was published
by Fraternal Press in 1958.

155. *BLACK PROFESSIONALS IN PREDOMINATELY WHITE INSTI-
TUTIONS OF HIGHER EDUCATION*. Edited by Melvin P.
Sikes and Paul E. Meacham. Austin, Texas, Hogg
Foundation for Mental Health, University of Texas,
1973, 135p.
Black professionals working in predominately white
academic institutions are listed by state and indexed
by name. Each entry generally provides the following

information: job title, school, address and educational
background. The data were collected through a mailed
survey initiated by the First National Congress of
Black Professionals in Higher Education in 1972.

156. *CONTEMPORARY BLACKS*. Detroit, Biography Publish-
      ing Center, 1975, 4v.
Two thousand in-depth biographic profiles of living
Blacks throughout the world are presented in this
four volume work. Pictures and portraits accompany
the entries which are arranged in alphabetical order
by individuals' last name. Future four volume units
will be issued periodically and will include up-dating
of the original volumes, more than 2,000 new profiles,
and a cumulative index to all volumes.

157. *DIRECTORY OF BLACK HISTORIANS, PH.D's AND OTHERS
      1975-1976: ESSAYS, COMMENTARIES AND PUBLICATIONS*.
      By Gossie Harold Hudson. Monticello, Illinois,
      Council of Planning Librarians, 1975, 196p. (Ex-
      change Bibliographies nos. 870-2).
This directory presents information on Blacks and others
currently teaching Black history. Over 500 individuals
are identified. The information given for each of these
teachers includes addresses, positions, degrees, and
thesis topics. There are several indexes which provide
data broken down by degree, field, sex, and location.
The directory also has a section of five essays by
historians writing on the field of Black history.

158. *FAMOUS FIRST BLACKS*. By Joan Horn. New York,
      Ace Books, 1976, 203p.
FAMOUS FIRST BLACKS is a comprehensive survey, in narrative and picture form, of 100 Black men and women who
have achieved a first in government, music, science, theater, education, sports, or many other fields. Contemporary and historical figures are covered. Some of the
biographees include Marian Anderson, Jesse Owens, Wilma
Rudolph, Duke Ellington, Gwendolyn Brooks, and Bill Cosby.

159. *GREAT NEGROES, PAST AND PRESENT*. By Russell L.
     Adams. 3rd rev. ed. Chicago, Afro-American Co.,
     1969, 212p.
The lives of over 175 important historical and contemporary Blacks (primarily American) are arranged chronologically (from 720 B.C. through 1967) with such broad
subject headings as science and industry, business, and
education. The biographical sketches include the usual
personal and occupational data and average a page in
length. Each biography is accompanied by footnotes giving references to articles and books by and about the
biographees as well as a portrait drawn by Eugene Wins-
low. Many of the subjects included are seldom written
about in other biographical sources, such as Ulysses Kay.

160. *HISTORICAL NEGRO BIOGRAPHIES*. By Wilhelmena S.
     Robinson. 2nd ed. New York, Publishers Co.,
     1968, 291p. (International Library of Negro
     Life and History).
HISTORICAL NEGRO BIOGRAPHIES is a collection of 500
biographical sketches of Black diplomats, explorers,
authors, etc. living between the 14th century and the
20th century in all parts of the world. The historical and cultural background of the Black is emphasized.
Arranged in chronological order, the average entry is
400 words. The volume is illustrated and includes a
bibliography. In addition to a name index, there is
an index by occupation. This volume is part of the
INTERNATIONAL LIBRARY OF NEGRO LIFE AND HISTORY set
(see Entry No. 88).

161. *IN BLACK AND WHITE: AFRO-AMERICANS IN PRINT: A
     GUIDE TO AFRO-AMERICANS WHO HAVE MADE CONTRIBU-
     TIONS TO THE UNITED STATES OF AMERICA FROM 1619
     TO 1975*. Edited by Mary Mace Spradling. 2nd ed.
     Kalamazoo, Michigan, Kalamazoo Library System,
     1976, 505p.
This is a listing of Black Americans who have contributed to American history and culture between 1619 and
1975. Popular entertainers and athletes along with
professionals and scholars are included. For each
biographee, information is given on birth and death

dates, occupation, and sources where additional data
can be obtained. The work is arranged alphabetically
and is supplemented by an occupation index. There is
also a list of books, magazines and newspapers analyzed
in preparing this publication.

162. *NATIONAL ROSTER OF BLACK ELECTED OFFICIALS*. Wash-
     ington, D.C., Joint Center for Political Studies,
     1969- . Irregular.
The *NATIONAL ROSTER OF BLACK ELECTED OFFICIALS* is a
census of Blacks holding elective offices in the United
States. In addition to names, the *ROSTER* identifies
for each entry the title of office, the jurisdiction
the official represents, a mailing address, and the
year in which the current term of office expires. The
office holders are listed in the following categories:
Federal, state, county, municipal, law enforcement, and
education. The 1975 edition lists nearly 3,000 Blacks
holding public elective office in the various states and
the District of Columbia. In the index, Black elected
officials are listed alphabetically by category of office
(e.g., Federal senators, state legislators, municipal
governing bodies, justices of the peace, local school
boards, chiefs of police, etc.).

163. *NEGRO HISTORIANS IN THE UNITED STATES*. By Earl
     E. Thorpe. Baton Rouge, Louisiana, Fraternal
     Press, 1958, 188p.
For annotation, see Entry No. 154.

164. *THE NEGRO VANGUARD*. By Richard Bardolph. New
     York, Rinehart, 1959, 388p.
The "vanguard" refers to the 1,000 "most celebrated
Negro Americans" between 1770 and 1959 chosen for inclusion in this source. Social commentary accompanies the
biographical sketches. The "Essay on Authorities" lists
other sources a researcher can use for additional biographical information. Bardolph's book was reprinted in
1972 by Negro University Press.

165. *NEGROES IN PUBLIC AFFAIRS AND GOVERNMENT*. Edited
     by Walter Christmas. Yonkers, New York, Educa-
     tional Heritage, 1966, 352p. (Negro Heritage
     Library).
NEGROES IN PUBLIC AFFAIRS AND GOVERNMENT is a biographical directory providing descriptions (one or more
pages each) of Black men and women working in five
areas: the United Nations, Congress, the judiciary,
the diplomatic corps and U.S. executive agencies. Both
contemporary and historical figures are included.
Numerous photographs and drawings illustrate the text.
Introductions precede each section and there is a four
page general bibliography. For each section, "Notes"
identify the sources (interviews, periodicals, newspapers, etc.) from which information was obtained. A
name index completes the work. Originally, two volumes
were planned, but only one has been issued to date.
The volume is part of the *NEGRO HERITAGE LIBRARY* set
(see Entry No. 93).

166. *PATHS TOWARD FREEDOM*. Edited by Frank Emory.
     Raleigh, North Carolina State University. To
     be published in 1976.
For annotation, see Entry No. 136.

167. *PROFILES OF NEGRO WOMANHOOD*. By Sylvia G.L.
     Dannett. Yonkers, Educational Heritage, 1964-6,
     2v. (Negro Heritage Library).
For annotation, see Entry No. 93.

168. *THE VOICE OF BLACK AMERICA: MAJOR SPEECHES BY
     NEGROES IN THE UNITED STATES, 1797-1971*. By
     Philip S. Foner. New York, Simon and Schuster,
     1972, 1215p.
For annotation, see Entry No. 258.

169. *WHO'S WHO AMONG BLACK AMERICANS, 1975/6-* .
     Northbrook, Illinois, Educational Communications,
     Inc., 1976- . Annual.
WHO'S WHO AMONG BLACK AMERICANS is planned to feature

complete biographies of high achieving and leading Blacks
at the local, community and national levels: professionals, celebrities, political figures, educators, businessmen, community organizers, etc. Over 10,000 biographical
sketches are to be included. They are to be arranged
alphabetically and indexed by career and geographical
location. The first edition of the source is scheduled
for publication in 1976.

170. *WHO'S WHO IN COLORED AMERICA; AN ILLUSTRATED
     BIOGRAPHICAL DIRECTORY OF NOTABLE LIVING PERSONS
     OF AFRICAN DESCENT IN THE UNITED STATES.* Yonkers,
     New York, Christian E. Burckel, 1927-50, 7v.
     Irregular.
Alphabetically arranged, *WHO'S WHO IN COLORED AMERICA*
identifies prominent Black Americans in all walks of
life. Inclusion is based upon two factors: either position (academic, religious, judicial, legislative, social,
military) or personal achievements. Only people living
at the time of the publication are included. The brief
entries include name, date and place of birth, marriage,
number of children, education, awards, publications,
positions held, current position and current address.
Many photographs accompany the biographical sketches.
The seven volumes in the series were issued irregularly
between 1927 and 1950.

171. *WORLD'S GREAT MEN OF COLOR.* By J.S. Rogers. Edited,
     with an introduction, commentary and new bibliogra-
     phical notes by John Henrik Clarke. New York,
     Macmillan, 1972, 2v.
Rogers' two volume biographical work was first published
in 1947 in a small private edition and was reprinted in
1972 by Macmillan. His purpose "was not to write highly
critical and psychoanalytical, or even literary essays,
but rather principally success stories, chiefly for
Negro youth." The 200 biographees (who are at least one-
eighth Black) span the years 300 B.C. to 1946 and are
arranged geographically. They include Hannibal, Alek-
sander Pushkin, Samuel Coleridge and Nat Turner. The
second volume has short entries of famous persons unrec-
ognized as part Black: e.g., Robert Browning, Beethoven

and Mohammed. Some photographs or portraits are included. The present edition (1972) has been expanded
somewhat from the original 1947 publication to include
an introduction, commentaries, and bibliographic notes.
There is no index.

Spanish Americans

172. *THE MEXICAN-AMERICAN DIRECTORY*. Edited by Arturo
      Palacios. Washington, D.C., Executive Systems
      Corporation, 1969/70- . Irregular.
The purposes of this compilation are to "provide sta-
ture to members of a minority culture by focusing attention on Mexican-Americans; provide public agencies
and the private sector with an appropriate vehicle by
which they may identify qualified professionals and
para-professionals; provide governmental agencies with
a compilation of personnel with expertise in the area
of Mexican-Americans; provide private community organizations with a compilation of personnel that can be used
for a coordinated effort between organizations for
recruitment and/or for consultant services." The listing
is not restricted to either Mexican-Americans or college
graduates; rather, it includes: 1) Mexican-Americans
who are prominent, distinguished or visible within
their communities or at the state and national levels,
regardless of academic degrees or credentials and 2)
a few people from other ethnic groups who have contributed to the Mexican-American community. The entries
are arranged alphabetically by surname and include
information provided by the respondents on: occupation,
birthplace and date, education, military service,
spouse, employment, memberships, awards and honors,
publications and addresses. Only one volume of the set
has been issued to date.

173. *NATIONAL DIRECTORY OF CHICANO FACULTY AND RESEARCH.*

By Renée Mares. Los Angeles, Aztlán Publications,
   1975, 175p.
Over 1,400 Chicano faculty and researchers are listed in
this directory.   Mexican researchers with an interest
in the Chicano are also included. For each biographee,
information is given on academic background, publications,
current and projected teaching, and research interests/
activities.

174. *NATIONAL ROSTER OF SPANISH-SURNAMED ELECTED OFFI-
       CIALS*. Compiled by Frank Lemus. Los Angeles,
       Aztlán Publications, 1974, 120p.
This directory includes over 2,000 names of Spanish
surnamed officials (Chicanos, Mexican-Americans, Puerto
Ricans, Latin Americans, Spanish Americans and Cuban
Americans) at all levels of government throughout 28
states in the United States. Its entries are arranged
by state and include the following information: name,
address, office, party affiliation, ethnic self identification, and last year of office. The listing is complete as of June, 1973. It is anticipated by the author
that the *ROSTER* will be periodically up-dated.

175. *SPANISH SURNAMED AMERICAN COLLEGE GRADUATES, 1971-
       72*. Prepared for the U.S. Cabinet Committee on
       Opportunity for the Spanish Speaking. Washington,
       D.C., G.P.O., 1971, 2 pts.
The Spanish surnamed graduates of over 800 colleges and
universities are listed alphabetically by state in this
directory intended to help employers interested in recruiting from this group.   Majors and graduation dates
are specified for each student. Tables are provided
which show the total number of graduates and the graduates' distribution by discipline.

176. *WHO'S WHO: CHICANO OFFICEHOLDERS, 1975-76*. By
       Arthur D. Martinez. Silver City, New Mexico,
       Bookstore, Western New Mexico University, 1976,
       225p.
Elected and appointed Chicano officeholders during the
1975-76 period are identified in this biographical

directory. Addresses and telephone numbers are included in each entry. Over 1,100 listings are provided.
The source is arranged by level of government (Federal,
state and local).

Women

177.   *AMERICAN INDIAN WOMEN*. By Marion E. Gridley.
       New York, Hawthorn Books, 1974, 178p.
Biographies and portraits of prominent American Indian
women past and present are included in this reference
work prepared by Marion Gridley, a prolific author of
books on American Indians. Some of the women included
in the source are Maria and Marjorie Tallchief, Susan
La Flesche Picotte, Sacajawea and Pocahontas. The
profiles are narrative, not chronological. Portraits
accompany the sketches. A two-page bibliography and
an analytic index complete the work.

178.   *THE AMERICAN WOMAN IN COLONIAL AND REVOLUTIONARY
       TIMES, 1565-1800; A SYLLABUS WITH BIBLIOGRAPHY*.
       By Eugenie A. Leonard and Sophie Drinker. Phila-
       delphia, University of Pennsylvania Press, 1962, 169p.
For annotation, see Entry No. 682.

179.   *AMERICAN WOMEN: FIFTEEN HUNDRED BIOGRAPHIES WITH
       OVER 1,400 PORTRAITS; A COMPREHENSIVE ENCYCLOPEDIA
       OF THE LIVES AND ACHIEVEMENTS OF AMERICAN WOMEN
       DURING THE NINETEENTH CENTURY*. Detroit, Gale
       Research Company, 1973, 2v.
For annotation, see Entry No. 197.

180.   *AMERICAN WOMEN: THE STANDARD BIOGRAPHICAL DICTION-
       ARY OF NOTABLE WOMEN: VOLUME III, 1939-40*. Edited
       by Durward Howes. Los Angeles, American Pub.,

1939; reprinted, Teaneak, New Jersey, Zephyrus,
1974, 1083p.
Biographical information of the who's who type covering
over 10,000 women living in the 1930s is found in this
reprint of the third and last volume of *AMERICAN WOMEN*.
A necrology list refers to women included in the first
and second volumes. The biographies (of such women as
Secretary of Labor Perkins and novelist Caroline Gordon)
were compiled from information supplied in questionnaires. Useful features of the book include a geographic index, an occupation index, a directory of women's
organizations, and statistical summaries of the age,
education, marital status and political affiliation
of the women included.

181. *BIOGRAPHICAL ENCYCLOPEDIA OF WOMEN*. Chicago,
     World Biography, 1975, 14v.
In-depth profiles of 12,438 living and deceased notable
women, who have made significant contributions to the
culture and life of the world, are presented in this
14 volume work. Arranged alphabetically, the entries
are between 500 and 3,500 words and each includes a
comprehensive, annotated bibliography. A subject index
and reference guide complete the source. The work is
profusely illustrated.

182. *BLACK WOMEN IN WHITE AMERICA: A DOCUMENTARY HIS-
     TORY*. Edited by Gerda Lerner. New York, Pantheon,
     1972, 630p.
For annotation, see Entry No. 262.

183. *CONTEMPORARY WOMEN*. Detroit, Biography Publish-
     ing Center, 1975, 4v.
CONTEMPORARY WOMEN contains profiles of over 2,000
living women throughout the world. The publishers
claim that "over 75 percent of the individuals represented are not included in any other reference source."
The entries are arranged alphabetically by the individual's last name. A typical profile is divided into
11 basic sections: personal, education, career, awards,
future ambitions, sidelights, avocational interests,

favorite and famous quotes, portrait, biographical
sources, bibliography. Over 2,400 pictures, photographs and illustrations supplement the text. Future
four volume units will be issued periodically and
will 1) up-date the previous volumes, 2) present more
than 2,000 new profiles, and 3) serve as a cumulative
index to all previously issued volumes.

184. *DIRECTORY OF WOMEN ATTORNEYS IN THE UNITED STATES*.
     Edited by Lee Ellen Ford. 3rd ed. Butler, In-
     diana, Ford Associates, 1974, 142p.
This mimeographed reference directory lists over 6,000
women attorneys in the United States. The only information provided covers name and address; to obtain
data on the lawyers' place of employment, education,
degrees, current position, etc., check *MARTINDALE-
HUBBELL LAW DIRECTORY* (Summit, New Jersey, Martindale-
Hubbell, 1943-). The *DIRECTORY OF WOMEN ATTORNEYS
IN THE UNITED STATES* is arranged alphabetically according to state of residence. A revision is planned for
every two years.

185. *FAMOUS AMERICAN WOMEN*. By Hope Stoddard. New
     York, Crowell, 1970, 461p.
Over 40 women important in American history and life
are described in this biographical source (Susan B.
Anthony, Mary Cassatt, Dorothea Dix, Lillian Gilbreth,
Margaret Chase Smith, Harriet Tubman, "Babe" Dedrikson
Zuharias, etc.). The publication is arranged alphabetically. Full page photographs of each woman accompany the sketches. Short bibliographies are provided
for each woman. There is an extensive general index
(21 pages).

186. *FAMOUS WOMEN: AN OUTLINE OF FEMININE ACHIEVEMENT
     THROUGH THE AGES WITH LIFE STORIES OF FIVE HUN-
     DRED NOTED WOMEN*. By Joseph Adelman. New York,
     The Pictorial Review, 1926, 328p.
Famous women of the world are described in this reference
source. The work is divided into 10 chapters; each
chapter deals with a different time period (e.g., 2100

B.C. to 1135 A.D.; 1860-1877; notable women living in
1925). About one-half page is devoted to a profile
of each biographee. There is an index in the front of
the source which classifies the women by activity (e.g.,
rulers, social leaders, reformers, educators, scientists,
authors, actresses, etc.). Sixteen full page paintings
and photographs of important women are included.

187. *FOREMOST WOMEN IN COMMUNICATIONS.* Edited by
      Barbara J. Love. New York, Bowker, 1970, 788p.
Short biographical sketches of over 8,000 women distinguished for their accomplishments and contributions to
communications are contained in this reference source.
The field of communications includes broadcasting, publishing, advertising, public relations, library science
and allied areas. The information for the sketches was
submitted by the subjects themselves. Entries are arranged alphabetically by name. Each sketch describes
present position, location, career history, professional
activities, achievements, honors, education, parents' names,
etc. A geographic index and a subject cross-index to
areas of professional concentration are appended.

188. *INDEX TO WOMEN OF THE WORLD FROM ANCIENT TO MODERN
      TIMES.* By Norma Ireland. Westwood, Massachusetts,
      Faxon, 1970, 573p. (Useful Reference Series of
      Library Books, Vol. 97).
For annotation, see Entry No. 708.

189. *INDIAN WOMEN OF NORTH AMERICA.* Edited by Keith
      Irvine. St. Clair Shores, Michigan, Scholarly
      Press, 1975, 382p. (American Indian Biography
      Series).
Biographies and portraits of 25 prominent American
Indian women past and present are included in this
reference work issued by the editors of the *ENCYCLO-
PEDIA OF INDIANS OF THE AMERICAS* (see Entry No. 30).
Some of the women included in the source are Dolly
Smith Akers (tribal leader elected to the Montana leg-
islature), Maria Tallchief (noted Osage ballet dancer)
and Sarah Winnemaucca (a Paiute called the "Indian Joan

of Arc"). Full page portraits accompany each profile.
INDIAN WOMEN OF NORTH AMERICA is one volume in the
AMERICAN INDIAN BIOGRAPHY SERIES; other titles include:
INDIAN WARRIORS OF NORTH AMERICA and *CONTEMPORARY AMER-
ICAN INDIAN LEADERS*.

190.   *A MINORITY OF MEMBERS: WOMEN IN THE U.S. CON-
       GRESS, 1917-1972.* By Hope Chamberlin. New York,
       Praeger, 1974, 374p.
The lives of 85 U.S. Congresswomen are documented in
this biographical reference source. The information
was obtained from interviews, diaries, letters, and
other personal documents. Claire Booth Luce, Shirley
Chisholm, Bella Abzug, and Margaret Chase Smith are
some of the women included. Arrangement is chronological. The biographical sketches vary in length from
less than one page to over 10 pages. Some photographs
are included. An alphabetical list of the Congresswomen, giving political party, state, and pertinent
dates for each, is appended.

191.   *NOTABLE AMERICAN WOMEN, 1607-1950: A BIOGRAPHI-
       CAL DICTIONARY.* Edited by Edward T. James and
       Janet W. James. Cambridge, Harvard University
       Press, 1971, 3v.
This three volume biographical dictionary was prepared
under the auspices of Radcliffe College and patterned
after the *DICTIONARY OF AMERICAN BIOGRAPHY* (which
covers only 700 women in its 15,000 entries). Nearly
1,400 women of distinction in all fields (artists,
musicians, political figures and wives of presidents)
living between 1607 and 1950 are included. The
articles vary in length from 400 to 7,000 words and
include bibliographies. Most of the signed entries
were written by scholars and experts, although there
is no list of contributors. Volume Three contains a
list of selected biographies classified by vocation.
The extensive preface to the source forms a concise
chronological history of American women.

192.   *PROFILES OF NEGRO WOMANHOOD.* By Sylvia G.L.

Dannett. Yonkers, Educational Heritage, 1964-6,
2v. (Negro Heritage Library).
Numerous illustrations (both drawings and photographs)
supplement the textual descriptions of Black American
women who made major contributions to their race and/or
their country during the last 300 years; volume one
covers the period 1619-1900 and volume two concentrates
on the 20th century. Each of the volumes is arranged
by subject (e.g., women in the Civil War, giants of
race advancement, educators, government officials, civil
rights activists, etc.), has bibliographies of general
biographical source material, includes a "Notes" section
which identifies sources from which information was
obtained, and concludes with a name index. This publication is part of the *NEGRO HERITAGE LIBRARY* (see Entry
No. 93).

193. *TWO THOUSAND WOMEN OF ACHIEVEMENT.* Edited by
      Ernest Kay. London, Melrose Press, 1969-72,
      4v.
This biographical reference work "exists to pay due
tribute and honour to those of distinguished achievement (whether professional, regional, national or
international) in many countries of the world." Entries from the United States predominate. Inclusion
is by invitation; respondents provide information to
the publishers through questionnaires. The profiles,
which are alphabetically arranged, range from 50 to
150 words in length. Most are accompanied by photographs. A companion four volume set, *TWO THOUSAND MEN
OF ACHIEVEMENT,* has been issued.

194. *UP FROM THE PEDESTAL; SELECTED WRITINGS IN THE
      HISTORY OF AMERICAN FEMINISM.* Edited by Aileen
      S. Kraditor. Chicago, Quadrangle Books, 1968,
      372p.
For annotation, see Entry No. 268.

195. *WHO'S WHO AND WHERE IN WOMEN'S STUDIES.* Edited
      by Tamar Berkowitz, Jean Mangi and Jane Williamson
      Old Westbury, New York, Feminist Press, 1974, 256p.

For annotation, see Entry No. 322.

196. *WHO'S WHO OF AMERICAN WOMEN; A BIOGRAPHICAL*
     DICTIONARY OF NOTABLE LIVING AMERICAN WOMEN.
     Chicago, Marquis-Who's Who, 1958/9- . Biennial.
WHO'S WHO OF AMERICAN WOMEN attempts to reflect "the
significant progress that women have made in all fields
of human endeavor, and it seeks to call attention to
women whose achievements have not, heretofore, been
recognized on this scale." Included are all women in
the latest edition of *WHO'S WHO IN AMERICA* (Chicago,
Marquis- Who's Who, 1899-) as well as others who are
"women outstanding as women" in business, politics,
the professions, science, the fine arts, entertainment,
and athletics. In most cases, the information is
supplied by the biographees. Arrangement is alphabetical by surname. The 25,000 entries cover such
matters as marital status, occupation, birthplace and
date, parentage, education, honors, family, career
history, associations, memberships, political and
religious affiliations, publications, and addresses.

197. *A WOMAN OF THE CENTURY, 1470 BIOGRAPHICAL SKET-*
     CHES ACCOMPANIED BY PORTRAITS OF LEADING AMERI-
     CAN WOMEN IN ALL WALKS OF LIFE. Edited by
     Frances Willard and Mary Livermore. Buffalo,
     Moulton, 1893, 812p.
This biographical directory is one of the basic sources
of information on nineteenth century American women.
The 1,470 profiles are alphabetically arranged and
range in length from 300 to 1,000 words. An informal
style of presentation is followed throughout. Photographs and an occupation index add to this reference
work. In 1901, the directory was revised and issued
under the title *PORTRAITS AND BIOGRAPHIES OF PROMINENT
AMERICAN WOMEN*. In 1973, the original work was reprinted under the title *AMERICAN WOMEN: FIFTEEN HUNDRED
BIOGRAPHIES WITH OVER 1,400 PORTRAITS; A COMPREHENSIVE
ENCYCLOPEDIA OF THE LIVES AND ACHIEVEMENTS OF AMERICAN
WOMEN DURING THE NINETEENTH CENTURY* (Detroit, Gale,
1973, 2v.).

198. *WOMAN'S RECORD; OR, SKETCHES OF ALL DISTINGUISHED
     WOMEN, FROM THE CREATION TO A.D. 1854.* Compiled
     by Sarah Hale. New York, Harper, 1855, 912p.
     Distributed by Source Book Press, 1971.
Dedicated to the "Men of America," *WOMAN'S RECORD* is a
compilation of over 2,500 biographical sketches of note-
worthy women from antiquity to the 1850s. The purpose
of the book is to help people "understand what God had
intended women should do; what she has done; and what
further advances are needed to fit her to perform well
her part." The book was prepared by Sarah Hale, 19th
century editor of *GODEY'S LADIES BOOK*. She includes a
lengthy preface to this directory in which she discusses
the superiority of women and presents selections from
the "choicest gems of thought, fancy, and feeling" of
female literature. Over 230 portraits illustrate the
text. The entries are arranged in four time periods
(creation to the birth of Christ; from Christ to 1500;
1500-1850; women of prominence in 1854). There is a
name index in the front of the volume.

199. *WOMAN'S WHO'S WHO OF AMERICA: A BIOGRAPHICAL
     DICTIONARY OF CONTEMPORARY WOMEN OF THE UNITED
     STATES AND CANADA, 1914-1915.* Edited by John
     William Leonard. New York, American Common-
     wealth, 1914, 961p. Reprinted by Gale Research,
     1975.
This biographical dictionary provides information on
women in North America during the time of the suffra-
gette movement. The usual biographical type information is supplemented by a statement of the biographees'
reactions to the suffrage movement. The work is arranged alphabetically by surname. An index providing
cross reference to married names is also included.

200. *WOMEN IN ANTIQUITY: AN ANNOTATED BIBLIOGRAPHY.*
     By Leanna Goodwater. Metuchen, New Jersey,
     Scarecrow Press, 1975, 171p.
For annotation, see Entry No. 731.

201. *WOMEN IN PUBLIC OFFICE: A BIOGRAPHICAL DIRECTORY*

AND STATISTICAL HANDBOOK. Compiled by the Eagleton Institute of Politics, Center for the American Women and Politics, Rutgers University. New York, Bowker, 1976, 455p.
Over 13,000 elected and appointed women officials--U.S. and state legislators, cabinet members, governors, mayors, commissioners, judges and councilwomen--are profiled in this directory. Arrangement is geographical: by state and within each state by level of office and name. The following biographical data are given: full name, current position and title, date elected or appointed, posts held on commissions and committees, past political positions, education, publications, place and date of birth, and home and office addresses. An appendix includes a statistical analysis of the data collected and a name index. Future editions plan to expand the coverage from state and local levels to presidential and Federal offices and women in Federal service.

202. *WOMEN IN THE UNITED STATES CONGRESS, 1917-1972: THEIR ACCOMPLISHMENTS, WITH BIBLIOGRAPHIES.* Littleton, Colorado, Libraries Unlimited, 1974, 184p.
The accomplishments of the 81 Congresswomen serving between 1917 and 1972 are chronicled in this biographical source. The emphasis is not on the lives of the women, but on their achievements in Congress. Edna Flannery Kelly, Maude Kee, and Shirley Chisholm are examples of the Congresswomen included. The source is arranged by house of Congress and then chronologically by term of office. The information provided includes party affiliation, state, years of congressional service, and a discussion of accomplishments during those years. A bibliography of books and articles provides additional information for each Congresswoman. In addition, a general bibliography of materials relating to women, women in politics, etc. is appended.

203. *WOMEN LAWYERS IN THE UNITED STATES.* Edited by Dorothy Fisch Thomashower. New York, Scarecrow Press, 1957, 747p.

This specialized biographical dictionary provides data
on 6,000 women lawyers practicing in the United States
during the 1950s. The amount and depth of information
varies greatly. The briefest entry gives only name,
place of admittance to the bar and an address. Generally, however, the following information is provided:
name, present position and type of practice, birthplace
and date, parentage, family, education, honors, where
and when admitted to the bar, professional experience,
professional memberships, publications, and addresses.
A geographical index, arranged by state, is appended.
An earlier work, *DIGEST OF WOMEN LAWYERS AND JUDGES*
(Louisville, Kentucky, Hunne Press, 1949, 480p.),
offers similar information about both lawyers and judges.

204. *WOMEN OF THE 80TH- CONGRESS*. Washington, D.C.,
        U.S. Women's Bureau, 1947- . Biennial.
A biennially published directory, this source contains
both photographs and brief sketches of the women who
have been elected to the Senate and the House of Representatives during that period. Included, also, is
a statistical table showing the number of women who have
served in Congress from 1917 to date. The title of this
work varies. Between 1947 and 1951, it was issued as
WOMEN IN THE ... CONGRESS. In 1953-4, it was published
as *WOMEN MEMBERS OF THE 83RD CONGRESS*.

205. *WOMEN OF THE WEST*. Compiled and edited by Max
        Binheim. Los Angeles, Publishers Press, 1928,
        223p.
Contained in this reference source are a series of
biographical sketches of living eminent women in 11
Western states: Arizona, California, Colorado, Idaho,
Montana, Nevada, New Mexico, Oregon, Utah, Washington,
and Wyoming. The biographees are arranged alphabetically within each state and there is an alphabetic
index of surnames. Some photographs of prominent
women in each state are included. Each entry provides
the following information: birthday, parentage, relatives, marital status, work history, publications,
memberships and addresses.

206. *WOMEN'S ORGANIZATIONS AND LEADERS DIRECTORY.*
Edited by Myra E. Barrer and Lester A. Barrer.
Washington, D.C., Today Publications and
News Services, 1973- . Annual.
This directory is a guide to over 20,000 women's organizations, their leaders and prominent individuals
active in the women's movement in the United States,
the Canal Zone, Guam, Puerto Rico, and the Virgin
Islands. Entries for the individuals listed include
name, address, telephone number, current occupation
and position, publications, and special interests/
activities in the women's movement. Organizational
entries include name, address, telephone numbers for
national, state, and local officers, chapters, committees, task forces, membership data, year founded,
number of chapters, publications, objectives, current
and proposed activities, and significant achievements.
Access is provided through the alphabetical arrangement
of the text and also through an entry number which
appears in the alphabetical index, the geographical
index, the subject area index, and the periodical
index.

207. *THE WORLD WHO'S WHO OF WOMEN.* Edited by Ernest
Kay. Cambridge, England, Melrose, 1973, 976p.
Nearly 7,000 biographies of women in all professions
throughout the world are included in this reference
work (politicians, actresses, singers, dancers, musicians, writers, lecturers, doctors, lawyers, scientists,
etc.). The entries are arranged alphabetically by last
name. Information for each entry includes: education,
career history, publications, honors, awards, and address. Portraits generally accompany the text. The
United States and England are emphasized. The data
presented in the source were gathered through questionnaires. Generally, the questionnaires were not returned
from non-English speaking countries and from many well
known feminists who refused inclusion. Consequently,
many prominent women (e.g., Ayn Rand, Shirley Chisholm,
Bella Abzug, Joyce Carol Oates, etc.) are not included.

Chapter 3

DOCUMENTARY SOURCES

Minorities

208. *THE ANNALS OF AMERICA: 1493-1973*. Edited by
Mortimer J. Adler, Charles Van Doren and others.
Chicago, Encyclopedia Britannica, 1968-1974, 22v.
This 22 volume publication presents a chronological
record of American life, action and thought between
1493 and 1973 through over 2,200 original writings
(laws, on-the-scene reports, reminiscences, stories,
transcriptions of dialogues, etc.) and 5,000 illustrations. Many of the selections are written by or
about minorities. The 18 textual volumes are arranged
in chronological order and contain (in addition to the
documents and illustrations) an introductory essay, a
10-20 page chronology of the period covered and a biographical index to the authors in the volume. Each of
the volumes presents approximately 100 documents which
cover a specific time period in American history (e.g.,
"Resistance and Revolution, 1775-83").

These selections are indexed by theme in the two volume
Conspectus section which is made up of 25 "Great Issues"
(e.g., law enforcement, rights of minorities, workers,
and urban America) and 50 subjects. There are essays
tracing each of the 25 "Great Issues" through American
history and each of these issues is further subdivided
into the 50 topics which refer to specific documents in
the textual volumes (the organization is similar to the
Encyclopedia Britannica's *GREAT BOOKS OF THE WESTERN
WORLD*). Cross references are made from each chapter of
the two volume Conspectus to relevant documents in the
ANNALS, from the *ANNALS* to articles in the *GREAT BOOKS*
series and from the *ANNALS* to articles in the *ENCYCLO-
PEDIA BRITANNICA* and *COMPTON'S ENCYCLOPEDIA*. There is,
however, no index to the people, places or events covered in the documents.

A one volume supplement is issued to the set annually.

Every five years, additional *ANNAL* volumes are planned.
While there is considerable similarity between the
ANNALS and *MAKERS OF AMERICA* (see Entry No. 215), there
is little overlap between the two sources.

209. *THE CIVIL RIGHTS ACT OF 1964.* Prepared by the
staff of the Bureau of National Affairs. Washington, D.C., B.N.A., 1964, 424p.
For annotation, see Entry No. 7.

210. *ETHNIC CHRONOLOGY SERIES: CHRONOLOGY AND FACT
BOOKS.* Dobbs Ferry, New York, Oceana Publica-
tions, 1971- . 16v.
For annotation, see Entry No. 11.

211. *FAIR EMPLOYMENT PRACTICE CASES.* Washington, D.C.,
The Bureau of National Affairs, Inc., 1969- .
Irregular.
Opinions of Federal and state courts and administrative
agencies under Federal and state laws relating to employment discrimination based on race, color, creed,
sex, national origin or age are reprinted in this set.
Court opinions are reported in full under the official
name of the cases. Preceding each opinion are summary
paragraphs which provide identification of the rulings
made by the court that decided the case. Digests of
the decisions of the Equal Opportunity Commission are
presented in a separate section. There is a parallel
table of cases (to the *LABOR RELATIONS REFERENCE MANUAL*)
as well as a table of cases. The set is kept up-to-date
by the looseleaf service *LABOR RELATIONS REPORTER: FAIR
EMPLOYMENT PRACTICE CASES* (see Entry No. 213).

212. *FAIR EMPLOYMENT PRACTICES MANUAL.* Washington, D.C.,
The Bureau of National Affairs, Inc., 1937- .
Weekly looseleaf service.
For annotation, see Entry No. 214.

213. *LABOR RELATIONS REPORTER: FAIR EMPLOYMENT PRACTICE*

CASES. Washington, D.C., The Bureau of National
Affairs, Inc., 1937- . Weekly looseleaf service.
This looseleaf service contains the full text of opinions of Federal and state courts under Federal and
state laws relating to employment discrimination based
on race, color, creed, sex, national origin, or age.
It also contains digests of decisions of the Equal
Employment Opportunity Commission. The contents of
this source are reprinted and bound periodically without change of page numbers as the publication *FAIR
EMPLOYMENT PRACTICE CASES* (see Entry No. 211).

214. *LABOR RELATIONS REPORTER: FAIR EMPLOYMENT PRAC-
     TICES MANUAL*. Washington, D.C., The Bureau of
     National Affairs, Inc., 1937- . Weekly loose-
     leaf service.
The *FAIR EMPLOYMENT PRACTICES MANUAL* combines the text
of Federal and state laws with editorial explanations
of the laws and court rulings interpreting them. Also
included are forms, charts, and directories relevant
to the equal employment area and a section reviewing
the policies and practices of companies and unions in
developing their own Fair Employment Practices Program.

215. *MAKERS OF AMERICA*. Edited by Wayne Moquin. Chi-
     cago, Encyclopedia Britannica, 1971, 10v.
MAKERS OF AMERICA is designed as a "documentary history
of the ethnic pluralism of America." Over 80 separate
ethnic, national and religious minorities are included.
More than 700 editorials, letters, excerpts from diaries, songs, sermons, magazine articles, etc. written
between 1536 and 1970 by and about the minority groups
are chronologically arranged. The selections are not
limited to writings of well-known persons, although
many famous names are included. Each of the selections
are reprinted in modern spelling; there are no facsimile
reproductions. There are, however, copies of over 1,000
photographs and drawings to illustrate the text.

Each volume contains a table of contents outlining four
to six chapter sections and each chapter is introduced
by a comprehensive essay. The tenth volume contains

five separate indexes (ethnic group, proper name, subject, illustration and author/source) and a bibliography of recommended readings. The set is quite similar to *THE ANNALS OF AMERICA* in organization, but fewer than 10 percent of the selections can be found in both works (see Entry No. 208).

216. *STATUTORY HISTORY OF THE UNITED STATES: CIVIL RIGHTS*. Edited by Bernard Schwartz. New York, Chelsea House in association with McGraw-Hill, 1970, 2v.

Volume 1 of this legislative history presents relevant documents through the Repeal Act of 1894. The second volume includes selections printed between 1900 and the Civil Rights Act of 1968. The source is chronologically arranged and contains edited legislative source material, congressional debates or congressional committee reports, court decisions relating to the legislation and informative introductory remarks. The index makes it easy to locate specific statutes or debates dealing with civil rights.

American Indians

217. *THE AMERICAN INDIAN AND THE UNITED STATES: A DOCUMENTARY HISTORY*. Edited by Wilcomb E. Washburn. New York, Random House, 1973, 4v.

This four volume compilation consists of 216 primary source documents which trace "the essence of the special relationship between the American Indian and the United States" from 1763 through 1973. The volumes are divided into five sections and each section is arranged in chronological order: 1) reports of the Commissioners of Indian Affairs; 2) congressional debates on Indian affairs; 3) laws, acts and ordinances; 4) major peace treaties; 5) judicial decisions affecting the Indian. Each section is introduced by a one or two page summary of the material and the reasons for including the sel-

ected documents. Similarly, each document is preceded
by a brief paragraph which describes its background.
An extensive 92 page general index completes the work.

218. *THE AMERICAN INDIAN 1492-1970: A CHRONOLOGY AND
      FACT BOOK.* Compiled and edited by Henry C. Dennis.
      Foreword by Robert L. Bennett. Dobbs Ferry, New
      York, Oceana Publications, 1971, 137p. (Ethnic
      Chronology Series no. 1).
For annotation, see Entry No. 20.

219. *A BIBLIOGRAPHY OF THE CONSTITUTIONS AND LAWS OF
      THE AMERICAN INDIANS.* By Lester Hargrett. Cam-
      bridge, Harvard University Press, 1947, 124p.
The constitutions, statutes, session acts and resolutions passed by the 13 "properly authorized bodies of
semi-independent and self-governing Indian tribes and
nations of the United States" cited in this bibliography have been reproduced on microfilm by KTO Microform
(the U.S. Division of Kraus-Thomson Organization Ltd.).
For a description of Hargrett's bibliography, see Entry
No. 462.

220. *A BIBLIOGRAPHY OF THE ENGLISH COLONIAL TREATIES
      WITH THE AMERICAN INDIANS INCLUDING A SYNOPSIS
      OF EACH TREATY.* By Henry F. De Puy. New York,
      AMS Press, 1972, 50p. (Reprint of a 1917 edition).
For annotation, see Entry No. 464.

221. *CHARTERS, CONSTITUTIONS, AND BY-LAWS OF THE IN-
      DIAN TRIBES OF NORTH AMERICA.* By George Emery Fay.
      Greeley, Colorado State College Museum of Anthro-
      pology, 1967-70, 9v. (Occasional Publications in
      Anthropology. Ethnology Series, no. 1-18).
Reproductions of charters, constitutions and by-laws
of present day Indians of North America make up this
nine volume set. The work is arranged by cultural and
geographic areas.

222. *CODE OF FEDERAL REGULATIONS. TITLE 25: INDIANS.*
      Prepared by the Office of the Federal Register,
      U.S. General Services Administration. Washington,
      D.C., G.P.O., 1975, 519p.
The *CODE OF FEDERAL REGULATIONS* (in 50 titles) is a
codification of the general and permanent rules published in the *FEDERAL REGISTER* by executive departments
and agencies of the Federal government. *TITLE 25* focuses on Indians. Chapter 1 covers rules issued by
the Bureau of Indian Affairs. The Indian Arts and
Crafts Board and the Indian Claims Commission are
covered in the remaining two chapters. The following
finding aids are provided at the end of *TITLE 25:*
parallel tables of statutory authorities and rules;
parallel tables of presidential documents; guide to
FEDERAL REGISTER finding aids; and a list of acts re-
quiring publication in the *FEDERAL REGISTER*. There is
also a separately published index to all 50 titles in
the *CODE*. The *CODE OF FEDERAL REGULATIONS* is kept up-
to-date by the individual issues of the *FEDERAL REGISTER*.

223. *THE CONSTITUTIONS AND LAWS OF THE AMERICAN INDIAN
      TRIBES.* Wilmington, Delaware, Scholarly Resour-
      ces Inc., 1973, Series I, 20v; Series II, 35v.
Reproduced in this 55 volume set are the written constitutions, treaties, acts, resolutions, and laws of American Indian tribes issued before 1906 (when tribal
governments in Indian Territory were abolished). Included in these two series are documents from the Creeks,
Muskogees, Chickesaws, Osages, Chactaws, Cherokees, etc.

224. *DECISIONS OF THE INDIAN CLAIMS COMMISSION.* New
      York, Clearwater Publishing Company, Inc., 1973,
      microfiche (The Library of American Indian Af-
      fairs).
The Indian Claims Commission was created on August 13,
1946 to serve as a tribunal for the hearing and deter-
mination of claims against the United States filed by
any Indian group. Nearly 400 petitions were filed with
the Commission. The claims consisted largely of "unconscionable consideration claims" arising from the cession
of aboriginal title lands. The claims are reproduced

by Clearwater Publishing Company in *EXPERT TESTIMONY BEFORE THE INDIAN CLAIMS COMMISSION: THE WRITTEN REPORTS* (see Entry No. 227). The decisions reached in these cases are reproduced in *DECISIONS OF THE INDIAN CLAIMS COMMISSION*. The decisions are accessed through the *INDEX TO THE DECISIONS OF THE INDIAN CLAIMS COMMISSION*; for a description of this source, see Entry No. 497.

225. *DOCUMENTS OF UNITED STATES INDIAN POLICY*. Edited by Francis Paul Prucha. Lincoln, University of Nebraska Press, 1975, 278p.

Excerpts from treaties, reports of Bureau of Indian Affairs officials, executive actions, congressional laws and court decisions focusing on Federal Indian policy between 1783 and 1973 are reproduced in this one volume collection. There is an introduction to each document. The source is indexed.

226. *DOCUMENTS RELATING TO INDIAN AFFAIRS, 1754-1765*. Edited by William McDowell, Jr. Columbia, University of South Carolina Press, 1970, 675p. (Colonial Records of South Carolina Series: No. 2).

DOCUMENTS RELATING TO INDIAN AFFAIRS is one volume in the *COLONIAL RECORDS OF SOUTH CAROLINA SERIES* prepared by the South Carolina Department of Archives and History. The source begins with a lengthy introduction which discusses the conditions of the Indians, the settlers, the traders, the colonies, and the European colonial powers between 1754-1765. The main body of the volume reprints documents relating to Indian affairs during the period covered. The major tribes represented in the documents are the Chactaws, Cherokees, Chickesaws, Creeks, Savannahs, and Tellicos. The documents cover diplomatic and commercial relations, relations between the Indians of the North and the South, and those between the Indian and the white man. There is an extensive index. This compilation serves as a sequel to McDowell's earlier work: *DOCUMENTS RELATED TO INDIAN AFFAIRS, MAY 21, 1750 - AUGUST 7, 1754* (Columbia, University of South Carolina Press, 1958).

227. *EXPERT TESTIMONY BEFORE THE INDIAN CLAIMS COM-
     MISSION: THE WRITTEN REPORTS.* New York, Clear-
     water Publishing Company, Inc., 1973, microfiche.
     (The Library of American Indian Affairs).
The Indian Claims Commission was created on August 13,
1946 to serve as a tribunal for the hearing and deter-
mination of claims against the United States filed by
any Indian group. Nearly 400 petitions were filed
with the Commission and are reproduced on microfiche
by the Clearwater Publishing Company. The claims consist largely of "unconscionable consideration claims"
arising from the cession of aboriginal title lands.
Format and quality of each claim varies. Most, however,
include maps or other illustrations. Many include extensive bibliographies and tables of contents. Some
are as short as 10 pages, but most of them are considerably longer; the longest is 5,000 pages. The reports
are accessed by using the *INDEX TO THE EXPERT TESTIMONY
BEFORE THE INDIAN CLAIMS COMMISSION:* for a description
of this source, see Entry No. 498.

228. *GREAT DOCUMENTS IN AMERICAN INDIAN HISTORY.* Edi-
     ted by Wayne Moquin and Charles Van Doren. New
     York, Praeger, 1973, 416p.
Nearly 100 primary source documents describing the history and life of American Indians are presented in this
compilation. The documents are selected from many
sources, but the majority of them are taken from government sources. The documents are arranged in
three sections: tribal life; Indian-white relations
from the early 17th century to the end of the 19th
century; pan-Indian efforts from 1900-1970. Explana-
tory headnotes and exact citations to original sources
are given for many of the documents. A short bibliography and a name index complete the book.

229. *GUIDE TO AMERICAN INDIAN DOCUMENTS IN THE CONGRES-
     SIONAL SERIAL SET: 1817-1899.* By Steven L. John-
     son. New York, Clearwater Publishing Company,
     Inc., 1976, 400p.
For annotation, see Entry No. 486.

230. *INDIAN AFFAIRS*. Edited by Thomas C. Cochran. Wilmington, Delaware, Scholarly Resources, Inc., 1972, 13v. (New American State Papers).
Government documents covering Indian relations included in the *NEW AMERICAN STATE PAPERS* issued between 1789 and 1960 are reprinted in this 13 volume set.

231. *INDIAN AFFAIRS: LAWS AND TREATIES*. Compiled and edited by Charles J. Kappler. Washington, D.C., G.P.O., 1904-41, 5v.
All laws, treaties, presidential proclamations and important court decisions related to Indian Affairs from the organization of the government to 1939 are reprinted in this five volume set. Volume 1 contains laws relating to individual tribes through 1902; an appendix has statistical information, spelling of Indian names, etc. Volume 2 contains treaties and agreements concluded between the United States and Indian tribes from 1778 to 1883, arranged chronologically. Volume 3 continues the compilation through 1913; volume 4 continues it through 1927; and volume 5 continues it through June 29, 1938. Each volume has a separate section for unratified treaties. Volumes 3 through 5 include annotations and citations from the opinions of the courts, the Secretary of the Interior, the Attorney General and the Comptroller of the Currency. There is a comprehensive index to the first four volumes in Volume 4. Volume 2 was published separately in 1972 by Interland Publishing Company under the title *INDIAN TREATIES, 1778-1883* (see Entry No. 232).

232. *INDIAN TREATIES, 1778-1883*. Compiled and edited by Charles J. Kappler. New ed. New York, Interland Publishing Company, 1972, 1099p.
The complete text of every (382) treaty and agreement concluded between the United States and Indian tribes from 1778 to 1883 is reprinted "as they were written and signed and ratified by all parties concerned." All documents are arranged in chronological order and indexed alphabetically. This source was originally published as volume 2 of Kappler's five volume *INDIAN*

AFFAIRS: LAWS AND TREATIES (see Entry No. 231).

233. *THIS COUNTRY WAS OURS: A DOCUMENTARY HISTORY OF
     THE AMERICAN INDIAN.* By Virgil J. Vogel. New
     York, Harper and Row, 1972, 473p.
Nearly 300 pages of this work are devoted to primary
source documents concerned with American Indian history
from 1492 to 1972. A variety of materials are represented: laws, treaties, official reports, letters,
court decisions, and party platforms. The documents
are arranged chronologically within five broad chapters:
1) Before Columbus came; 2) From discovery to the Revolutionary War; 3) From the Revolutionary War to the Civil
War; 4) From the Civil War to the present; 5) The Indian
in perspective. Each chapter contains a concise introduction. The documents represent a variety of subjects
and points of view, from the Royal Proclamation of King
George closing the West to white settlement in 1763
to President Harrison's version of the Wounded Knee
massacre to political party platform statements relating to Indians. One-third of the book is a bibliography and a series of appendices. The extensive
bibliography lists books pertaining to Indian history
and culture. The appendices include short biographies
of famous Indians, basic chronologies, and a list of
audio-visual aids, museums, government agencies, Indian organizations and publications concerned with
Indians. There is a general index.

234. *UNITED STATES CODE ANNOTATED. TITLE 25: INDIANS.*
     St. Paul, Minnesota, West Publishing Co., 1963;
     1976 pocket supplement, 253p.
TITLE 25 of the *UNITED STATES CODE ANNOTATED* contains the
"laws of a general and permanent nature relating to Indians,
including all amendments and enactments..." The general Indian laws relating to property, mineral rights,
and allotments are contained in this volume, and Chapter 14 embodies the bulk of legislation terminating
Federal supervision over certain Indian tribes and
authorizing the distribution of tribal and judgment
funds to their respective members. Only laws currently
in effect at the time of the volume's publication are

included here. References are made throughout the work to statutes and court decisions. Historical notes and cross references to related subjects are also provided. A separate index to the text of the laws contained in *TITLE 25* is included. The work is kept up to date with pocket supplements. The text of laws relating to Indians currently in force can also be found in the *UNITED STATES CODE. TITLE 25: INDIANS* (Washington, D.C., G.P.O., 1971; Supplement, 1974).

Asian Americans

235. *THE CHINESE IN AMERICA 1820-1973: A CHRONOLOGY AND FACT BOOK.* By William L. Tung. Dobbs Ferry, New York, Oceana Publications, 1974, 150p. (Ethnic Chronology Series no. 14).
For annotation, see Entry No. 54.

236. *THE JAPANESE IN AMERICA 1843-1973: A CHRONOLOGY AND FACT BOOK.* Compiled and edited by Masako Herman. Dobbs Ferry, New York, Oceana Publications, 1974, 152p. (Ethnic Chronology Series no. 15).
For annotation, see Entry No. 57.

237. *THE KOREANS IN AMERICA 1882-1974: A CHRONOLOGY AND FACT BOOK.* Compiled and edited by Hyung-Chan Kim and Wayne Patterson. Dobbs Ferry, New York, Oceana Publications, 1974, 147p. (Ethnic Chronology Series no. 16).
For annotation, see Entry No. 58.

Black Americans

238. *AFRO-AMERICAN HISTORY SERIES.* With new introductions and notes by Maxwell Whiteman. Wilmington, Delaware, Scholarly Resources Inc., 1972,
10v.
Included in this 10 volume set are reproductions of
slave narratives, writings by Black intellectuals,
selections from Black drama and poetry, excerpts from
convention pamphlets, etc.

239. *THE AFRO-AMERICANS: SELECTED DOCUMENTS.* Edited
by John H. Bradey, Jr., August Meier and Elliott
Rudwick. Boston, Allyn and Bacon, 1972, 751p.
Presented in this compilation are 67 documents covering
such topics as slavery, Black workers, urban ghettos
and racial conflict. These selections, written by
such notables as Douglass, Dubois, Turner, Washington,
Hughes, Garvey and Sojourner Truth, are preceded by a
short introduction. There is no index.

240. *AMERICAN NEGRO FOLKLORE.* By J. Mason Brewer.
New York, Quadrangle/New York Times Book Co.,
1968, 448p.
This anthology is divided into 10 sections: Tales; The
Negro's Religion; Songs; Personal Experiences; Superstitions; Proverbs; Rhymes; Riddles; Names; and Children's
Rhymes and Pastimes. A brief introduction precedes each
of these sections. Sources are cited for the folklore.
Musical notations accompany the songs. Illustrations
are included. There is an index. A paperback reprinting
of this work was issued by Quadrangle in 1974.

241. *THE BLACK BOOK.* By Middleton Harris with Morris

Levitt, Roger Furman and Ernest Smith. New
York, Random House, 1973, 198p.
The *BLACK BOOK* reproduces handbills, old newspaper
articles, advertisements, sheet music, photographs,
and poems created by Blacks or describing the Black
experience in America. The work is arranged in chronological order. Historical narrative puts the documents in perspective.

242. *BLACK WOMEN IN WHITE AMERICA: A DOCUMENTARY
     HISTORY*. Edited by Gerda Lerner. New York,
     Pantheon, 1972, 630p.
For annotation, see Entry No. 262.

243. *BLACKS IN AMERICA 1492-1900: A CHRONOLOGY AND
     FACT BOOK*. Compiled by Irving J. Sloan. 3rd
     rev. ed. Dobbs Ferry, New York, Oceana Publi-
     cations, 1971, 149p. (Ethnic Chronology Series
     no. 2).
For annotation, see Entry No. 72.

244. *THE BOOK OF NEGRO HUMOR*. Selected and edited by
     Langston Hughes. New York, Dodd, Mead, 1965,
     265p.
Included in this collection are prose and poetry selections which represent the "best of American Negro
humor." The selections are taken from the Cool
Comics; commedians such as Jackie Mabley, Dan Burley,
and Dick Gregory; jokes and jive; dialect tales; and
the works of many authors (James Baldwin, Arno Bon-
temps, Zora Neal Hurston, Ted Poston, Richard Wright
and others).

245. *THE CIVIL RIGHTS ACT OF 1964*. Prepared by the
     staff of the Bureau of National Affairs. Wash-
     ington, D.C., B.N.A., 1964, 424p.
For annotation, see Entry No. 7.

246. *CIVIL RIGHTS AND THE AMERICAN NEGRO; A DOCU-*

MENTARY HISTORY. Edited by Albert P. Blaustein
and Robert L. Zangrando. New York, Trident
Press, 1968, 671p.
Unlike other civil rights compilations (e.g., *CIVIL
RIGHTS RECORD,* Entry No. 247), considerable attention
is paid to the Negroes' legal position prior to the
Civil War in this documentary history. Extracts from
appropriate court decisions and legislation supplement
the authors' narrative. Special chapters describing
the social thought of the era provide historical perspective for the documents.

247. *THE CIVIL RIGHTS RECORD, BLACK AMERICANS AND
THE LAW, 1849-1970.* By Richard Bardolph. New
York, Crowell, 1970, 558p.
The purpose of this source is to narrate, in chronological order, the Negro's struggle for civil rights in
the courts, state legislatures and the U.S. Congress
from Reconstruction times through 1970. Official documents (presidential speeches, party platforms, court
decisions, laws, etc.) are presented without major
modifications. The reader can trace the history of
"Jim Crow" laws, school segregation, prohibition of
interracial marriage, busing of students and labor
force participation. Information notes describe the
contemporary social, political and legal climate in
which these civil rights events occurred. There is an
index to court cases as well as a general index to the
information presented.

248. *A DOCUMENTARY HISTORY OF THE NEGRO PEOPLE IN THE
UNITED STATES.* Edited by Herbert Aptheker. Se-
caucus, New York, Citadel Press, 1951-   , 3v.
Aptheker's documentary history is planned as a three
volume work. The first volume, published in 1951,
covers the period 1661 to 1910. The second volume
continues the coverage to 1932. The third volume, covering 1932 through the end of World War II, is soon to
be published. The documents, which are arranged chronologically under descriptive titles, include descriptions of working conditions and racism, voting, commun-
ism, lynching, and Pan-Africanism. Commentaries

precede these groups of documents (which are reprints
of newspaper and journal articles, letters and other
writings). Sources of the documents and their location in repositories are indicated. There is an index
to names and subjects in volume 2.

249. *ENCYCLOPEDIA OF BLACK FOLKLORE AND HUMOR.* Edited
      by Henry D. Spalding. Illustrated by Rue Knapp.
      Middle Village, New York, Jonathan David Publi-
      shers, Inc., 1972, 589p.
For annotation, see Entry No. 83.

250. *EYEWITNESS: THE NEGRO IN AMERICAN HISTORY.* 3rd
      edition. By William L. Katz. New York, Pitman,
      1974, 554p.
Excerpts from letters, articles, addresses, essays,
etc. are brought together in this source to provide
an eyewitness view of Afro-American life from the
16th century through the 1960's. Historical background is provided for the documents. There are
numerous illustrations and an index. The first edition of this work was issued in 1967.

251. *GREAT DOCUMENTS IN BLACK AMERICAN HISTORY.* Edi-
      ted by George Ducas, with Charles Van Doren.
      Introduction by C. Eric Lincoln. New York,
      Praeger, 1970, 321p.
Ducas has assembled 22 basic documents in Black American history ranging from John Woolman's "Some Consi-
derations on the Keeping of Negroes (1754)" to LeRoi
Jones' "The Legacy of Malcolm X, and the Coming of
Age of the Black Nation (1966)." Long passages are
taken from the works of Douglass, Turner, Washington,
DuBois and Richard Wright. Each document is preceded
by a statement which places the item in historical
perspective. Illustrations of important individuals
and events are included. There is a brief index.

252. *I TOO AM AMERICAN. DOCUMENTS FROM 1619 TO THE
      PRESENT.* New York, United Publishers Co., 1970,

304p. (International Library of Negro Life and History).

Nearly 300 addresses, letters, speeches, essays and other materials portray within three chronological sections the struggle of Black Americans for freedom. Most of the documents are taken from nongovernmental sources (e.g., Douglass' 1848 letter to his former master, Richard T. Greener's 1880's speech supporting the northern migration of Blacks), although some laws and court cases are included. Introductory notes provide background for the speeches. Repository locations are indicated. A detailed table of contents and index complete the source. This documentary history is one volume in the *INTERNATIONAL LIBRARY OF NEGRO LIFE AND HISTORY* set (see Entry No. 88).

253. *IN THEIR OWN WORDS: A HISTORY OF THE AMERICAN NEGRO, 1619-1966.* By Milton Meltzer. New York, Crowell, 1964-1967, 3v.

This three volume work presents the story of American Negroes in their own words--through letters, diaries, journals, autobiographies, speeches, resolutions, newspapers, pamphlets, etc. The volumes are chronologically arranged (1619-1865; 1865-1916; 1916-1966) and span the time when Blacks served as slaves in colonial America to their participation in the civil rights movement in the 1960's. Each document is preceded by a brief introduction. In addition, the volumes each contain a calendar of Negro history, a reading list and a subject index.

254. *JUDICIAL CASES CONCERNING AMERICAN SLAVERY AND THE NEGRO.* Edited by Helen T. Catterall. New York, Octagon Press, 1968, 5v.

Court cases dealing with American slavery or Negro affairs prior to 1875 are arranged chronologically by state. Abbreviated quotations of facts followed by an abbreviated version of the judicial opinion make up the entries for each case. Volume 1 presents English cases; volume 2 covers the oldest colonies and early American cases; the states, Canada and Jamaica are treated in the succeeding three volumes.

This edition is a reprint of the original set published between 1926 and 1937 by Negro University Press.

255. *LABOR AND SLAVERY*. Edited by Thomas C. Cochran.
Wilmington, Delaware, Scholarly Resources, Inc.,
1973, 7v. (New American State Papers).
Documents dealing with labor and slavery issued be-
tween 1789 and 1860 are reproduced from the *NEW AMER-
ICAN STATE PAPERS* in this seven volume set.

256. *THE NEGRO AMERICAN; A DOCUMENTARY HISTORY*. Edited
by Leslie H. Fishel, Jr. and Benjamin Quarles.
New York, Morrow, 1970, 608p.
Over 200 documents portraying the role of Blacks in
American history from 1500-1965 are arranged chronologically within subject subdivisions. There are
numerous illustrations. Subject and title indexes
complete the source.

257. *THE NEGRO IN AMERICAN HISTORY*. Edited by Mortimer Adler, Charles Van Doren and George Ducas.
Rev. ed. Chicago, Encyclopedia Britannica, 1972,
3v.
This reference work contains 195 primary source materials written by 144 different authors covering over
400 years of American history (back to 1567) reprinted
in chronological order. Each document is accompanied
by an introduction which describes the historical
circumstances surrounding it. Volume 1 covers "Black
America 1928-1971;" volume 2 deals with "A Taste of
Freedom 1854-1927;" volume 3 documents "Slaves and
Masters 1567-1854." Photographs and illustrations are
included. There is a general index to all three volumes. Each volume has a separate list of authors
which provides very brief biographical information.
Many of the selections included here can also be
found in *THE ANNALS OF AMERICA* (Entry No. 208), a
20 volume set from the same publisher.

258. *THE VOICE OF BLACK AMERICA: MAJOR SPEECHES BY*

NEGROES IN THE UNITED STATES, 1791-1971. By
Philip S. Foner. New York, Simon and Schuster,
1972, 1215p.
Speeches by Black Americans are presented in six chron-
ologically arranged sections, covering the period 1791
to 1971. Included are selections from Sojourner Truth,
Booker T. Washington, Langston Hughes, Marcus Garvey,
Paul Robeson, John Hope Franklin, Martin Luther King,
Jr., Whitney M. Young, Jr., Dick Gregory, Malcolm X,
James Baldwin, Adam Clayton Powell, Stokely Carmichael,
Edward Brooke, H. Rap Brown, Eldridge Cleaver, and
Julian Bond, among others. Each speech is preceded
by biographical and introductory notes which place
the selection in its historical framework. Explana-
tory footnotes are provided wherever necessary. Although some speeches are presented in their entirety,
the majority have been extracted. The first section
of the publication opens with the earliest published
speech of a Black American--Price Hall's Masonic ser-
mon of June 24, 1797 and the last section closes with
the Legacy of George Jackson by Angela Davis, August,
1971. A subject index completes the work.

Spanish Americans

259. *A DOCUMENTARY HISTORY OF THE MEXICAN AMERICANS.*
Edited by Wayne Moquin and Charles Van Doren.
Introduction by Feliciano Rivera. New York,
Praeger, 1971, 413p.
The history of the Mexican American people from 1536
to 1970 is presented through 65 documents (treaties,
official reports, excerpts from early manuscripts and
journals, letters, essays by modern historians, etc.).
The work is arranged chronologically and further divided into five chapters that represent significant epochs
in the Mexican American experience. Additional readings
(both fiction and non-fiction) are recommended.

260. *THE PUERTO RICANS 1493-1973: A CHRONOLOGY AND FACT BOOK.* Compiled and edited by Francesco Cordasco. Dobbs Ferry, New York, Oceana Publications, 1973, 137p. (Ethnic Chronology Series no. 11).
For annotation, see Entry No. 109.

261. *THE SPANISH IN AMERICA 1513-1974: A CHRONOLOGY AND FACTBOOK.* Compiled and edited by Arthur A. Natella, Jr. Dobbs Ferry, New York, Oceana Publications, 1975, 139p. (Ethnic Chronology Series no. 12).
For annotation, see Entry No. 111.

Women

262. *BLACK WOMEN IN WHITE AMERICA: A DOCUMENTARY HISTORY.* Edited by Gerda Lerner. New York, Pantheon, 1972, 630p.
This anthology covers a wide range of topics dealing with the struggle of Black women in white America: in education, employment, slavery, liberation, etc. Each topical section connects pertinent documents (memoirs, essays, bills of sale, speeches, letters, etc.) with biographical data about the women quoted. Items range from a bill of sale for a female slave to contemporary remarks made by female Black leaders such as Shirley Chisholm. There is a critical bibliography on pages 615-30.

263. *DISCRIMINATION AGAINST WOMEN; CONGRESSIONAL HEARINGS ON EQUAL RIGHTS IN EDUCATION AND EMPLOYMENT.* Edited by Catharine R. Stimpson. New York, Bowker, 1973, 558p.
For annotation, see Entry No. 114.

264. *FEMINISM: THE ESSENTIAL HISTORICAL WRITINGS*.
      Edited by Miriam Schneir. New York, Random
      House, 1972, 360p.
The works in this anthology are arranged chronologically and range from 1776, the earliest, to 1929--
the dates which define the boundaries of "old feminism."
The majority of the selections included here are by
Americans, although authors who were born in England,
France, Germany, Norway, Scotland, Russia and Poland
also appear. Historical sketches place each document
in perspective. There is no index.

265. *HISTORY OF WOMAN SUFFRAGE*. Edited by Susan B.
      Anthony, Elizabeth Cady Stanton and I. H. Harper.
      Cincinnati, Collectors' Editions, 1971, 6v.
      (Source Library of the Women's Movement).
Volumes one through three are made up of an "immense
grab-bag" of news clippings, speeches and letters.
Campaigns and convention dates, speakers and committees
and the progress of the suffrage movement in the various
states are recorded in the remaining volumes. This is
a reprint of an 1881 edition.

266. *JOURNAL OF REPRINTS OF DOCUMENTS AFFECTING WOMEN*.
      Edited by Myra E. Barrer. Washington, D.C.,
      Today Publications and News Service, Inc., 1976-
      Quarterly.
Key documents focusing on equal rights and equal opportunities for women are reprinted in this quarterly
journal. Included are laws, legislation, government
rules and regulations, government administrative memor-
anda, and judicial decisions concerning women. In
addition, in the first two years of publication, the
JOURNAL will reprint almost every document issued
during the past 10 years which has been instrumental
in changing the status and role of women throughout
society. Historical background notes accompany each
document. The *JOURNAL* contains a general index
of individuals, organizations, cases and subject areas
as well as an alphabetical index of documents.

267. *SISTERHOOD IS POWERFUL: AN ANTHOLOGY OF WRITINGS*
      FROM THE WOMEN'S LIBERATION MOVEMENT. Edited by
      Robin Morgan. New York, Random House, 1970,
      602p.
Writings from psychiatrists and Ph.D.s, Blacks and
Mexican-Americans, teenagers and middle-aged women
make up this comprehensive compilation of writings
on the women's movement. Articles, poems, photographs
and manifestos are all represented in the source. Some
very important documents are presented, including the
WITCH manifesto and the NOW Bill of Rights. The anthology is arranged by subjects, which range from psychological oppression to changing consciousness. A bibliography on the women's rights movement (prepared by
Lucinda Cisler) and a list of who's who in the movement
complete the publication.

268. *UP FROM THE PEDESTAL; SELECTED WRITINGS IN THE*
      HISTORY OF AMERICAN FEMINISM. Edited by Aileen
      S. Kraditor. Chicago, Quadrangle Books, 1968,
      372p.
Three hundred years of American thought on the political and social status of women are presented in 70
chronologically arranged documents. The editor, Aileen
Kraditor, chose materials "representing the principal
emphases of the feminist movement in each period,
opting for unity over comprehensiveness." Documents
which recently have been published or republished are
excluded. Biographical information is appended to
each of the documents included.

269. *WE, THE AMERICAN WOMEN--A DOCUMENTARY HISTORY*.
      By Beth Millstein and Jeanne Bodin. New York,
      Jerome S. Ozer, Publisher, 1976, 221p.
WE, THE AMERICAN WOMEN is a documentary history of
American women from the earliest settlements to the
1970s. Over 125 documents and 60 drawings and
photographs are included. Each chapter consists of a
narrative discussing the status of women in that
particular time in history plus the relevant documents.
Included are materials relating to Abigail Adams,
Dorothea Dix, Jane Addams, Margaret Sanger, Margaret

Mead, Betty Friedan, Deborah Champion (who rode through
the British lines to carry a message to General Washington), Ernestine Rose (one of the founders of the
women's rights movement in the mid-19th century), etc.
An index and bibliography complete this publication.

270. *WOMEN LAW REPORTER*. Washington, D.C., Women Law
     Reporter, Inc., 1974- . Bi-weekly.
For annotation, see Entry No. 128.

Chapter 4

DIRECTORIES

Minorities

271. *A CHANCE TO GO TO COLLEGE. A DIRECTORY OF 800*
     COLLEGES THAT HAVE SPECIAL HELP FOR STUDENTS
     FROM MINORITIES AND LOW INCOME FAMILIES. New
     York, College Entrance Examination Board, 1971,
     248p.
Descriptive information on over 800 American colleges
and universities which offer special help or programs
for students from minority or low income families are
described in this directory. The information was
gathered from a questionnaire administered by the
publisher and includes: name of college or university,
address, admission requirements, fees, opportunities
for the disadvantaged, etc. There is an index.

272. *CIVIL RIGHTS: A CURRENT GUIDE TO THE PEOPLE,*
     ORGANIZATIONS, AND EVENTS. By Joan Martin
     Burke. 2nd ed. New York, Bowker, 1974, 266p.
     (A CBS News Reference Book).
For annotation, see Entry No. 132.

273. *CIVIL RIGHTS DIRECTORY, 1975.* Prepared by the
     U.S. Commission on Civil Rights Clearinghouse.
     Rev. ed. Washington, D.C., G.P.O., 1975, 224p.
     (CHP No. 15).
For annotation, see Entry No. 133.

274. *DIRECTORY FOR REACHING MINORITY GROUPS.* Prepared
     by the U.S. Department of Labor Apprenticeship
     and Training Bureau. Washington, D.C., G.P.O.,
     1970- . Irregular.
Organizations and individuals interested in providing
minority groups with information on job training and

opportunities are listed in this directory. The National Association for the Advancement of Colored People, the National Urban League, and the Bureau of Indian Affairs are examples of organizations included. The entries are arranged geographically (by state and city) and include the following information: names, addresses, telephone numbers. A supplementary list of Black fraternities, sororities and institutions of higher education is included.

275. *DIRECTORY OF MINORITY MEDIA.* Prepared by the U.S. Office of Minority Business Enterprise, U.S. Department of Commerce. Washington, D.C., G.P.O., 1973, 89p.

Minority newspapers, periodicals, magazines, newsletters, radio and television stations are listed in this directory of minority media. "The media is slanted toward only one type of audience--the minority group community." This publication is arranged into two sections: newspapers-periodicals and radio-TV stations. Each section is subdivided by the specific minority group (American Indians, Blacks, Orientals and Spanish speaking). The name and address is given for each listing. There is a statistical summary of minority consumer expenditures included in the source.

276. *DIRECTORY OF ORGANIZATIONS SERVING MINORITY COMMUNITIES.* Prepared by the U.S. Department of Justice. Washington, D.C., G.P.O., 1971, 88p.

Federal agencies, private organizations, colleges and universities, newspapers, and radio and television broadcasters serving women, Black, Spanish American, American Indian and Oriental communities are listed in this source. Section one lists the names and addresses of the main offices of Federal agencies and private organizations with nation-wide affiliation serving minority groups. The second section arranges entries by state, subdivided by type of organization and group served.

277. *DIRECTORY OF PRIVATE PROGRAMS FOR MINORITY BUSI-*

NESS ENTERPRISE. Prepared by the U.S. Office
of Minority Business Enterprise. Washington,
D.C., G.P.O., 1969- . Annual.
This directory lists over 350 private, national, and
municipal programs which provide assistance to minority businesses. The following information is provided
for each entry: name, address, telephone number, officials, and functions. There is an institutional
index. The publication has also been issued under the
title *DIRECTORY OF PRIVATE PROGRAMS ASSISTING MINORITY
BUSINESSES.*

278. *DIRECTORY OF SPECIAL PROGRAMS FOR MINORITY GROUP
     MEMBERS: CAREER INFORMATION SERVICES, EMPLOY-
     MENT SKILLS BANKS, FINANCIAL AID SOURCES.* Edited
     by Willis L. Johnson. Garrett Park, Maryland,
     Garrett Park Press, 1975, 400p.
Intended as a guide to employment and assistance programs for minorities (including women), this directory lists programs available through 750 national and
local organizations, 300 Federally supported projects,
and hundreds of individual colleges and universities.
It includes scholarships, employment services, Federal
assistance programs, women's career counseling, college
and univeristy awards, and talent banks. Appendices
are included for specific programs: Upward Bound,
Talent Search, Special Services, Opportunities Industrialization Centers, and the National Urban League.
Summaries for each entry include information on address,
application procedures, deadlines and qualifications.
In addition, there is a glossary, a selective bibliography of sources, and indexes to the organizations
and programs in the publication. Approximately 50
percent more opportunities are listed here than in the
first edition. A third edition is planned.

279. *ENCYCLOPEDIC DIRECTORY OF ETHNIC NEWSPAPERS AND
     PERIODICALS IN THE UNITED STATES.* By Lubomyr
     Wynar. 2nd ed. Littleton,Colorado, Libraries
     Unlimited, 1975, 260p.
For annotation, see Entry No. 423.

280. *ENCYCLOPEDIC DIRECTORY OF ETHNIC ORGANIZATIONS
IN THE UNITED STATES*. By Lubomyr R. Wynar.
Littleton, Colorado, Libraries Unlimited, 1975,
440p.
Based on information gathered in a questionnaire survey between 1973 and 1975, this directory describes
1,500 organizations (religious, fraternal, political,
educational, professional, scholarly, youth, etc.)
representing 73 ethnic groups (Albanian, Chinese,
Dutch, Irish, Polish, etc.). Because Black, Chicano,
Jewish and American Indian groups are listed in other
directories, they are included only selectively
here. Each entry includes the following information:
address, phone, officers, publications, meetings,
memberships, and goals. A separate section provides
a selective listing of major multi-ethnic and research-
oriented non-ethnic organizations involved in the study
of ethnicity. An essay on "The Nature of Ethnic Organizations" and an alphabetical index of organization
names complete the work.

281. *GRADUATE AND PROFESSIONAL SCHOOL OPPORTUNITIES
FOR MINORITY STUDENTS*. Princeton, New Jersey,
Educational Testing Service, 1969- . Biennial.
Designed to "assist minority students in their search
for graduate school opportunities," this survey provides capsule summaries of schools and professions
offering programs of aid for minority students in all
fields, including business, law, medicine, and general
graduate education. Over 700 programs are described
(application fee, tests used, application dates, number of students, number of minority students, number
of minority students receiving aid, and number of minority faculty). The publication is arranged in two main
sections: by type of graduate school and by graduate
program to be pursued within the school. In addition,
separate sections are included on sources of funds for
minority students and qualifying examinations for
entrance to graduate and professional schools. During
1969 and 1970 the publication was issued under the
title *GRADUATE STUDY OPPORTUNITIES FOR MINORITY GROUP
STUDENTS*.

282. *GRADUATE STUDY OPPORTUNITIES FOR MINORITY GROUP
     STUDENTS*. Princeton, New Jersey, Educational
     Testing Service, 1969-1970. Annual.
For annotation, see Entry No. 281.

283. *HIGHER EDUCATION AID FOR MINORITY BUSINESS; A
     DIRECTORY OF ASSISTANCE AVAILABLE TO MINORITIES
     BY SELECTED COLLEGIATE SCHOOLS OF BUSINESS*. Pre-
     pared by the U.S. Office of Minority Business
     Enterprise. Washington, D.C., G.P.O., 1970,
     103p.
Published to help the minority person "sharpen his
means of competition" in the business field, this
directory identifies higher education aid for minority
businesses. The source is arranged in three parts.
The first section lists schools at which some type of
financial aid is earmarked for minority students interested in business careers. The second section
describes the institutions of higher education which
have special business programs (e.g., management assistance, recruitment, etc.) for minority group
members. The final section is a geographical list
of schools.

284. *MINORITY BUSINESS OPPORTUNITIES: A MANUAL ON
     OPPORTUNITIES FOR SMALL AND MINORITY GROUP
     BUSINESSMEN AND PROFESSIONALS IN HUD PROGRAMS*.
     Prepared by the U.S. Department of Housing and
     Urban Development. Washington, D.C., G.P.O.,
     1970, 398p.
This manual has been prepared to assist "small and
minority group entrepreneurs and professionals who
are interested in participating in Federally assisted
housing, development, planning, construction and related programs." The manual is divided into four
major parts. Part 1 is organized by profession. The
type of work available under a number of programs,
qualifications required, fees, pertinent facts, and
the persons to contact are given. Part 2 consists of
opportunities for entrepreneurship. Part 3 contains a
summary of Federal programs listed in the manual. Part
4 is a listing of resources (associations, programs,

publications, etc.) to assist minority professionals.
Appendices include information on mortgage applications
and lists of Federal government regional and area offices.

285. *NATIONAL DIRECTORY OF MINORITY MANUFACTURES.*
Prepared by the Office of Minority Business Enterprise, Department of Commerce. Washington,
D.C., G.P.O., 1974, 121p.
This directory lists manufacturing companies that are
at least partially owned by a minority individual
(American Indian, Black, Oriental, Mexican, Cuban,
Puerto Rican, Central or South American). For each
company, the following information is provided: name
of firm, owner, address, date established, ethnic
ownership, government contract, number of employees,
annual sales, SIC, and type of product. Five separate
indexes are provided: alphabetical company index;
alphabetical product description index; geographic
index, by city within state; standard industrial classification index (numerical); and Federal supply classification index (numerical).

286. *NATIONAL MINORITY BUSINESS DIRECTORY.* Minneapolis, Minnesota, National Minority Business Campaign, 1972, 100p.
Issued originally (1969) as the *NATIONAL BLACK BUSINESS
DIRECTORY,* this listing was expanded in 1972 to include
other minorities (Indians, Mexican-Americans, Puerto
Ricans, etc.). A brief abstract on each firm is given,
indicating services offered, number of employees, sales
or assets, square footage of office space, and founding
date. In addition, Standard Industrial Classification
numbers and sketches of famous minority Americans are
included. Most information was obtained directly from
the 1,600 firms listed.

287. *NATIONAL ROSTER OF MINORITY PROFESSIONAL CONSUL-
TING FIRMS.* Prepared for the U.S. Office of
Minority Business Enterprise. Washington, D.C.,
1971- . Irregular.

Minority professional consulting firms (those owned by
a majority of minority group members) are listed alphabetically and indexed by region, state, and function
in this directory. There is a separate section which
covers company capability statements. The definition
of a consulting firm used in this source is a business
which "aims to perform professional, analytic, scientific or technical work and which delivers as an end
product a report, plan, study or other document rather
than tangible goods or property."

288. *NATION-WIDE ROSTER OF PROFESSIONAL MINORITY CON-
      SULTING FIRMS*. Washington, D.C., U.S. Environ-
      mental Protection Agency, 1973- . Irregular.
Prepared by the Environmental Protection Agency in
their efforts to increase minority participation in
the Agency's procurement programs, the roster lists
the names and capabilities of several hundred minority
professional consulting firms. The areas represented
range from accounting to data processing to urban
planning. The firms are listed by capabilities and
each description includes their names, addresses,
telephone numbers and representatives. There is an
alphabetical index to the firms.

289. *REGISTRY OF MINORITY CONTRACTORS AND HOUSING
      PROFESSIONALS*. Prepared by the U.S. Department
      of Housing and Urban Development. Washington,
      D.C., G.P.O., 1973, 12v.
There are 12 volumes in this directory of minority
construction contractors and housing professionals.
Each volume covers selected cities in different states
(e.g., Volume 1: Connecticut, Maine, Massachusetts,
New Hampshire, Rhode Island and Vermont; Volume 10:
Alaska, Idaho, Oregon and Washington). The volumes
are divided into two sections. The first section is
arranged by metropolitan area and lists contractors
and their telephone numbers. The second section describes the businesses listed in section one, indicating
the founding year, number of employees, minority groups,
etc.

290. *SPECIAL CATALOG OF FEDERAL ASSISTANCE PROGRAMS FOR MINORITY BUSINESS ENTERPRISES*. Prepared by the Office of Minority Business Enterprise. Washington, D.C., G.P.O., 1970- . Irregular.
This catalog provides a "comprehensive description of selected, relevant programs designed to assist minority entrepreneurs, minority group members interested in new business opportunities, and supporting organizations and groups." Its objective is to provide aid in identifying types of assistance available, determining eligibility requirements for specific programs and indicating new sources of additional information on these programs. Federal assistance and construction opportunity programs are listed by agency. For each program the following information is given: name of program, who is eligible to apply, how to apply, the nearest field office of the agency involved and its national headquarters. In addition, each description includes a section which focuses on a series of references designed to aid the reader in exploring other data relative to that program. An appendix contains information on OMBE affiliates, MBO committees, regional and local Federal offices. There is an index of programs.

American Indians

291. *AMERICAN INDIAN MEDIA DIRECTORY*. Washington, D.C., American Indian Press Association, 1974- Annual.
This directory is compiled by the American Indian Press Association. It lists Indian-owned communications media enterprises: Indian presses, Indian radio stations, Indian music, Indian television stations, Indian films and Indian theaters. Each entry includes a description of activities, addresses, and costs.

292. *FEDERAL AND STATE INDIAN RESERVATIONS AND INDIAN*

TRUST AREAS. Prepared by the Commerce Department.
Washington, D.C., G.P.O., 1974, 604p.
Information is provided on the land status, history,
culture, government, tribal economy, climate, transportation, and mailing address of over 300 Indian and
Eskimo native villages and reservations supervised
either on the Federal or state level in this directory. The entries are arranged by state.

293. *A GUIDE TO AMERICA'S INDIANS: CEREMONIES, RE-
     SERVATIONS, AND MUSEUMS*. By Arnold Marquis.
     Norman, University of Oklahoma Press, 1974,
     267p.
For annotation, see Entry No. 32.

294. *THE OFFICE OF INDIAN AFFAIRS, 1824-1880: HISTOR-
     ICAL SKETCHES*. By Edward E. Hill. New York,
     Clearwater Publishing Company, 1974, 246p. (The
     Library of American Indian Affairs).
The historical sketches contained in this book "were
originally prepared to enable researchers to locate
correspondence contained in Microcopy 234, *LETTERS
RECEIVED BY THE OFFICE OF INDIAN AFFAIRS, 1824-1880*
(National Archives and Records Service). The sketches
provide brief histories of the 100 agencies, superintendencies and field units of the Office of Indian
Affairs for that period." The following information
is provided for each field office: all locations;
dates of operation; tribes served; names of all agents
and superintendents with dates of appointment; access
to correspondence contained in National Archives Microcopy 234; etc. The sketches are arranged by agency
name. There are two indexes which provide access to
this reference work: the tribal index is arranged
alphabetically by tribes and important bands and the
agency and superintendency responsible for their
supervision; the jurisdictionary index lists agencies
and superintendencies alphabetically and gives years
of operation, years the reports were received for
filing, a file heading, microfilm reel reference number,
and a page citation to the sketch. Since there are
962 reels in Microcopy 234, these two indexes operate

as helpful locators for researchers.

295. *REFERENCE ENCYCLOPEDIA OF THE AMERICAN INDIAN.*
By Barry T. Klein and Dan Icolari. 2nd ed. Rye,
New York, Todd Publications, 1973-4, 2v.
For annotation, see Entry No. 50.

296. *A REFERENCE RESOURCE GUIDE OF THE AMERICAN IN-*
DIAN. By George A. Gill. Tempe, Center for
Indian Education, Arizona State University, 1974,
187p.
The purpose of this directory is to indicate all "resource materials and data concerning all aspects of our
First American." Separate chapters list government
agencies, tribal councils and Indian organizations,
Indian action groups, religious groups, Indian arts
and crafts organizations, monuments and parks, museums,
libraries, book publishers, audio-visual materials,
university and college Indian programs, Indian self-
help programs, etc. Most of the chapters are subdivided
by geographic location. Brief identification information accompanies many entries.

Black Americans

297. *THE AFRO-AMERICAN PRESS AND ITS EDITORS.* By I.
Garland Penn. New York, Arno, 1969, 565p.
(American Negro--His History and Literature,
Series No. 2).
This is a reprint of the 1891 edition. It reviews
Black magazines and newspapers published between 1827
and 1891. In addition, it provides biographical sket-
ches and portraits of Black editors. Also covered are
such topics as opinions about the press and Afro-Amer-
ican women in journalism.

298.   *BLACK LIST: THE CONCISE AND COMPREHENSIVE REFER-*
       ENCE GUIDE TO BLACK JOURNALISM, RADIO AND TELE-
       VISION, EDUCATIONAL AND CULTURAL ORGANIZATIONS
       IN THE U.S.A., AFRICA AND THE CARIBBEAN. 2nd ed.
       New York, Panther House, 1975, 2v.
This is a two volume reference set; volume 1 concentrates
on Afroamerica (U.S.A.) and volume 2 on Africa, the
Caribbean, and Latin America. Descriptions are provided for newspapers, periodicals, broadcasting stations,
colleges and universities, publishers, book clubs,
bookstores, advertising and public relations firms,
and literary agents in these areas. Specific information given on each organization includes: address,
person to whom correspondence should be addressed, and
principal officers. The African, Caribbean and Latin
American volume also includes information on embassies
and permanent missions to the U.N. The editor has
included a short essay showing the Black employment
rate of the major TV networks, and offering critiques
of the networks' hiring and editorial policies. An
earlier edition, issued in 1971, was entitled *BLACK*
LIST: THE CONCISE REFERENCE GUIDE TO PUBLICATIONS AND
BROADCASTING MEDIA OF BLACK AMERICA, AFRICA AND THE
CARIBBEAN (New York, Panther House, 1971, 289p.).

299.   *THE BLACK WOMAN IN AMERICAN SOCIETY: A SELECTED*
       ANNOTATED BIBLIOGRAPHY. By Lenwood G. Davis.
       Boston, G.K. Hall, 1975, 159p.
One-third of this publication contains directory and
statistical information. For complete annotation, see
Entry No. 692.

300.   *CIVIL RIGHTS DIRECTORY, 1975.* Prepared by the U.S.
       Commission on Civil Rights Clearinghouse. Rev. ed.
       Washington, D.C., G.P.O., 1975, 224p. (CHP no. 15).
For annotation, see Entry No. 133.

301.   *DIRECTORY OF AFRO-AMERICAN RESOURCES.* Edited
       by Walter Schatz. New York, Bowker, 1970, 485p.
Over 2,000 U.S. organizations and institutions holding
research materials in Afro-American studies are listed

in this directory. Included are all types of libraries, public and private agencies, and civil rights organizations. The book is arranged geographically by state and city and then by institution. The following information is provided for each entry: full name, address, telephone number, chief officer, publications, statement of purpose, and a description of the collection. Each collection is identified by subject matter, physical facilities, scope, and content. There is a bibliography of secondary source materials which lists bibliographies and directories. Indexes to institutions, collections and personnel are provided.

302. *DIRECTORY OF NATIONAL BLACK ORGANIZATIONS*. Compiled by Charles L. Sanders and Linda McLean. New York, AFRAM Associates, 1972, 115p.

Over 200 Black organizations are identified in this directory. The organizations are arranged within eight topical categories (educational, religious, civic, political, professional, etc.). Private profit-making organizations are included. The following information is provided for each organization: address, telephone number, key staff, purpose, programs, membership criteria, action techniques, publications, awards and scholarships, date founded, and informational contact. Descriptions can be found for such organizations as the Black Librarians Caucus, the Second World Black Festival of Arts and Culture, and the Union of Black Episcopalians. There is an index of organizations. Revised editions are planned.

303. *DIRECTORY OF PREDOMINATELY NEGRO COLLEGES AND UNIVERSITIES IN THE UNITED STATES OF AMERICA (FOUR YEAR INSTITUTIONS ONLY)*. Washington, D.C., G.P.O., 1966- . Irregular.

One page is devoted to each of the predominately Black academic institutions included here. Information is provided on the school's address, phone number, administrators, current enrollment, degrees offered, number of degrees granted, objectives and affiliations. The colleges and universities are arranged alphabetically and indexed by geographic location. Both private and public institutions are included.

304. *NATIONAL BLACK BUSINESS DIRECTORY*. Minneapolis, Minnesota, National Minority Business Campaign, 1969, 89p.
For annotation, see Entry No. 286.

305. *SURVEY OF BIBLIOGRAPHIC ACTIVITIES OF U.S. COLLEGES AND UNIVERSITIES ON BLACK STUDIES*. By Gail Juris and others. St. Louis, Pius XII Library, St. Louis University, 1971, 60p. (Bibliographic Series, no. 7).
For annotation, see Entry No. 624.

Spanish Americans

306. *DIRECTORY OF CONSULTANTS ON MIGRANT EDUCATION*. Prepared by the U.S. Office of Education. Washington, D.C., G.P.O., 1970, 90p.
Included in this directory are "national and state lists for migrant education programs under Title I, Elementary and Secondary Education Act, Public Law 89-10, as amended." Consultants and consulting firm experts in the field of migrant education are listed alphabetically by state. For each consultant, the following information is given: name, address, telephone number, and areas of specialization. There is a separate section containing a national list of consultants.

307. *DIRECTORY OF SPANISH ORGANIZATIONS IN THE UNITED STATES*. Prepared by the U.S. Cabinet Committee on Opportunity for the Spanish Speaking. Washington, D.C., G.P.O., 1971, 231p.
Over 200 Spanish organizations in the United States are

identified in this directory. They are listed by state, city and name of organization. The following information is provided: name, address, telephone number, principal officers, scope, date founded, ethnic membership, frequency of meetings, objectives, and availability of literature about the organization. The same information is furnished for six national organizations which are listed in a separate section. A subject and name index is appended. The publication was issued in 1970 under the title *DIRECTORY OF SPANISH SPEAKING COMMUNITY ORGANIZATIONS*.

308. *DIRECTORY OF SPANISH SPEAKING COMMUNITY ORGANIZA-TIONS*. Prepared by the U.S. Cabinet Committee on Opportunity for the Spanish Speaking. Washington, D.C., G.P.O., 1970, 224p.
For annotation, see Entry No. 307.

309. *1969 DIRECTORY OF MIGRANT HEALTH PROJECTS ASSISTED BY PUBLIC HEALTH SERVICE GRANTS*. Washington, D.C., U.S. Health Services and Mental Health Administration, 1969, 178p.
Migrant health projects are listed by grant number under each of the 36 states covered. At the beginning of each of these state sections, a map shows all the migrant-populated counties and the counties that provide health care and sanitation services. For each project, the following information is given: name of project, sponsor, directory, span of migrant season, number of migrant counties serviced, the location of family health service centers, and the health services provided.

Women

310. *THE BLACK WOMAN IN AMERICAN SOCIETY: A SELECTED, ANNOTATED BIBLIOGRAPHY*. By Lenwood G. Davis.

Boston, G. K. Hall, 1975, 159p.
One-third of this publication contains directory and
statistical information. For complete annotation,
see Entry No. 692.

311. *CHICAGO WOMEN'S DIRECTORY: ARTICLES AND LISTINGS.*
      Chicago, Inforwomen, 1974, 225p.
Focusing on survival, health, schools, employment,
children, law, media and women in general, this directory lists agencies, groups, and pertinent literature.
Essays on issues of interest and concern to women (the
Equal Rights Amendment, the welfare system, etc.) are
also included. There is a "Listings Index" and a
table of contents which serves as a subject index. The
publication is bi-lingual (English-Spanish).

312. *CONTINUING EDUCATION PROGRAMS AND SERVICES FOR
      WOMEN.* Compiled by Jean Wells. Washington,
      D.C., G.P.O., 1974, 167p.
Nearly 500 programs designed by educational organizations for adult women are listed in this directory.
Colleges providing these special courses of study are
arranged alphabetically by state. The schools are indexed by types of courses/programs offered. A résumé
of Federal funds for continuing education programs and
a bibliography on continuing education complete the
source. This compilation revises the directories of continuing education programs issued by the U.S. Government Printing Office in 1968 and in 1971.

313. *GOING STRONG/NEW COURSES, NEW PROGRAMS.* Edited
      by Deborah Silverton Rosenfelt. Old Westbury,
      New York, Feminist Press, 1973, 256p. (Female
      Studies VII).
Rosenfelt describes 60 new courses and new programs
in women studies. Included are syllabi and bibliographies relating to the courses and the subject of
the women's movement. Syllabi are presented in the
area of Third World women and women in non-western
societies: La Chicana in the United States; Women
in African History; American Indian, African Women;

Race, Sex and Ethnic Groups in America. In addition,
Rayna Reiter's bibliography "Anthropological Perspectives on Women" and Lise Vogel's selected bibliography
of "Women, Art and Feminism" are included.

314. *GUIDE TO WOMEN'S ORGANIZATIONS: A HANDBOOK ABOUT
     NATIONAL AND INTERNATIONAL GROUPS.* By Ellen
     Anderson. Washington, D.C., Public Affairs
     Press, 1950, 167p.
This book "represents the first comprehensive guide to
women's organizations." Its chief objective is to
describe those national and international groups which
were in active operation in the late 1940s. Included
are women's organizations and those in which women and
the interests of women are of major importance. The
source is arranged alphabetically by association and
indexed by subject. The following information, obtained through questionnaires, is given for each
organization: name, founding date, executives, address,
number of chapters, purpose, affiliations, publications,
etc.

315. *INTERNATIONAL DIRECTORY OF WOMEN'S ORGANIZATIONS.*
     Issued by the National Council of Women of the
     United States. New York, Research and Action
     Association, 1963, various pagings.
The name, objectives, founding date, officers, addresses,
membership, affiliations, etc. are given for numerous
international and American women's organizations. For
an earlier listing of similar scope, see Mary E. Torrance
Buchanan's *WORLD DIRECTORY OF WOMEN'S ORGANISATIONS*
(Entry No. 328). To up-date these listings, use the
ENCYCLOPEDIA OF ASSOCIATIONS (Detroit, Gale, 1975, 3v.).

316. *MEDIA REPORT TO WOMEN INDEX/DIRECTORY.* Washing-
     ton, D.C., Media Report to Women, 1975, 225p.
One section of this publication includes a directory of
women's media groups and individual media women. For
complete annotation, see Entry No. 119.

317. *THE NEW WOMAN'S SURVIVAL CATALOG.* Edited by
      Kirsten Grimstad and Susan Rennie. New York,
      Coward, McCann and Geoghegan, Inc., 1973, 250p.
"This book catalogues and documents activities...
aimed explicitly at the development of an alternative
woman's culture." Using the style of the *WHOLE EARTH
CATALOG,* it describes and evaluates publishers, day
care centers, radio/tv stations, speakers' bureaus,
and other projects, enterprises and resources that
have come into existence with the changing role of
women. The information is organized into nine chapters; abortion, communication, self-defense, health,
work and money, justice, and continuing education are
among the topics reviewed. Cartoons, posters and
photographs accompany most topics. For a sequel to
this publication, see *THE NEW WOMAN'S SURVIVAL SOURCE-
BOOK* (Entry No. 120).

318. *THE NEW WOMAN'S SURVIVAL SOURCEBOOK.* Edited by
      Kirsten Grimstad and Susan Rennie. New York,
      Knopf, 1975, 245p.
For annotation, see Entry No. 120.

319. *THE NEW YORK WOMAN'S DIRECTORY.* Prepared by
      the Womanpower Project. New York, Workman
      Publishing Co., 1973, 262p. (Guides to New
      York Series).
The Womanpower Project is a group of 25 New York-area
women who have compiled this guide to a variety of
services and businesses for and run by women in the
New York City area (medical, legal, psychological,
financial and others). Short essays cover such topics
as finding a job, a day-care center, a place to live,
etc. The names and addresses of appropriate services
and businesses are given. "Each chapter of the directory attempts to give you an idea of the situation of
women working in male-dominated professions in New
York City."

320. *NORTH AMERICAN REFERENCE ENCYCLOPEDIA OF WOMEN'S
      LIBERATION.* Edited by William White, Jr. Phila-

delphia, North American, 1972, 194p. (North
American Reference Library).
For annotation, see Entry No. 121.

321. *A PRACTICAL GUIDE TO THE WOMEN'S MOVEMENT*. Edited by Deena Peterson. New York, Women's Action
Alliance, 1975, 213p.
Names, addresses, and descriptions of women's organizations in such categories as abortion, family, media,
older women and lesbianism are provided in this directory. Also listed are a number of women's periodicals,
newsletters and newspapers.

322. *WHO'S WHO AND WHERE IN WOMEN'S STUDIES*. Edited
by Tamar Berkowitz, Jean Mangi and Jane William-
son. Old Westbury, New York, Feminist Press,
1974, 256p.
This is an up-to-date directory of college level women's
studies courses and faculty. Nearly 5,000 women's
studies courses are listed by instructor, by institution,
and by department. The work is divided into three main
lists and a section on women's studies programs. List I
details 4,900 courses taught in colleges and universities.
The entries list faculty members by name, title of course,
and years in which taught. List II organizes this same
information alphabetically by name of teacher; entries
indicate the name of department, institution, titles
of courses or course taught. List III reorganizes the
same data under specific names of the appropriate
departments (e.g., American Studies, Anthropology,
Economics/Business). The entries in this section list
titles of courses and teachers. Similar but more
selective lists of women's studies courses can be found
in Deborah Silverton Rosenfelt's *FEMALE STUDIES VII:
GOING STRONG--NEW COURSES, NEW PROGRAMS* (see Entry No.
313) and Lora H. Robinson's *WOMEN'S STUDIES: COURSES
AND PROGRAMS FOR HIGHER EDUCATION* (Washington, D.C.,
American Association for Higher Education, 1973, 34p.).

323. *WOMANHOOD MEDIA: CURRENT RESOURCES ABOUT WOMEN*.
By Helen Wheeler. Metuchen, New Jersey, Scare-

crow Press, 1972, 335p.
For annotation, see Entry Nos. 724 and 725.

324. *WOMEN IN CALIFORNIA: A GUIDE TO ORGANIZATIONS
AND INFORMATION SOURCES*. By Diana A. de Noy-
elles and Joan Dickson Smith. Claremont,
California, Center for Public Affairs, the Claremont Colleges, to be published in 1976.
This is a comprehensive, descriptive directory of
California state and local public agencies and citizens
and professional organizations concerned with women's
rights and problems. An annotated bibliography on
women in California is included. The publication,
prepared by a librarian in the Los Angeles County
Public Library system and an administrator of the
Center for California Public Affairs, will be issued
in 1976.

325. *WOMEN'S MOVEMENT MEDIA: A SOURCE GUIDE*. By
Cynthia Ellen Harrison. New York, Bowker, 1975,
269p.
The services and products of over 500 organizations
are described in this directory. Included are publishers of feminist materials, women's research centers,
library research collections, local and national women's
organizations, government agencies, and special interest
services (speakers' bureaus, birth control centers, etc.).
The organizations are grouped into five categories,
based on the type or main interest of the group. Each
entry includes the following information: a brief
profile, address, telephone number, a sampling of published titles (including brochures and pamphlets as
well as books and periodicals), and a list of AV items.
Four indexes—groups by name, by subject, by geographical area, and by media—complete the work. The publisher claims that this is "the most comprehensive
directory of all to the services, publications, products, activities offered by the women's movement in
the U.S. and Canada today."

326. *WOMEN'S ORGANIZATIONS AND LEADERS DIRECTORY*.

Edited by Myra E. Barrer and Lester A. Barrer.
Washington, D.C., Today Publications and News
Services, 1973- . Annual
For annotation, see Entry No. 206.

327. *WOMEN'S YELLOW PAGES; THE ORIGINAL SOURCE BOOK
      FOR WOMEN*. Boston, Boston Women's Collective,
      Inc., 1973, 159p.
The purpose of this book is to provide "a vehicle for
putting women in contact with people, organizations,
and agencies who can help them meet their needs, both
in crisis and in daily life." Some of the topics
covered are: perspectives on aging and agelessness,
welfare, self-defense, law and women, and health. One
section consists of an alphabetical list of women's
groups. Coverage is focused on the Boston area. For
each group, the address, contact, and a short description of its services are given. There is an index.

328. *WORLD DIRECTORY OF WOMEN'S ORGANISATIONS*. Com-
      piled and edited by Mary Buchanan. London,
      World Directory of Women's Organisations, 1953,
      222p.
This is a listing of women's organizations operating
around in the world in the early 1950s. "No organisation has been entered unless the information about
it has [come] either from the organisation itself or
from its international headquarters, or from an equally
reliable source." The directory is arranged by country
and then alphabetically by organization. The following
information is provided for each entry: name, address,
founding date, officers, purpose, membership, member
country, international conferences, and affiliation.
The publication was reprinted in 1973.

Chapter 5

STATISTICAL SOURCES

Minorities

329. *AGE OF THE FOREIGN-BORN WHITE POPULATION BY
   COUNTRY OF BIRTH: 1930 CENSUS OF POPULATION.
   SPECIAL REPORTS.* Prepared by the U.S. Bureau
   of the Census. Washington, D.C., G.P.O.,
      1933, 77p.
Statistics are presented on foreign born whites by
country of birth, sex, and age. Text and tables
cover median age of foreign born, immigration into
the United States, mortality rates, etc. The data
were compiled for only 12 states (those which constitute 47 percent of the foreign born whites in the
Unites States). For related statistics, see *NATIONAL
ORIGIN AND LANGUAGE* (Entry No. 341).

330. *COLOR AND SEX OF MIGRANTS: 1940 CENSUS OF POPU-
   LATION. FINAL REPORTS.* Prepared by the U.S.
   Bureau of the Census. Washington, D.C., G.P.O.,
      1943, 490p.
This statistical compilation is the third volume in
the four volume set entitled *INTERNAL MIGRATION,
1935 TO 1940* (Washington, D.C., G.P.O., 1943-1946,
4v). It presents statistics on the color and sex
of migrants in various locations. Tables display
data on in- and out-migration and net migration for
cities of 100,000 or more inhabitants, states, and
regions. Also included are data covering immigrants
from foreign countries and U.S. possessions.

331. *COLOR, RACE AND TENURE OF FARM OPERATOR: CENSUS
   OF AGRICULTURE. GENERAL REPORTS. STATISTICS BY
   SUBJECTS.* Prepared by the U.S. Bureau of the
   Census. Washington, D.C., G.P.O., 1910-   .
   Every five years.

This publication is a reprint of a chapter of the Census of Agriculture's special report, *STATISTICS BY SUBJECTS*. It contains an introduction, followed by tabular sections containing statistics on the color and tenure of farm operators for the United States, for geographical divisions, and for states. This report has been issued under various titles: *STATISTICS OF FARMS, CLASSIFIED BY RACE, NATIVITY, AND TENURE OF FARMERS* (1914, 86p.); *FARM STATISTICS BY COLOR AND TENURE OF FARMER* (1923, 103p.); *STATISTICS BY COLOR AND TENURE OF FARM OPERATOR* (1933, 153p.) and *COLOR, RACE AND TENURE OF OPERATOR* (1940, 100p.).

332. *DIRECTORY OF PUBLIC ELEMENTARY AND SECONDARY SCHOOLS IN SELECTED DISTRICTS: ENROLLMENT AND STAFF BY RACIAL/ETHNIC GROUP.* Prepared by the U.S. Department of Health, Education and Welfare. Washington, D.C., G.P.O., 1969- . Biennial.
Information on the racial/ethnic composition of public and full time classroom teachers assigned to one school in over 8,000 school districts is provided annually in this publication. School districts and individual schools are listed alphabetically by state. Each entry includes information on the district name, city, enrollment (total, white, Black, other), and instructional staff (total, white, Black, and other). The report is based on data collected in The Elementary and Secondary School Civil Rights Survey. When the publication was first issued, it was entitled *DIRECTORY: PUBLIC SCHOOLS IN LARGE DISTRICTS WITH ENROLLMENT AND STAFF, BY RACE.*

333. *DIRECTORY: PUBLIC SCHOOLS IN LARGE DISTRICTS WITH ENROLLMENT AND STAFF, BY RACE.* Prepared by the U.S. Department of Health, Education and Welfare. Washington, D.C., G.P.O., 1969- . Biennial.
The current title of this publication is *DIRECTORY OF PUBLIC ELEMENTARY AND SECONDARY SCHOOLS IN SELECTED DISTRICTS: ENROLLMENT AND STAFF BY RACIAL/ETHNIC GROUP.* For annotation, see Entry No. 332.

334. *EQUAL EMPLOYMENT OPPORTUNITY REPORT.* Prepared
by the U.S. Equal Employment Opportunity Commission. Washington, D.C., G.P.O., 1966- .
Annual.
The private sector employment situation of American
Indians, Blacks, Orientals, Spanish Americans, and
women is quantitatively described in annual multi-
volume reports. Data are obtained entirely from
employer submitted forms to the EEOC - Labor Department Joint Reporting Committee. All states (except
Hawaii) are included. Contents are organized into
a U.S. summary and regional reports (New England,
West, North, Central, Mountain, Pacific, etc.). Data
are displayed for nine occupational categories (professionals, technicians, laborers, service workers,
salesworkers, etc.). Male and female employees are
shown separately for each minority. No report was
issued for 1968 or 1972.

335. *ETHNIC GROUPS: 1970 CENSUS OF POPULATION. SUB-
JECT REPORTS.* Prepared by the U.S. Bureau of
the Census. Washington, D.C., G.P.O., 1973,
7v.
Issued as part of the subject reports of the 1970
Census of Population, this series presents data on
selected population, socioeconomic and housing char-
acteristics of different ethnic groups. The follow-
ing reports in this series have been issued: *NATIONAL
ORIGIN AND LANGUAGE* (Entry No. 341), *NEGRO POPULATION*
(Entry No. 372), *PERSONS OF SPANISH ORIGIN* (Entry No.
381), *PERSONS OF SPANISH SURNAME* (Entry No. 382),
PUERTO RICANS IN THE UNITED STATES (Entry No. 383),
AMERICAN INDIANS (Entry No. 350), and *JAPANESE, CHI-
NESE AND FILIPINOS IN THE UNITED STATES* (Entry No.
359).

336. *HOUSING OF SELECTED RACIAL GROUPS: 1970 CENSUS
OF HOUSING. SUBJECT REPORTS.* Prepared by the
U.S. Bureau of the Census. Washington, D.C.,
G.P.O., 1973, 132p.
Data on selected racial groups cross-classified by
various housing and household characteristics are

presented in this report from the 1970 Census of
Housing. The racial groups include American Indian,
Japanese, Chinese, Filipino, Korean, and others.
Data are shown for the United States by inside and
outside standard metropolitan statistical areas and
regions. The statistics distinguish between owner-
occupied and renter-occupied housing units.

337. *IMMIGRANTS AND THEIR CHILDREN, 1850-1950: 1950
     CENSUS OF POPULATION. MONOGRAPH.* Prepared by
     E.P. Hutchinson for the U.S. Bureau of the
     Census. Washington, D.C., G.P.O., 1956, 482p.
The composition and geographic distribution of first
and second generation immigrants are described in this
1950 CENSUS MONOGRAPH. Relevant data are reproduced
from each decennial census from 1850 to 1950. Appendix tables display statistics for the foreign born
population in the United States between 1850 and 1950
by country of birth and for labor force participants
in 1950 (both male and female) by nativity, parentage,
and country of origin.

338. *MINORITIES AND WOMEN IN STATE AND LOCAL GOVERN-
     MENT.* Washington, D.C., U.S. Equal Opportunity
     Commission, 1973- . Annual.
The data in this report are based on statistics filed
by state and local governments in accordance with the
Equal Employment Opportunity Act of 1972. Analysis of
the data on the employment of minorities and women in
state and local government is made by race/ethnic
group and sex, function of government, salary group,
and job category. Excluded are employees of public
elementary and secondary school systems or higher
educational institutions. Similar statistics for
Federal minority and women employees can be found in
Entry Nos. 339, 405. Information on employment of
women and minorities in private industry can be
found in Entry No. 334.

339. *MINORITY GROUP EMPLOYMENT IN THE FEDERAL GOVERN-
     MENT.* Prepared by the U.S. Civil Service Commis-

sion. Washington, D.C., G.P.O., 1969- .
Annual.
Statistics on full-time Federal civilian employment
for designated minority groups (American Indians,
Asian Americans, Blacks, and Spanish Americans) are
presented by agency, pay system, and grade or salary
level groupings. The source is arranged by Federal
agency. For similar data on the state and local
levels, see the annual *MINORITIES AND WOMEN IN STATE
AND LOCAL GOVERNMENT* (Entry No. 338). For private
sector information, see *EQUAL EMPLOYMENT OPPORTUNITY
REPORT* (Entry No. 334).

340. *MINORITY-OWNED BUSINESSES: ALL MINORITIES.*
      Prepared by the U.S. Bureau of the Census.
      Washington, D.C., G.P.O., 1969- . Irregular.
This survey was initiated in 1969 and repeated again
in 1972 (as part of the 1972 Economic Censuses). The
publication includes data on the number of minority
owned firms, gross receipts and number of paid employees distributed geographically by industry, size of
firm, and legal form of organization. Maps, figures
and tables are included. For a list of other volumes
in the series, see Entry No. 347.

341. *NATIONAL ORIGIN AND LANGUAGE: 1970 CENSUS OF
      POPULATION. SUBJECT REPORTS.* Prepared by
      the U.S. Bureau of the Census. Washington,
      D.C., G.P.O., 1973, 505p.
Statistics for the United States and selected standard
metropolitan statistical areas (SMSAs) on the social
and economic characteristics of immigrants and their
children for selected countries of origin are presented
in this census publication. Tables 1-9 include data on
the social and economic characteristics of the native
population of native parentage, cross-classified by
race, the native population of foreign or mixed parentage, and the foreign-born population for the United
States and its regions. Tables 10-14 present similar
characteristics by country of origin. Tables 15 and
16 provide data for SMSAs with a total foreign stock
population of 250,000. Tables 17 and 18 include

information at the national level for the social and
economic characteristics of the foreign-born population by years of immigration. Table 19 presents
detailed statistics on the mother tongue for the
United States. Table 20 indicates, for persons in
families which the head or wife are of foreign stock,
the nativity and parentage classified for family
members. The statistics are based on the 1970 Census
of Population. Related earlier publications include
for 1960, *NATIVITY AND PARENTAGE* and *MOTHER TONGUE OF
THE FOREIGN BORN;* for 1950, *NATIVITY AND PARENTAGE;*
for 1940, *NATIVITY AND PARENTAGE OF THE WHITE POPULA-
TION;* for 1910 to 1930, *COUNTRY OF BIRTH OF FOREIGN-
BORN, COUNTRY OF ORIGIN OF THE FOREIGN WHITE STOCK,*
and *MOTHER TONGUE OF THE FOREIGN WHITE STOCK.*

342. *NONWHITE POPULATION BY RACE: SOCIAL AND ECONOMIC
     STATISTICS FOR NEGROES, INDIANS, JAPANESE, CHI-
     NESE, AND FILIPINOS: 1960 CENSUS OF POPULATION.
     SUBJECT REPORTS.* Prepared by the U.S. Bureau of
     the Census. Washington, D.C., G.P.O., 1963, 255p.
Statistics (from the 1960 Census of Population) on the
social and economic characteristics of each of the nonwhite races are presented in this report: Blacks, Indians, Japanese, Chinese, and Filipinos. Detailed
quantitative data and cross relationships are provided
for the national, regional, local and standard metropolitan statistical areas. Information is provided
for nativity, residence in 1955, years of school completed, marital status, relationship to head of household, family composition and characteristics, employment
status, hours worked, weeks worked in 1959, occupation,
and income. Data for 1960 on racial composition for the
U.S., SMSAs, municipalities, and counties is also given
in Volume 1 of the Census of Population's *CHARACTERIS-
TICS OF THE POPULATION.* Similar data are presented
for tracted areas in the 1960 Census of Population's
CENSUS TRACTS. Comparable earlier statistics are
available in *NONWHITE POPULATION BY RACE* (1950, 189p.);
CHARACTERISTICS OF THE NONWHITE POPULATION BY RACE
(1943, 112p.); and *COLOR OR RACE, NATIVITY, AND PAREN-
TAGE* (for the 1910 through 1930 censuses).

343.   *PROFESSIONAL WOMEN AND MINORITIES; A MANPOWER*
       RESOURCE SERVICE. By Betty M. Vetter and
       Eleanor L. Babco. Washington, D.C., Scientific
       Manpower Commission, 1975, 656p.
For annotation, see Entry No. 402.

344.   *RACIAL AND ETHNIC ENROLLMENT DATA FROM INSTITU-*
       TIONS OF HIGHER EDUCATION. Prepared by the U.S.
       Department of Health, Education, and Welfare.
       Washington, D.C., G.P.O., 1968- . Biennial.
This biennial report presents racial and enrollment
data for institutions of higher education which
respond to the HEW Civil Rights Survey of Institutions of Higher Education. American Indian, Black,
Oriental, Spanish surnamed, total minority and all
other students at each institution and branch or
campus are quantitatively described. The survey is
divided into three major sections: enrollment by
level of institution (undergraduate, graduate, professional), enrollment by location, and historical
comparisons (1968-1972).

345.   *SPECIAL REPORT ON FOREIGN-BORN WHITE FAMILIES*
       BY COUNTRY OF BIRTH OF HEAD WITH AN APPENDIX
       GIVING STATISTICS FOR MEXICAN, INDIAN, CHINESE,
       AND JAPANESE FAMILIES: 1930 CENSUS OF POPULA-
       TION. FINAL REPORTS. Prepared by the U.S.
       Bureau of the Census. Washington, D.C., G.P.O.,
       1933, 217p.
Statistics on families are presented for foreign-born
white stock in the United States as a whole and in
states, cities and divisions. In addition, data are
provided for Mexican, Indian, Chinese, and Japanese
families. For related statistics, see *NATIONAL ORI-*
GIN AND LANGUAGE (Entry No. 341).

346.   *STUDY OF SELECTED SOCIO-ECONOMIC CHARACTERISTICS*
       OF ETHNIC MINORITIES BASED ON THE 1970 CENSUS.
       Prepared by the U.S. Department of Health, Educ-
       ation, and Welfare. Washington, D.C., G.P.O.,
       1974, 4v.

This series of reports analyzes socio-economic
data on major ethnic minorities (Spanish Americans,
Asian Americans and American Indians) and their sub-
groups in the United States (see Entry Nos. 349, 357,
376). Data are selected from various 1970 publications. Population, family, education, employment,
and income characteristics are emphasized. The last
volume of the four volume set presents statistics
for the major ethnic minorities (including Blacks)
in the 10 H.E.W. regions.

347. *SURVEY OF MINORITY-OWNED BUSINESS ENTERPRISES.*
     Prepared by the U.S. Bureau of the Census.
     Washington, D.C., G.P.O., 1969- . Irregular.
The *SURVEY OF MINORITY-OWNED BUSINESS ENTERPRISES* is
conducted to determine the extent of business ownership by specific minority groups. It provides data
on businesses owned by Blacks, Spanish-Americans,
American Indians, Asian Americans, women, etc. The
survey includes all industries listed in the Standard
Industrial Classification (SIC) system, with the following exceptions: railroad transportation; offices
of physicians, surgeons, dentists, dental surgeons,
osteopathic physicians and chiropractors; health and
allied services; legal services; nonprofit organizations; agricultural production; U.S. Postal Service;
private households; and public administration. The
current survey (1972) is the second study in a series
initiated in 1969 and was taken as part of the 1972
Economic Censuses. Final detailed statistics are
issued in separate, paperbound reports: *MINORITY-
OWNED BUSINESSES: BLACK* (see Entry No. 367); *MINORITY-
OWNED BUSINESSES: SPANISH ORIGIN* (see Entry No. 380);
MINORITY-OWNED BUSINESSES: ALL MINORITIES (see Entry
No. 340) and *WOMEN-OWNED BUSINESS* (see Entry No. 409).

348. *YEARBOOK OF EQUAL EDUCATIONAL OPPORTUNITY, 1975-
     76.* Chicago, Marquis Academic Media/Marquis
     Who's Who, 1975, 479p.
For annotation, see Entry No. 15.

Asian Americans

349. *AMERICAN INDIANS.* Prepared by the U.S. Depart-
      ment of Health, Education and Welfare. Washing-
      ton, D.C., G.P.O., 1974, 100p.
Prepared as part of the *STUDY OF SELECTED SOCIO-ECONO-
MIC CHARACTERISTICS OF ETHNIC MINORITIES BASED ON THE
1970 CENSUS* (see Entry No. 346), this volume analyzes
data on American Indians, with separate sections for
California, Oklahoma, Washington, Arizona, New Mexico,
and South Dakota. Alaskan Indians, Eskimos and Aleuts
are covered in another part of the work. Included are
12 charts and 28 tables which focus on the population,
family, education, employment, and income characteristics of these groups.

350. *AMERICAN INDIANS: 1970 CENSUS OF POPULATION.
      SUBJECT REPORTS.* Prepared by the U.S. Bureau
      of the Census. Washington, D.C., G.P.O,, 1973,
      192p.
This census report presents statistics on the American
Indian population in 1970. The statistics are arranged
by various social and economic characteristics for the
United States as a whole, selected states, standard
metropolitan statistical areas (SMSAs), Indian tribes
and identified reservations. Table 1 presents data
for the American Indian population classified by sex
and urban-rural residence for the United States,
regions, divisions, and states. Tables 2-10 contain
data on characteristics such as age, family composition,
marital status, school enrollment, employment status,
occupation, income in 1969, and housing for the United
States, regions, and selected states. In tables 11-15,
statistics on social, economic, and housing characteristics are given for selected SMSAs, Indian tribes,
and identified reservations. Tables 16 and 17 show

the age and sex distributions for all the reservations
and tribes identified in the 1970 census. Table 18
presents a cross-classification of mother tongue by
age and sex for all Indians and all those living on
identified reservations. The data included in this
publication are based on the 1970 Census of Population and are extracted from *CHARACTERISTICS OF THE
POPULATION*. Similar statistics for 1960 and 1950 are
included in *NONWHITE POPULATION BY RACE* (see Entry No.
342).

351. *CENSUS OF NON-RESERVATION CALIFORNIA INDIANS,
      1905-1906*. By C.E. Kelsey. Berkeley, Depart-
      ment of Anthropology, University of California,
      1971, 118p.
The Kelsey census provides an actual count of the
number of American Indians in each of the 45 counties
in California. The data are broken down by land holdings and racial composition. For each county, the
names of the individual Indians living there and the
number in each family are given. This is a reprint
of a census done by Kelsey when he was a special agent
for the California Indians.

352. *THE EDUCATION OF AMERICAN INDIANS*. Prepared for
      the Subcommittee on Indian Education of the Com-
      mittee on Labor and Public Welfare, United States
      Senate. Washington, D.C., G.P.O., 1969, 3v.
This committee print focuses on American Indian education. Volume 1 is a compilation of statutes relating
to American Indian education from 1897 to 1964. Volume
2 contains field investigations and research reports
on the educational problems in the Southwest, West,
Northwest, North, Midwest and East. Volume 3 is a
compendium of Federal boarding school evaluations and
the problems associated with the schools.

353. *INDIAN POPULATION IN THE UNITED STATES AND ALASKA,
      1910*. Prepared by the U.S. Bureau of the Census.
      Washington, D.C., G.P.O., 1915, 285p.
"This report presents the statistics of the Indian

population of the United States collected at the Fifteenth Decennial Census, taken as of April 1, 1930, with comparisons as far as practicable with the census of 1920, and with the special enumeration of Indians made as part of the Census of 1910." Text and tables are devoted to the following subjects: residence location, stock and tribe, admixture of blood, age distribution, marital condition, school attendance, illiteracy, inability to speak English, occupations, and industry groups, etc. An abridged version of this publication was issued in 1913 under the title *STATISTICS OF THE INDIAN POPULATION--NUMBER, TRIBES, SEX, AGE, FECUNDITY, AND VITALITY* (Washington, D.C., G.P.O., 1913, 25p.).

354. *THE INDIAN POPULATION OF THE UNITED STATES AND ALASKA, 1930*. Prepared by the U.S. Bureau of the Census. Washington, D.C., G.P.O., 1937, 238p. Detailed tables and diagrams, supplemented by brief descriptive analyses, are provided for the following 12 topics: Indian population by states and counties; Indians by stock and tribe; classification by admixture of blood; age distribution; marital condition; school attendance; illiteracy; inability to speak English; composition of the Indian population of counties and cities; occupations; Indian farm operators and farms; Indian population of Alaska.

355. *REPORT ON INDIANS TAXED AND INDIANS NOT TAXED IN THE UNITED STATES (EXCEPT ALASKA): 1890 CENSUS OF POPULATION. FINAL REPORTS*. Washington, D.C., G.P.O., 1894, 683p. The Indian population prior to 1890 is described in this census publication. Data are presented on Indians by sex, location, stock and tribe, children, English ability, education, marital status, etc. In addition, a historical review of Indian affairs in the United States is provided, including descriptions of Indian conditions, Indian wars, legal status, reservations, crops, etc. One section of the source includes a "Census of Indians in the Dominion of Canada, 1890."

356. *STATISTICS CONCERNING INDIAN EDUCATION*. Washington, D.C., U.S. Bureau of Indian Affairs, 1960- . Annual.

Tables and maps showing the number of Indian children enrolled in schools operated by the Bureau of Indian Affairs are included in this publication. Information is presented on the types and locations of schools, enrollment, grades, graduates, educational programs, etc.

Asian Americans

357. *ASIAN AMERICANS*. Prepared by the U.S. Department of Health, Education, and Welfare. Washington, D.C., G.P.O., 1974, 159p.

Issued as the second volume in the *STUDY OF SELECTED SOCIO-ECONOMIC CHARACTERISTICS OF ETHNIC MINORITIES BASED ON THE 1970 CENSUS* (see Entry No. 346), this publication analyzes data on Americans of Japanese, Chinese, Filipino, Korean, and Hawaiian descent. Population, family, education, employment and income characteristics are emphasized. Local analyses are provided for Hawaii and California (all groups), New York City (Chinese and Koreans), San Francisco (Chinese), and Honolulu and Los Angeles (Koreans) in 16 charts and 51 tables.

358. *CHINESE AND JAPANESE IN THE UNITED STATES, 1910: 1910 CENSUS. GENERAL REPORTS*. Prepared by the U.S. Bureau of the Census. Washington, D.C., G.P.O., 1914, 50p.

This report contains "practically all the available data about the Chinese and Japanese in the United States compiled at the Census of 1910. A large part of this material has been previously published in the population volumes of the Thirteenth Census and the bulletins for individual states and cities...The agricultural statistics, however, are practically all published here for the first time, since previous publications gave only the number of Chinese and Japanese farmers." Statistics are given for the total number of Chinese and Japanese in the United States and Hawaii, urban/rural distribution, marital status, age, sex, school attendance, occupation, language background, etc. Similar statistics for 1880 to 1900 can be found in the third *SPECIAL CENSUS BULLETINS* of the Twelfth (1900) Census: *DISTRIBUTION OF THE CHINESE AND JAPANESE POPULATION IN WESTERN STATES AND TERRITORIES BY COUNTIES: 1880 TO 1900*.

359. *JAPANESE, CHINESE AND FILIPINOS IN THE UNITED STATES: 1970 CENSUS OF POPULATION. SUBJECT REPORTS.* Prepared by the U.S. Bureau of the Census. Washington, D.C., G.P.O., 1973, 181p. This report presents statistics on the Japanese, Chinese, Filipino, Korean and Hawaiian populations, cross-classified by various social and economic characteristics for the United States, regions, selected states, standard metropolitan statistical areas (SMSAs), and cities. Table 1 presents data for the Japanese population for the United States, regions, divisions, and states. Tables 2-10 contain data on such characteristics as age, sex, family composition, marital status, school enrollment, employment status, occupation, income in 1969, and housing for the United States, regions, and selected states. In tables 11-15, statistics on social, economic, and housing characteristics are given for selected SMSAs and cities. Identical statistics are shown for the Chinese in tables 16-30 and for the Filipinos in tables 31-45. Social and economic data are presented for Hawaiians in tables 46 and 47 and for Koreans in tables 48 and 49. The data are based on the 1970 Census of Population. Similar statistics are presented for 1960 in *NONWHITE POPULATION BY RACE,* for 1950 in *NONWHITE POPULATION BY RACE,* and for 1940 in *CHARACTERISTICS OF THE NONWHITE POPULATION BY RACE*.

Black Americans

360. *THE AMERICAN NEGRO REFERENCE BOOK.* Edited by
     John P. Davis. Englewood Cliffs, New Jersey,
     Prentice-Hall, 1966, 969p.
Over 100 statistical tables are included in this
publication. For complete annotation, see Entry No.
63.

361. *BLACK AMERICANS: A CHARTBOOK.* Washington, D.C.,
     G.P.O., 1971, 141p.
Information on the progress and problems of urban
Blacks in recent years is presented in tabular and
graphic form. Migration and population, employment
and unemployment, income, poverty, vital statistics,
family, health, housing, crime, and citizenship are
the major subjects covered. Trends in labor force
participation and educational attainment are projected to 1980.

362. *THE BLACK WOMAN IN AMERICAN SOCIETY: A SELECTED
     ANNOTATED BIBLIOGRAPHY.* By Lenwood G. Davis.
     Boston, G.K. Hall, 1975, 159p.
One-third of this publication contains directory and
statistical information. For complete annotation, see
Entry No. 692.

363. *CHANGING CHARACTERISTICS OF THE NEGRO POPULATION:
     1960 CENSUS OF POPULATION. MONOGRAPH.* By Daniel
     O. Price. Washington, D.C., U.S. Bureau of the
     Census, 1970, 263p.
The purpose of this study is to describe the changes
in the demographic characteristics and economic status
of the Negro population of the United States since 1870,

with particular emphasis on the period 1940-1960.
The data in this compilation were taken primarily
from the decennial censuses of population between
1870 and 1960. Trends in population distribution,
income, employment, occupational composition, education, marital patterns, family and voting are examined. Wherever possible, data on whites and Negroes
are compared. There is a considerable amount of
narrative material accompanying the graphic (tabular,
chart) presentations. A subject index is provided.

364. *CHICAGO NEGRO ALMANAC AND REFERENCE BOOK*.
      Compiled by Ernest R. Rather. Chicago, Chi-
      cago Negro Almanac Publishing Co., 1972,
      256p.
Current and historical information on Blacks in
Chicago is presented both descriptively and statistically in this source. For a more detailed description, see Entry No. 74.

365. *THE EBONY HANDBOOK*. Compiled by Ebony editors
      and Doris E. Saunders. Chicago, Johnson Publi-
      shing Co., 1974, 553p.
Over 100 statistical tables supplement the text of
this publication. For a complete annotation, see
Entry No. 81.

366. *FEDERAL AGENCIES AND BLACK COLLEGES*. Prepared
      by the U.S. Department of Health, Education,
      and Welfare. Washington, D.C., G.P.O., 1970-
      Annual.
Federal aid to 115 Black colleges and universities
is described in this annual report. Tables cover
Federal funds obligated by agency and program;
Black institutions receiving Federal funds by state,
institution, agency and program; distribution of
Federal funds to Black colleges by control and level;
and total Federal obligations to colleges and universities by agency.

367. *MINORITY-OWNED BUSINESSES: BLACK*. Prepared by
      the U.S. Bureau of the Census. Washington, D.C.,
      G.P.O., 1969- . Irregular.
This survey was initiated in 1969 and repeated again
in 1972 (as part of the 1972 Economic Censuses). The
publication includes data on the number of Black firms,
gross receipts, and number of paid employees distributed
geographically by industry, size of firm and legal form
or organization of firm. Maps, figures and tables are
included. For a list of other volumes issued in the
series, see Entry No. 347.

368. *THE NEGRO FARMER IN THE UNITED STATES: 1930 CEN-
      SUS OF AGRICULTURE*. Prepared by the U.S. Bureau
      of the Census. Washington, D.C., G.P.O., 1933,
      84p.
The Black rural population in 1930 is described in text
and statistical tables. This population is compared to
the Black American population as a whole and the total
racial distribution of farm operators. The geographic
distribution of Black farmers, the tenure of Black
farmers, and the value of their lands and buildings
are quantitatively described. The data for 1930 are
compared with relevant data from the Census of Agriculture for 1910 and 1920.

369. *THE NEGRO HANDBOOK*. Compiled and edited by
      Florence Murray. New York, W. Malliet and Com-
      pany, 1942-9. Biennial.
This handbook provides factual and statistical information on financial, political, artistic, and religious
developments in Black America between 1942 and 1949.
For a complete annotation, see Entry No. 91.

370. *NEGRO IN THE ARMED FORCES: A STATISTICAL FACT
      BOOK*. Prepared by the U.S. Office of the Secre-
      tary of Defense. Washington, D.C., 1971, 259p.
This report statistically describes Black participation
in the U.S. Armed Forces between 1962 and 1972. The
data are analyzed by military service, grade, sex,
reenlistments, etc.

371. *NEGRO POPULATION, 1790-1915.* Prepared by Dr.
John Cummings. Washington, D.C., U.S. Bureau
of the Census, 1918. Reprinted by Kraus, 1969,
844p.

NEGRO POPULATION, 1790-1915 is a reprint of a 1918
census report that "provides a wealth of information
on every facet of Negro life susceptible of statistical
study": growth of population, migration, sex, age,
marital status, fertility, intermixture with other
races, mortality, education, economic conditions, etc.
Statistic data on the white population is included in
some tables for comparison. The report is divided into
four major periods: (1) colonial and revolutionary
period, 1619-1789; (2) slavery in the U.S., 1790-1865;
(3) first generation of freedom, 1865-1915; (4) second
generations since beginning of massive northward migration in 1915. Regular decennial censuses, other previously published and unpublished census data and
special original compilations of data were drawn on
in preparing this survey. A subject index is provided.
Current statistical data on this topic are included in
NEGRO POPULATION for the 1970 census (See Entry No.
372.

372. *NEGRO POPULATION: 1970 CENSUS OF POPULATION.
SUBJECT REPORTS.* Prepared by the U.S. Bureau
of the Census. Washington, D.C., G.P.O., 1973,
207p.

This report presents statistics on the Black population in 1970, cross-classified by various social and
economic characteristics for the United States, regions, selected states, standard metropolitan statistical areas (SMSAs) and cities. Table 1 presents
data for Blacks classified by sex and urban-rural residence for the U.S., regions, divisions and states.
Tables 2 through 10 contain data on characteristics
such as age, family relationships, marital status,
school enrollment, employment status, occupations,
income in 1969, and housing. In tables 11 to 15,
statistics on social, economic, and housing characteristics are given for selected SMSAs and cities. A
major portion of this information also appears in
Volume 1 of the 1970 Census of Population publication,

CHARACTERISTICS OF THE POPULATION. Similar data are
given for each tracted area in the Census of Population's *CENSUS TRACTS*. In addition, the 1970 Census
of Housing's *HOUSING CHARACTERISTICS FOR STATES, CITIES
AND COUNTIES* (volume 1) presents data on the characteristics of housing units with Black heads of household
for state, SMSAs, municipalities, and counties. Earlier
related data can be found in *NONWHITE POPULATION BY RACE*
(see Entry No. 342).

373. *NEGRO YEAR BOOK: AN ANNUAL ENCYCLOPEDIA OF THE
      NEGRO*. By Monroe N. Work. Tuskegee, Alabama,
      Tuskegee Institute Department of Records and
      Research, 1912-52, 11v. Irregular.
Many statistical tables supplement this publication's
factual description of Negro life. For a complete
annotation, see Entry No. 94.

374. *NEGROES IN THE UNITED STATES, 1920-32*. Prepared
      by Charles E. Hall. Washington, D.C., U.S. Bureau
      of the Census, 1935, 845p.
This report supplements *NEGRO POPULATION, 1790-1915*
(Entry No. 371). Each of its 20 chapters provides
introductory information and explanations of terms,
followed by a tabular presentation of the data. The
appendix gives characteristics of the Negro population
by counties according to the 1930 census. Some of the
statistics included here can be found in tables which
have been published elsewhere, but most of the material
is otherwise unavailable.

375. *THE SOCIAL AND ECONOMIC STATUS OF THE BLACK POPU-
      LATION IN THE UNITED STATES: CURRENT POPULATION
      REPORTS. SPECIAL STUDIES*. Prepared by the U.S.
      Bureau of the Census. Washington, D.C., G.P.O.,
      1966- . Annual.
Prepared by the Bureau of the Census, this report presents data on the socioeconomic and demographic characteristics of Black Americans from the Current Population Surveys, the Censuses of Population and Housing,
the Annual Housing Surveys, other government sources,

146

and private agencies. Subjects include: the growth
and distribution of the Black population, the income
levels of families, employment, labor force participation, occupation, Black-owned businesses, school
enrollment and educational attainment, characteristics
of postsecondary students, structure and other characteristics of the family, health, housing, voter registration and participation, elected officials, criminal
victimization, jail inmates, and capital punishment.
Statistics on Black and white populations are compared
for each subject covered.

Spanish Americans

376. *AMERICANS OF SPANISH ORIGIN*. Prepared by the
     U.S. Department of Health, Education and Welfare.
     Washington, D.C., G.P.O., 1974, 118p.
Data on Mexican Americans, Puerto Ricans, and Cuban
Americans are presented in this report which is part
of the *STUDY OF SELECTED SOCIO-ECONOMIC CHARACTERIS-
TICS OF ETHNIC MINORITIES BASED ON THE 1970 CENSUS*
(See Entry No. 346). Local analyses are included for
Mexican Americans in California, Arizona, New Mexico,
Colorado, Illinois, and Texas; for Puerto Ricans in
Illinois, Connecticut, New Jersey, and New York; and
for Cuban Americans in Florida, New York and New Jer-
sey. Family, education, employment and income char-
acteristics of these groups are emphasized in 15
charts and 38 tables.

377. *CHARACTERISTICS OF THE SPANISH SURNAME POPULA-
     TION BY CENSUS TRACT; FOR SMSA'S: 1970 CENSUS
     OF POPULATION. SUPPLEMENTARY REPORT*. Prepared
     by the U.S. Bureau of the Census. Washington,
     D.C., G.P.O., 1974, 939p.
Issued in five parts, this report presents data for
persons of Spanish surname in the standard metropoli-

tan statistical areas (SMSAs) of the five Southwestern
states: Arizona, California, Colorado, New Mexico, and
Texas. Information is provided for persons of Spanish
surname living in census tracts of 400 or more persons
of Spanish surname within SMSAs in each state as of
April 1, 1970. Cross tabulations of the data are presented by age, sex, relationship to head of household,
type of household, school enrollment, years of school
completed, residence in 1965, employment status, family
income, and poverty status.

378. *CHILENOS IN CALIFORNIA: A STUDY OF THE 1850,*
1852 AND 1860 CENSUS. By Carlos U. Lopez. San
Francisco, R & E Research Associates, 1973, 87p.
All persons who declared their country of origin to be
"Chile" in the 1850, 1852 and 1860 censuses are listed
in this computer produced reprint. Last names are
listed just as they appeared in the census rolls. First
names are also listed without spelling corrections.
The sex, age, county of residence and profession for
each of these individuals is provided. The census in
which they were listed is also indicated.

379. *EMPLOYMENT PROFILES OF SELECTED LOW-INCOME AREAS.*
N.Y.--PUERTO RICAN POPULATION OF SURVEY AREA:
1970 CENSUS OF POPULATION. Prepared by the U.S.
Bureau of the Census. Washington, D.C., G.P.O.,
1972, 284p.
This report presents statistics from the Census Employment Survey (CES) conducted as part of the overall
program of the 1970 Census of Population and Housing.
Tables A to N present general demographic characteristics of the Puerto Rican population of New York by the
most important labor force and socio-economic factors.
Tables 1 - 18 of the detailed characteristics' tables
show current labor force and employment status statistics by specific demographic characteristics. Tables
19 - 31 present the same detailed demographic characteristics by work experience of the population in the
last 12 months. Information on job training and work
history of the population is presented in tables 32 -
39. Detailed statistics on family income and migration

patterns in this area are presented in tables 40 - 54.

380. *MINORITY-OWNED BUSINESSES: SPANISH ORIGIN.* Pre-
      pared by the U.S. Bureau of the Census. Washing-
      ton, D.C., G.P.O., 1969- . Irregular.
This survey was initiated in 1969 and repeated again
in 1972 (as part of the 1972 Economic Census). The
publication includes data on the number of Spanish
American owned firms, gross receipts, and number of
paid employees distributed geographically by industry,
size of firm and legal form of organization. Maps,
figures, and tables are included. For a list of other
volumes in the series, see Entry No. 347.

381. *PERSONS OF SPANISH ORIGIN: 1970 CENSUS OF POPU-
      LATION. SUBJECT REPORTS.* Prepared by the U.S.
      Bureau of the Census. Washington, D.C., G.P.O.,
      1973, 199p.
This report presents statistics for persons of Spanish
origin, cross-classified by various social and economic
characteristics for the United States, regions, selected
states, standard metropolitan statistical areas (SMSAs),
and places. Selected housing characteristics are also
given. Table 1 presents data for the Spanish origin
population by type of origin cross-classified by sex
and urban-rural residence for the United States, regions,
divisions, and states. Table 2 shows data by race for
the total Spanish origin population with the same area
detail as Table 1, excluding urban-rural residence.
Tables 3 through 12 contain data on characteristics
such as age, race, household relationships, marital
status, education, employment status, occupation,
income in 1969 and housing. Most of these tables include data by urban-rural residence for the United
States and selected states. In tables 13 through 17,
statistics on social, economic and housing characteristics are given for 29 SMSAs with 50,000 or more
persons of Spanish origin and 31 places with 25,000
or more persons of Spanish origin. For each of the
selected SMSAs and places, data are shown separately
for the Spanish origin groups (Mexican, Puerto Rican,
or Cuban) with 25,000 or more persons. The data are

based on statistics collected by the 1970 Census of
Population. Related statistics are included in the
census report *PERSONS OF SPANISH SURNAME* (see Entry
No. 382). The data included here are up-dated by an
annual report, *PERSONS OF SPANISH ORIGIN IN THE U.S.*
(Prepared by the Bureau of the Census. Washington,
D.C., G.P.O., 1973- . Annual).

382. *PERSONS OF SPANISH SURNAME: CENSUS OF POPULATION.*
      SUBJECT REPORTS. Prepared by the U.S. Bureau of
      the Census. Washington, D.C., G.P.O., 1950- .
      Every 10 years.
Social, economic, and housing data for persons of
Spanish surname in Arizona, California, Colorado, New
Mexico and Texas are presented in this census publication. Information is also provided for selected
standard metropolitan statistical areas (SMSAs) and
places within the five states. Tables 1 through 13
present data for the five Southwestern states generally
by urban-rural residence; various social and economic
characteristics for persons of Spanish surname are
shown. Tables 1 through 3 also include data for SMSAs
and places with 25,000 or more persons of Spanish surname. Table 13 shows housing characteristics for
households with heads having Spanish surnames. Tables
14 through 18 present data for SMSAs with 25,000 or
more persons of Spanish surname and places with 10,000
or more such persons; tables 14 through 17 also show
social and economic data for these persons and table 18
shows data on their housing. Table 19 presents estimates
of the number of persons of Spanish surname for counties
and for all places of 10,000 or more inhabitants in the
five states. The data are based on the 1970 Census of
Population. Related statistics for 1970 can be found
in *PERSONS OF SPANISH ORIGIN* (see Entry No. 381). *PER-*
SONS OF SPANISH SURNAME has been issued as a subject
report of the Census of Population since 1950.

383. *PUERTO RICANS IN THE UNITED STATES: CENSUS OF*
      POPULATION. SUBJECT REPORTS. Prepared by the
      U.S. Census of Population. Washington, D.C.,
      G.P.O., 1960- . Every 10 years.

Based on data collected in the 1970 Census of Population, this report details selected social, economic and housing characteristics for persons of Puerto Rican parentage for the United States, regions, divisions, states, and selected standard metropolitan statistical areas (SMSAs) and cities. Table 1 shows statistics by urban and rural residence for the United States, regions, divisions, and states and table 3 shows statistics for the United States as a whole. Tables 2 and 4 through 10 include data for states with 10,000 or more Puerto Ricans, Tables 11, 15, 19, 23, and 27 provide data for SMSAs with 25,000 or more Puerto Ricans. Tables 12, 16, 20, 26 and 28 display data for SMSAs with 10,000 or more Puerto Ricans. Tables 13, 17, 21, 25, and 29 contain statistics for cities with 25,000 or more Puerto Ricans. Tables 14, 18, 22, 26, and 30 focus on cities with 5,000 to 25,000 such persons. Comparable data are available for 1950 in *PUERTO RICANS IN THE CONTINENTAL UNITED STATES*.

384. *SPANISH NAME PEOPLE IN THE SOUTHWEST AND WEST: SOCIOECONOMIC CHARACTERISTICS OF WHITE PERSONS OF SPANISH SURNAME IN TEXAS, ARIZONA, CALIFORNIA, COLORADO, AND NEW MEXICO*. By Robert Harris Talbert. Fort Worth, Texas, Leo Potishman Foundation, Texas Christian University, 1955, 90p.

Data concerning white persons of Spanish surname in Texas and four other Southwestern states are analyzed in this report based on statistics gathered in the 1950 Census of Population and Housing. Quantitative information is presented on education, marital and economic status, and housing. There is a subject index and a selected bibliography.

385. *SPANISH SURNAMED AMERICAN EMPLOYMENT IN THE SOUTHWEST*. Prepared by Fred H. Schmidt for the Colorado Civil Rights Commission under the auspices of the U.S. Equal Employment Opportunity Commission. Washington, D.C., G.P.O., 1970, 247p.

This study presents statistical information on the job patterns characterizing Spanish surnamed Americans in the Southwestern part of the United States (Arizona, California, Colorado, New Mexico, and Texas). Tabular data describe occupational distribution by job category, union arrangement, unemployment rates, employment growth, etc. Also included are sections which provide a historical background and an analysis of job discrimination patterns for these people. Reports on Spanish surnamed American employment in New York and Chicago are planned for future publication.

386. *A STATISTICAL PROFILE OF THE SPANISH-SURNAME POPULATION OF TEXAS*. By Harley L. Browning and S. Dale McLemore. Austin, Bureau of Business Research, University of Texas, 1964, 83p.
The main features and characteristics of the Spanish-surnamed population in Texas are compared with those of the Anglo and nonwhite for 1950 and 1960. These characteristics include: size and distribution of the population, age and sex composition, fertility and mortality rates, educational attainment, employment by occupation and industry, and income. The data included in this publication were taken from two reports published in 1950 and 1960 by the Bureau of the Census under the title *PERSONS OF SPANISH SURNAME* (see Entry No. 382).

Women

387. *AGE AT FIRST MARRIAGE: CENSUS OF POPULATION. SUBJECT REPORTS*. Prepared by the U.S. Bureau of the Census. Washington, D.C., G.P.O., 1960- . Every 10 years.
This report presents detailed statistics for the United States on characteristics of persons over 13 years of age by age of first marriage. Tables 1 through 19

display data on personal and socio-economic characteristics (marital status, race, sex, education,
occupation, etc.) of persons 14 years old and over
by age at first marriage. Tables 20-22 present
average annual rates of first marriage per 1,000
single persons 14 to 79 years old in 1968 and 1969,
by income, age, sex, education, and race. Most of
the statistics describe the United States and urban
areas. Some tables analyze data by type of residence
and regions. Rates of first marriage by age are shown
for States and the District of Columbia. The statistics
included in this publication are based on the decennial
Census of Population and also appear in the census publication *CHARACTERISTICS OF THE POPULATION*. Related
data can be found in *MARITAL STATUS* (see Entry No. 398).
In the 1950 census reports, statistics on age at which
current marital status was entered for women in selected age groups and duration of marriage were presented
in *DURATION OF CURRENT MARITAL STATUS* (1955, 55p.) and
FERTILITY (see Entry No. 394).

388. *BIRTH, STILLBIRTH, AND INFANT MORTALITY STATIS-
      TICS FOR THE CONTINENTAL UNITED STATES, THE
      TERRITORY OF HAWAII, THE VIRGIN ISLANDS, 1915-
      1936*. Prepared by the U.S. Bureau of the Census.
      Washington, D.C., G.P.O., 1917-1938. Annual.
Issued under various titles *(BIRTH STATISTICS FOR THE
BIRTH REGISTRATION AREA OF THE UNITED STATES* and *BIRTH,
STILLBIRTH, AND INFANT MORTALITY STATISTICS FOR THE
BIRTH REGISTRATION AREA OF THE UNITED STATES)*, this
annual presents statistics on births, still births, and
infant mortality analyzed by sex, color, nativity, and
age of mother, etc. Data are presented for the U.S.,
states, cities, and rural districts. Statistics for
the Virgin Islands and Hawaii are included in a separate section. The series ceased publication with the
1936 data and was continued by *VITAL STATISTICS OF THE
UNITED STATES* (Prepared by the U.S. Bureau of the Census. Washington, D.C., G.P.O., 1939- . Annual).

389. *THE BLACK WOMAN IN AMERICAN SOCIETY: A SELECTED,
      ANNOTATED BIBLIOGRAPHY*. By Lenwood G. Davis.

Boston, G.K. Hall, 1975, 159p.
One-third of this publication contains directory and
statistical information. For complete annotation, see
Entry No. 692.

390. *CHILDSPACING: 1960 CENSUS OF POPULATION. SUBJECT
     REPORTS.* Prepared by the U.S. Bureau of the Cen-
     sus. Washington, D.C., G.P.O., 1968, 185p.
National statistics on births to women by successive
ages and successive intervals since marriage, on intervals between births, and on birth rates for past
years are presented in this census report. Some
regional statistics (primarily for the South) are also
presented. The tabulations are based on the fertility
histories of women as obtained from reported birth
dates of their children who were present in the home
and from estimates of birth dates for those children
who had died or left home. The data are shown by
demographic, social, and economic characteristics of
women and their families. Among the characteristics
shown are race, marital status, age at first marriage,
education, occupation and income of the husband, and
labor force participation of the women. The statistics are based on data collected in the 1960 Census
of Population. Earlier data can be found in *FERTILITY*
(see Entry No. 394). Recent statistics on fertility
are presented in *WOMEN BY NUMBER OF CHILDREN EVER BORN*
(see Entry No. 407).

391. *COLOR AND SEX OF MIGRANTS: 1940 CENSUS OF POPU-
     LATION. FINAL REPORT.* Prepared by the U.S.
     Bureau of the Census. Washington, D.C., G.P.O.,
     1943, 490p.
For annotation, see Entry No. 330.

392. *EMPLOYMENT AND FAMILY CHARACTERISTICS OF WOMEN:
     1940 CENSUS OF POPULATION. FINAL REPORTS.*
     Prepared by the U.S. Bureau of the Census.
     Washington, D.C., G.P.O., 1943, 212p.
Data on the labor force status of women according to
employment and family status (e.g., marital status,

number and age of children, color, education, occupation) are presented in this report. The statistics included here are based on tabulations of samples taken from 1940 census returns and published as part of *THE LABOR FORCE* (1943, 6v.). Similar, earlier information is included in *MARITAL CONDITION OF OCCUPIED WOMEN* for 1920 (1923, 180p.) and for 1930 (1932, 72p.). Since 1940, related data can be found in such decennial census publications as *CHARACTERISTICS OF THE POPULATION; FAMILIES; EMPLOYMENT STATUS AND WORK EXPERIENCE;* and *OCCUPATIONAL CHARACTERISTICS*.

393. *EQUAL EMPLOYMENT OPPORTUNITY REPORT*. Prepared
      by the Equal Employment Opportunity Commission.
      Washington, D.C., G.P.O., 1966- . Annual.
For annotation, see Entry No. 334.

394. *FERTILITY: 1950 CENSUS OF POPULATION. SUBJECT
      REPORTS*. Prepared by the U. S. Bureau of the
      Census. Washington, D.C., G.P.O,, 1955, 188p.
Statistics presented on fertility are analyzed by
color, marital status, age, location, education,
occupation, etc. in 1950. Data are also included on
number of children ever born by age, color, marital
status, and location. The tabulations are based on
data collected in the 1950 Census of Population. Related census data for 1940 were published in five
volumes as *DIFFERENTIAL FERTILITY, 1940 and 1910;*
the five volumes were titled: *FERTILITY BY DURATION
OF MARRIAGE* (1947, 338p.); *FERTILITY FOR STATES AND
LARGE CITIES* (1943, 281p.); *STANDARDIZED FERTILITY
RATES AND REPRODUCTION RATES* (1944, 40p.); *WOMEN BY
NUMBER OF CHILDREN EVER BORN* (1945, 410p.); and
WOMEN BY NUMBER OF CHILDREN UNDER 5 YEARS OLD (1945,
265p.). Other statistics can be found in the census
publications *PROPORTION OF CHILDREN IN THE UNITED
STATES* (1905, 27p.); *RATIO OF CHILDREN TO WOMEN*
(1920 *CENSUS MONOGRAPH XI*, 1931, 242p.); *CHILDSPACING*
(see Entry No. 390); *WOMEN BY CHILDREN UNDER 5 YEARS
OLD* (see Entry No. 406); and *WOMEN BY NUMBER OF CHILDREN EVER BORN* (see Entry No. 407).

395. *THE FERTILITY OF AMERICAN WOMEN: 1950 CENSUS OF POPULATION. MONOGRAPH.* Prepared by Wilson H. Grabill, Clyde B. Kiser, and Pascal K. Whelpton for the U.S. Department of the Census. Washington, D.C., G.P.O., 1958, 162p.
Emphasizing census data from 1910, 1940 and 1950, this monograph traces reproductive trends in the United States. The fertility rate is analyzed by such factors as location, age, race, occupation, education, income, and other socioeconomic characteristics. Data are included on the number of children ever born, the number of children under five years of age, the number of birth registrations, and the prevalence of contraceptive practice. A bibliography of materials dealing with the fertility of American women is provided. An earlier, related census monograph publication is *RATIO OF CHILDREN TO WOMEN, 1920. A STUDY IN THE DIFFERENTIAL ROLE OF NATURAL INCREASE IN THE UNITED STATES: 1920 CENSUS OF POPULATION. MONOGRAPH.* (By Warren S. Thompson for the U.S. Bureau of the Census. Washington, D.C., G.P.O., 1931, 242p.). For up-to-date statistics on fertility, see *WOMEN BY NUMBER OF CHILDREN EVER BORN* (Entry No. 407).

396. *HANDBOOK ON WOMEN WORKERS.* Issued by the U.S. Women's Bureau. Washington, D.C., G.P.O., 1948- . Irregular.
Information on the earnings, income, employment and education of women in the labor force is presented in this periodically revised handbook. In addition to the statistical compilations, a legal survey (a report on women in each state), a directory of "organizations of interest to women," and an extensive, annotated bibliography covering such topics as counseling, family status, and education can be found in this source. The title of the *HANDBOOK* varies. Between 1948 and 1952, it was issued as the *HANDBOOK OF FACTS ON WOMEN WORKERS*. The latest edition of the *HANDBOOK ON WOMEN WORKERS* came out in 1975.

397. *MARITAL STATUS AND LIVING ARRANGEMENTS: CURRENT POPULATION REPORTS. POPULATION CHARACTERISTICS.*

Prepared by the U.S. Bureau of the Census.
Washington, D.C., G.P.O., 1947- . Annual.
Issued under various titles (*CHARACTERISTICS OF
SINGLE, MARRIED, WIDOWED, AND DIVORCED PERSONS IN
1947; MARITAL STATUS, NUMBER OF TIMES MARRIED, AND
DURATION OF PRESENT MARITAL STATUS: APRIL 1948;
MARITAL STATUS AND HOUSEHOLD CHARACTERISTICS; MARITAL
STATUS, ECONOMIC STATUS, AND FAMILY STATUS: MARCH
1957; MARITAL STATUS AND FAMILY STATUS*), this annual
presents "detailed statistics on the marital status
and living arrangements of the noninstitutional population of the United States." Included in the reports
is information on the marital status of persons over
13 years of age, analyzed by race, sex, age, presence
of parents for persons under 18 years old, and household headship by marital status for regions. The
data displayed in each report are taken from the annually conducted Current Population Survey.

398. *MARITAL STATUS: CENSUS OF POPULATION. SUBJECT
REPORTS*. Prepared by the U.S. Bureau of the
Census. Washington, D.C., 1950- . Every 10
years.
Statistics are presented on the family status of
persons over 13 years old, by marital status, age,
sex, income, race, location, etc. Data are also
provided for the duration of marriage, analyzed by
age, offsprings, education, race, etc. This series
was first issued in 1950, in two parts: *MARITAL
STATUS* (1953, 68p.) and *DURATION OF CURRENT MARITAL
STATUS* (1955, 55p.). Similar data can be found in
the general final reports of the decennial census
(*CHARACTERISTICS OF THE POPULATION*), in the annual
series issued as part of the Current Population Report
series, *MARITAL STATUS AND LIVING ARRANGEMENTS* (see
Entry No. 397), and in volume 3 of the *VITAL STATISTICS
OF THE UNITED STATES* (Rockville, Maryland, U.S. Public
Health Service, 1939- . Annual).

399. *MARRIAGE AND DIVORCE, 1922-1932: VITAL STATIS-
TICS. SPECIAL REPORTS*. Prepared by the U.S.
Bureau of the Census. Washington, D.C., 1925-

1934. Annual.
These annual reports, covering the years from 1922
through 1932, contain text and tables on the number
of marriages, divorces and annulments, divorces
contested and not contested, divorces by cause, annulments by duration of marriage, etc. The contents of
each of these reports varies. The data were collected
from records of selected states cooperating with the
Census Bureau and from county offices. The series
ceased with the report covering 1932. Volume 3 of
the *VITAL STATISTICS OF THE UNITED STATES* (Rockville,
Maryland, U.S. Public Health Service, 1939- . Annual)
has provided equivalent information annually since 1937.
Earlier compilations issued by the Bureau of the Census
also cover the same topic: *MARRIAGE AND DIVORCE, 1916*
(1919, 47p.) and *MARRIAGE AND DIVORCE 1867-1906* (1908-
1909, 2v.).

400. *MARRIAGE AND LIVING ARRANGEMENTS: CENSUS OF POP-
     ULATION. SUBJECT REPORTS.* Washington, D.C.,
     G.P.O., 1950- . Every 10 years.
Included in this series of reports issued as part of
the decennial Census of Population are *FAMILY COMPOSI-
TION, PERSONS BY FAMILY CHARACTERISTICS, MARITAL STATUS*
(see Entry No. 398), and *AGE AT FIRST MARRIAGE* (see
Entry No. 387).

401. *MINORITIES AND WOMEN IN STATE AND LOCAL GOVERN-
     MENT.* Washington, D.C., U.S. Equal Opportunity
     Commission, 1973- . Annual
Analysis of data on the employment of minorities and
women in state and local government is made in this
annual by race/ethnic group and sex, function of
government, salary group, and job category. For a
complete annotation, see Entry No. 388.

402. *PROFESSIONAL WOMEN AND MINORITIES; A MANPOWER
     RESOURCE SERVICE.* By Betty M. Vetter and Eleanor
     L. Babco. Washington, D.C., Scientific Manpower
     Commission, 1975, 656p.
Data on the supply of manpower in the professions

(with special emphasis on women and minorities) are
presented in this publication. No original statistics are supplied; data are extracted from compilations
produced by the Bureau of the Census, Department of
Labor, U.S. Office of Education, and the National
Science Foundation. The book is arranged by academic
discipline and provides information on professionals
and on graduate degrees in the various disciplines.
Semi-annual updates are planned.

403.   A STATISTICAL PORTRAIT OF WOMEN IN THE UNITED
       STATES: CURRENT POPULATION REPORTS. SPECIAL
       STUDIES. Prepared by the U.S. Bureau of the
       Census. Washington, D.C., G.P.O., 1976, 90p.
This report presents a statistical portrait showing
"the role of women in the United States during the
20th century." Data are from government sources:
surveys, decennial censuses, vital statistics, and
administrative records. Selected data are provided
in a historical framework, beginning in 1950, or
earlier if statistics are available. The analyses
trace trends among women in the areas of population
growth and composition, longevity, mortality and health,
residence and migration, marital and family status,
fertility, education, labor force participation, occupation and industry, work experience, income and
poverty status, voting and public office holding,
and crime and victimization. Comparisons of Black
and white women are discussed separately, and recent
data are included for women of Spanish origin.

404.   STATISTICS OF WOMEN AT WORK BASED ON UNPUBLISHED
       INFORMATION FROM THE SCHEDULES OF THE TWELFTH
       CENSUS: 1900. Prepared by the U.S. Bureau of
       the Census. Washington, D.C., 1907, 399p.
Statistics are provided on women employed in various
occupations (domestic work, dressmaking, textile work,
clerical activities, education, etc.). The data are
analyzed by geographic distribution, race, parentage,
age, marital status, family relationship, earlier
census figures, etc.

405. *STUDY OF EMPLOYMENT OF WOMEN IN THE FEDERAL GOVERNMENT*. Prepared for the Federal Women's Program by the U.S. Civil Service Commission. Washington, D.C., G.P.O., 1967- . Annual.
This study presents statistical information on full-time Federal civilian white collar employees. The statistics are analyzed by general schedule and equivalent grades, by special occupational groups and by pay schedules. Similar data for the state and local levels can be found in the annual *MINORITIES AND WOMEN IN STATE AND LOCAL GOVERNMENT* (see Entry No. 338).

406. *WOMEN BY CHILDREN UNDER 5 YEARS OLD: 1960 CENSUS OF POPULATION. SUBJECT REPORTS*. Prepared by the U.S. Bureau of the Census. Washington, D.C., G.P.O., 1968, 140p.
This report presents statistics on the fertility of women in the United States as measured by the number of their own children under five years old present in the household. Some data on children five to nine years old are also presented. The data are shown by demographic, social, and economic characteristics of the women and their families. Among the characteristics shown are: age, race, nativity, country of origin, education, marital status, age at first marriage, occupation, income in 1959, and housing characteristics. Most of the statistics are based on the 1960 Census of Population. Earlier data can be found in *FERITLITY* (see Entry No. 394). Recent statistics on fertility are presented in *WOMEN BY NUMBER OF CHILDREN EVER BORN* (see Entry No. 407).

407. *WOMEN BY NUMBER OF CHILDREN EVER BORN: 1970 CENSUS OF POPULATION. SUBJECT REPORTS*. Prepared by the U.S. Bureau of the Census. Washington, D.C., G.P.O., 1973, 379p.
Detailed statistics for the United States and its regions regarding the number of children ever born to women 15 years old and over are presented in this report. The data are cross-classified by numerous social and economic characteristics of women and their families. Tables 1-21 present data on children

160

ever born analyzed by age, race, ethnic group, urban-rural residence, and residence in 1965. Tables 22-43 emphasize cross-tabulations by marital status and marital history. The economic details of occupation and income are covered in tables 44-57. Tables 58-64 relate primarily to housing and household characteristics. Tables 65-67 show the data available regarding children born to single women who are otherwise regarded as childless in the detailed tables of this report. The statistics are based on the 1970 Census of Population. Earlier related data can be found in the 1960 census reports *WOMEN BY NUMBER OF CHILDREN EVER BORN, CHILDSPACING* (see Entry No. 390), and *WOMEN BY CHILDREN UNDER 5 YEARS OLD* (see Entry No. 406); and the 1950 census report *FERTILITY* (see Entry No. 394).

408. *WOMEN IN PUBLIC OFFICE: A BIOGRAPHICAL DIRECTORY AND STATISTICAL HANDBOOK.* Compiled by the Eagleton Institute of Politics, Rutgers University. New York, Bowker, 1976, 455p.
For annotation, see Entry No. 201.

409. *WOMEN-OWNED BUSINESS, 1972.* Prepared by the U.S. Bureau of the Census. Washington, D.C., G.P.O., 1976, 277p.
The 1972 survey of women-owned businesses is a special project funded by the Office of Minority Business Enterprise. Basic data presented in the publication were obtained from the administrative records of the 1972 Economic Censuses. Information is presented by industry, geographic area, employment size, receipts' size and legal form of organization. Maps supplement the statistical tables. Minority firms owned by women are also included. Coverage is the same as that for other publications in the *1972 SURVEY OF MINORITY-OWNED BUSINESS ENTERPRISES* (see Entry No. 347).

410. *WOMEN'S RIGHTS ALMANAC, 1974.* Edited by Nancy Gager. Bethesda, Maryland, Elizabeth Cady Stanton Publishing Co., 1974, 620p.
A variety of statistical and factual information is

provided on the women's movement. For a complete
annotation, see Entry No. 131.

Chapter 6

MINORITIES

(Indexes, Abstracts, Bibliographies, etc.)

411. *AMERICAN ETHNIC GROUPS: A SOURCEBOOK.* By Jack
F. Kinton. 4th ed. Aurora, Illinois, Social
Science and Sociological Resources, 1974, 206p.
This sourcebook on American ethnic groups includes
citations to print (books, articles, periodicals and
reference works) and non-print materials on American
Indians, Asians, European immigrant groups, Spanish-
speaking Americans and Blacks. The objective of the
bibliography is to expose "present and future social
scientists to minority studies--ethnic and racial,
theoretical and empirical." Included are major works
from the fields of sociology, anthropology, and American history. Lists of minority studies' centers and
lists of films on ethnic groups are also identified
in the source.

412. *AMERICAN MAJORITIES AND MINORITIES: A SYLLABUS
OF UNITED STATES HISTORY FOR SECONDARY SCHOOLS.*
By Warren J. Halliburton and William Loren
Katz. New York, Arno Press, 1970, 219p.
Commissioned by the Education Programs Department of
the NAACP, this publication presents 38 units of
multi-racial and multi-ethnic American history to
help teachers prepare their daily lesson plans. Each
of the units includes: factual information, a concep-
tual framework, and an annotated bibliography (of
readings for students and audio-visual materials for
classroom use). The source is designed to help
teachers integrate the contributions made by Blacks,
Indians, Mexican-Americans, Puerto Ricans and other
minorities into their regular course of study in
American history for junior and senior high schools.
Katz has also prepared a similar source for American
Negro history; see Entry No. 625.

413. *A BIBLIOGRAPHY OF DOCTORAL RESEARCH ON MINORITIES:
RACIAL, RELIGIOUS AND ETHNIC.* Ann Arbor, Michigan, Xerox University Microfilms, 1972, 55p.
This bibliography is a guide to more than 500 dissertations accepted at American universities and published
by Xerox University Microfilms between 1938 and 1970.
The major source used in compiling this bibliography

was *DISSERTATION ABSTRACTS INTERNATIONAL* (Ann Arbor,
Michigan, University Microfilms, 1938-   ). The dissertations are listed alphabetically by author; each
entry includes the name of the author, the full title
of the dissertation, the name of the accepting institution, the date of completion, the University Microfilms' order number and the page/volume reference for
DISSERTATION ABSTRACTS INTERNATIONAL. The dissertations cover every aspect of study relating to racial,
ethnic and religious minorities both in the United
States and around the world. Dissertations on Blacks,
however, are generally excluded from this listing;
for these citations, see Earle H. West's *A BIBLIOGRAPHY
OF DOCTORAL RESEARCH ON THE NEGRO 1933-1966* (Entry No.
565.

414. *BIBLIOGRAPHY OF IMMIGRATION IN THE UNITED STATES,
      1900-1930.* By William Ralph Janeway. Columbus,
      Ohio, H.L. Hedrick, 1934, 105p. Reprinted by R
      & E Research Associates, 1972.
The aim of this bibliography is to include "the more
important books, documents and periodical material
published between the years 1900 to 1933, which were
the years in which the subject of immigration was most
widely discussed." It is aimed primarily toward the
undergraduate student. This list is arranged by subject (e.g., alien stream and its control, immigrant
backgrounds and cultural heritages, social adjustments,
etc.) and subdivided alphabetically by format (books,
periodicals, references, etc.) and/or author. In depth
coverage is provided for Mexican-American and other
Central and South American as well as Asian immigrants.

415. *A BIBLIOGRAPHY OF NORTH AMERICAN FOLKLORE AND
      FOLKSONG.* By Charles Haywood. 2nd rev. ed.
      New York, Dover Publications, Inc., 1961, 2v.
Volume 1 of this two volume set has a very extensive
section on the folklore of the Negro and a few references for Chinese, Japanese and Spanish Americans.
Volume 2 is entitled *THE AMERICAN INDIANS NORTH OF
MEXICO, INCLUDING THE ESKIMOS.* For a complete annotation, see Entry No. 461.

416. *BIBLIOGRAPHY ON ETHNICITY AND ETHNIC GROUPS.*
Compiled and edited by Richard Kolm for the
U.S. National Institute on Mental Health.
Washington, D.C., G.P.O., 1973, 250p.
The emphasis of this bibliography is on "materials
dealing with the situation of immigrant ethnic groups,
their psychological adjustments and conditions affecting acculturation; and materials dealing with patterns
of ethnic behavior, identity, family life, and communications structure." The nearly 2,000 citations are
arranged alphabetically by author in two major sections:
annotated entries and unannotated entries. Most
references were published since the end of World War
II. A subject index is included.

417. *BIBLIOGRAPHY ON RACISM.* Prepared by the U.S.
National Institute on Mental Health. Washington,
D.C., G.P.O., 1972, 160p.
All materials relating to racism available from the
computerized information files of the National Clearinghouse for Mental Health Information are listed in
this bibliography. Articles, books and reports are
cited. An abstract accompanies each citation. The
work is indexed by author and subject.

418. *CULTURALLY DISADVANTAGED: A BIBLIOGRAPHY AND
KEYWORD-OUT-OF-CONTEXT (KWOC) INDEX.* By Robert
E. Booth and others. Detroit, Wayne State
University Press, 1967, 803p.
Nearly 1,500 books, journal articles and reports are
listed by key word (or descriptors) derived from either
the titles of the materials or the body of their texts.
The citations cover everything from conformity to
library service to self-concept. No item is more
recent than 1965. Semi-annual supplements are planned.

419. *DOCUMENT AND REFERENCE TEXT (DART): AN INDEX TO
MINORITY GROUP EMPLOYMENT.* Ann Arbor, Institute of Labor and Industrial Relations, University of Michigan-Wayne State University, 1967,
602p. *SUPPLEMENT,* 1971.

DART is a computer produced literature index based on
the full title key-word-in-context (KWIC) indexing
system. Over 4,000 books and articles describing employment and social problems faced by Blacks, Spanish-
speaking, American Indians, Oriental Americans and
women are arranged by key word. There are no annotations. Author and institutional sponsor indexes are
provided. In the appendices, there are listings of
agencies administering fair employment practices acts
and organizations concerned with minority group employment. The supplement issued in 1971 follows the same
organization and content as the original edition.

420. *THE ECONOMICS OF MINORITIES: A GUIDE TO INFORMA-*
     TION SOURCES. By Kenneth L. Gagala. Detroit,
     Gale Research Company, 1976, 212p. (Economics
     Information Guide Series, no. 2).
Research on the economic conditions of non-white people
(Blacks, Mexican-Americans, Native Americans, Puerto
Ricans) in the United States is presented and briefly
summarized in this bibliography. The bulk of the
material cited was published during the period 1965
to the summer of 1974. The source is organized by
subject (e.g., description and causes of Black economic
inequality, the psychology of race, economic development
of Black community, American Indians, etc.). Books,
articles, government documents, some reports and occasional unpublished materials are cited. The entries are
annotated. Title and subject indexes are provided.

421. *THE EDUCATION OF THE MINORITY CHILD: A COMPRE-*
     HENSIVE BIBLIOGRAPHY OF 10,000 SELECTED ENTRIES.
     By Meyer Weinberg. Chicago, Integrated Educa-
     tion Associates, 1970, 530p.
Mexicans, Indians, Blacks and other North American
ethnic minorities are represented in this unannotated
bibliography of 10,000 references on the education of
minority children. In addition to including literature on the minority child, Weinberg presents selections which concentrate on the classroom teachers,
compensatory education, student involvement, recent
educational innovations, etc. Listed are primary

sources, scientific studies, Black periodicals,
congressional transcripts, public hearings, books,
articles, and dissertations. The citations are arranged in 24 sections (e.g., history; the Black woman;
Indian Americans; school organization, social
conditions, etc.). One of the major sections, "The
American Scene," emphasizes current educational issues
and situations in 42 states, plus the District of
Columbia. Another important section covers Afro-
American studies and explores such issues as culturally fair textbooks and the organization of Black
studies programs. A separate section lists 250 bibliographies relating to the field of education generally
and the minority child specifically.

422. *THE EMERGING MINORITIES IN AMERICA: A RESOURCE
      GUIDE FOR TEACHERS*. Edited by the Santa Barbara
      County Board of Education. Santa Barbara, Calif-
      ornia, ABC-Clio, 1973, 256p.
For annotation, see Entry No. 135.

423. *ENCYCLOPEDIC DIRECTORY OF ETHNIC NEWSPAPERS AND
      PERIODICALS IN THE UNITED STATES*. 2nd ed. By
      Lubomyr R. Wynar. Littleton, Colorado, Libraries
      Unlimited, 1975, 260p.
In this encyclopedic directory, over 900 ethnic newspapers and periodicals are arranged in two categories
under each of the 43 ethnic groups covered: publications in native language (410) and bilingual (207);
publications in English (286). Within each section,
titles are again arranged alphabetically. Information
provided for each item includes name, address, editor,
language of publication, sponsoring organization,
circulation, frequency and subscription price. Brief
descriptive annotations delineate the scope, content
and purpose of the publications. An added feature of
the directory is its introductory article, "The
Ethnic Press in the United States and Its Bibliographic
Control." Ethnic press is defined as newspapers and
periodicals published in a foreign language or in
English but addressing themselves to a national group.
Statistical tables (giving such information as the

distribution of ethnic press by type, frequency and circulation) are included in the introduction and the appendix. There is a title index.

424. *EQUAL OPPORTUNITY IN EMPLOYMENT*. Prepared by
      the U.S. Civil Service Commission. Washington,
      D.C., G.P.O., 1971, 135p. (Personnel Bibliogra-
      phy Series, No. 38). Revised, 1973, 170p.
      (Personnel Bibliography Series no. 49).
Materials received in the Civil Service Commission
Library are listed in this annotated bibliography.
The 1971 edition includes 1969-1970 acquisitions; the
1973 publication concentrates on 1971 and 1972. The
entries are classified into various subject chapters:
minority groups, older workers, women, etc. Each chapter also contains a list of bibliographies on its topic.

425. *THE EQUALITY OF EDUCATIONAL OPPORTUNITY; A
      BIBLIOGRAPHY OF SELECTED REFERENCES*. By Fran-
      cesco Cordasco, Mauri Hillson and Eugene Busshio-
      ni. Totowa, New Jersey, Rowman and Littlefield,
      1973, 139p.
The bibliographic portion of this source lists over
400 books, articles, and government documents "selected
from the vast literature spawned in the 1960s (and
extending into the next decade) which deals with the
American schools and the children of the poor; with
the so called 'minority child'...; with the surging
restiveness of community involvements; the desegregation of urban schools; with multifarious educational
experiments and failing innovative designs; and with the
twin themes of alienation and disaffection." This
section is preceded by a short bibliographic essay
which cites works dealing with poverty in general,
bibliographic aids, and guides to programs for the
disadvantaged. Other parts of the work contain an
essay on education for the poor and relevant Federal
programs from 1785 to the 1960s, a bibliography of
education for Puerto Ricans on the mainland, and a
summary of *HEW's 1969 URBAN EDUCATION TASK FORCE REPORT*.

426. *ETHNIC BIBLIOGRAPHICAL GUIDES*. New York, Burt
     Franklin Originals, 1974- .
The purpose of this series is to "provide concise,
yet comprehensive, introductions to the literature
for each ethnic community on such diverse subjects as:
social backgrounds, the adjustment process, genera-
tional and social class factors, as well as historical,
cultural and religious influences." Each volume is
prepared by a leading scholar and includes an introduction, hundreds of critically annotated entries, and
a selection of scarce and important documents. Only
one volume, Francesco Cordasco's *THE ITALIAN-AMERICAN
EXPERIENCE,* has been issued to date.

427. *ETHNIC CHRONOLOGY SERIES: CHRONOLOGY AND FACT
     BOOKS*. Dobbs Ferry, New York, Oceana Publica-
     tions, 1971- . 16v.
For annotation, see Entry No. 11.

428. *ETHNIC GROUPS IN OHIO WITH SPECIAL EMPHASIS ON
     CLEVELAND: AN ANNOTATED BIBLIOGRAPHICAL GUIDE*.
     By Lubomyr R. Wynar and associates. Cleveland,
     Cleveland State University Ethnic Studies Dev-
     elopment Program, 1975, 254p.
This guide "constitutes a selective listing of the
English language materials on ethnic groups in the
United States, with special emphasis on Ohio. Materials in non-English languages dealing with individual
ethnic groups are excluded." Indians, Appalachians,
Blacks, Chinese, Japanese, and Ukrainians are among
the 31 major ethnic groups in Ohio that are covered.
The annotated entries consist mostly of monographs
and are arranged by individual ethnic group. A section of general works on ethnicity and a section of
reference books are included. The appendix contains
a directory of ethnic archival holdings and ethnic
newspapers in Cleveland, Ohio; the Ohio network of
American history research centers; and statistics
on the ethnic population in the United States, Ohio,
and Cleveland. An author index and an index to institutions with archival holdings are included.

429. *ETHNIC INFORMATION SOURCES OF THE UNITED STATES:*
      A GUIDE TO ORGANIZATIONS, AGENCIES, FOUNDATIONS,
      INSTITUTIONS, MEDIA, COMMERCIAL AND TRADE BODIES,
      GOVERNMENT PROGRAMS, RESEARCH INSTITUTES, LIBRA-
      RIES AND MUSEUMS, RELIGIOUS ORGANIZATIONS, BANK-
      ING FIRMS, FESTIVALS AND FAIRS, TRAVEL AND TOURIST
      OFFICES, AIRLINES AND SHIP LINES, BOOKDEALERS
      AND PUBLISHERS' REPRESENTATIVES, AND BOOKS,
      PAMPHLETS AND AUDIOVISUALS ON SPECIFIC ETHNIC
      GROUPS. Edited by Paul Wasserman and Jean Morgan.
      Detroit, Gale Research, 1976, 770p.
Sources of information about ethnic groups are identified and described. Both organizational and bibliographic sources available in the United States are covered.
All identifiable ethnic groups are considered, except
for Blacks, American Indians and Eskimos. For each
ethnic group, information sources are listed under 26
major headings, including foundations, museums, cultural
and educational organizations, magazines, newspapers
and newsletters, radio programs, books, pamphlets,
and audio-visual material. There are indexes to the
organizations and publications.

430. *ETHNIC STUDIES BIBLIOGRAPHY.* Pittsburgh, Univ-
      ersity Center for International Studies, Univer-
      sity of Pittsburgh, 1976- . Annual.
The purpose of this bibliography is to identify
journal articles dealing with ethnic studies. Produced from a computer-based information system, *ETHNIC*
STUDIES BIBLIOGRAPHY examines and analyzes ethnic studies literature found in nearly 120 journals. Part I
of the bibliography consists of five indexes: author,
subject, geographic area, proper names (e.g., organizations, laws, sub-national geographic areas, etc.), and
journal. Part II contains document descriptions of the
relevant articles; the information given for each
entry includes author, title, journal citation, abstract
of contents, names of special features (figures, tables,
etc.), names of cited persons, key subject descriptors,
and proper names.

431. *ETHNIC STUDIES IN HIGHER EDUCATION: STATE OF THE*

ART AND BIBLIOGRAPHY. By Winnie Bengelsdorf,
with the assistance of Susan Norwitch and Louise
Vrande. Washington, American Association of
State Colleges and Universities, 1972, 260p.
The purpose of this reference source is to "identify
and summarize recent material on Ethnic Studies in
higher education and to determine the state of the
art or trend of these studies." Separate sections
cover Asian-Americans, Blacks, Chicanos, Indians,
Puerto Ricans, white ethnic groups and programs in
the multi-ethnic or cross-cultural field." Monographs, articles, periodicals, and research completed
or pending are cited. Most of the entries are annotated. There are separate chapters on multi-ethnic
teacher training efforts, minority enrollment and
minority opportunities. An index completes the source.

432. *GUIDE TO MEDIA AND MATERIALS ON ETHNIC AMERICAN
     MINORITIES.* By Harry A. Johnson. New York,
     Bowker, to be published in 1976.
Media relevant to the needs of Spanish, Indian, Asian
Americans, and Afro-Americans are listed and described.
Entries are arranged by minority group and subdivided
by form of media. A list of selected paperbound pub-
lications on minorities and other ethnic groups in
America is also included.

433. *HUMAN RELATIONS AREA FILES.* Prepared by George
     P. Murdock and others. New Haven, Connecticut.
     Human Relations Area Files, 1949- .
For annotation, see Entry No. 494.

434. *INVENTORY OF RESEARCH IN RACIAL AND CULTURAL
     RELATIONS.* Chicago, Committee on Education,
     Training and Research in Race Relations of the
     University of Chicago, 1948-1953. Annual.
Books, journal articles, government documents, pamphlets, dissertations and research in progress issued
between 1948 and 1953 are listed in this bibliography.
The entries are arranged alphabetically by author and
indexed by subject. Lengthy annotations are included.

The publication ceased with volume five ("The Committee is no longer financially able to continue the undertaking."). This final volume contains, in addition to the annotated bibliography, a cumulated index for the entire period of the *INVENTORY*'s existence, proceedings of the Conference on Research in Race Relations cosponsored by the Committee and the National Association of Intergroup Relations Officials, and a general report on the status of research in the field.

435. *KNOWING AND EDUCATING THE DISADVANTAGED: AN
     ANNOTATED BIBLIOGRAPHY*. Alamosa, Colorado,
     Center for Cultural Studies, Adams State College,
     1965, 460p.
This bibliography, sponsored by the U.S. Office of
Education, was compiled to aid the planning, research,
and demonstration projects related to the education of
agricultural migratory adults. The citations (to books,
articles and audio-visual materials) are listed by
author or title and indexed by topic (e.g., acculturation, bilingualism, etc.). Emphasis is on Mexican
Americans and Indians. A separate section lists
publishers, resource/service sources, and A-V producers.

436. *MINORITY BUSINESS ENTERPRISE: A BIBLIOGRAPHY*.
     Prepared by the U.S. Department of Commerce.
     Washington, D.C., G.P.O., 1973, 231p.
This bibliography, "intended to serve as a basis for
what it is hoped will ultimately evolve into a comprehensive and useful resource tool for all pertinent
references on minority business enterprise," is arranged
in five sections: bibliographies; books and monographs;
journal articles, reports and speeches; pertinent directories; periodical titles. Over 1,400 citations are
included. Annotations are provided for each item. When
available, purchase information is included. There is
a subject index.

437. *MINORITY GROUPS AND HOUSING; A BIBLIOGRAPHY,
     1950-1970*. By Byrl N. Boyce and Sidney Turoff.
     Morristown, New Jersey, General Learning Press,

1972, 202p.
This is a bibliography of research materials which deal
with the findings, problems and issues relating to the
housing of minorities in the United States (segregation,
socio-economic characteristics, fair housing trends,
etc.). Books, pamphlets, articles, periodicals, government documents, films, unpublished papers, theses, and
dissertations are cited. The materials are listed in
several sections: community and group action/integra-
tion and discrimination; housing brokerage and development finance; housing costs and values; legislation;
legal action; public housing and urban renewal; reference books; and relevant organizations. The commentary
preceding each section generally refers to the items
cited there. Subject and author indexes complete the
work, which is an updated and expanded version of an
earlier bibliography: *MINORITY GROUPS AND HOUSING, A
SELECTED BIBLIOGRAPHY, 1950-1967* (By Stephen D. Messner. Storrs, Connecticut, University of Connecticut,
1968, 58p.).

438. *MINORITY STUDIES: A SELECTIVE, ANNOTATED BIBLIO-
     GRAPHY OF WORKS ON NATIVE AMERICANS, SPANISH
     AMERICANS, AFRO-AMERICANS, AND ASIAN AMERICANS.*
     By Priscilla Oaks. Boston, G.K. Hall, 1976,
     285p.
Easily obtainable books (particularly paperbacks and
reprints) are listed in this bibliography of basic
ethnic studies materials. The items are arranged by
ethnic groups (Native Americans, Afro-Americans,
Spanish Americans and Asian Americans) and subdivided
by subject. Each entry is critically annotated. Works
by ethnic authors are stressed. Emphasis is placed on
autobiographical works and primary source material.
There is an index for titles and authors.

439. *POVERTY, RURAL POVERTY AND MINORITY GROUPS LIVING
     IN RURAL POVERTY: AN ANNOTATED BIBLIOGRAPHY.*
     Prepared by the Institute for Rural America.
     Lexington, Kentucky, Spindletop Research, 1969,
     159p.
The purpose of this selective, annotated bibliography

is "to aid individuals who are engaged in research on
the subject of poverty in the United States." It
contains entries for each of a number of topics (e.g.,
assimilation of Indians, life patterns of migrants,
Negro marriage and the family, discrimination against
Spanish Americans) under three headings: Poverty in the
United States; Rural Poverty; and Minority Groups Living
in Rural Poverty. Included in this bibliography are
a large number of government publications, books,
and journal articles. There is no index, but there is
a detailed table of contents. The publication is the
product of research and bibliographic activities conducted by the Institute for Rural America for Spindle-
top Research, Inc.

440. *RESEARCH ANNUAL ON INTERGROUP RELATIONS.* Edited
      by Melvin M. Tumin. Chicago, Quadrangle Books,
      1965- . Annual.
This bibliography represents an outgrowth of Tumin's
1957 publication, *SEGREGATION AND DESEGREGATION* (New
York, Anti-Defamation League of B'nai B'rith, 1957,
112p.) and its supplement, *SEGREGATION AND DESEGREGA-
TION; A DIGEST OF RECENT RESEARCH, 1956-1959* (New York,
Anti-Defamation League, 1960, 32p.). It briefly annotates research (especially unpublished studies)
which examines the attitudes and relationships of
"groups that were ethnic, racial, religious or national
in character." A classified arrangement is employed.
Addresses for the cited researchers and their organizations are provided. There is an author index.

441. *SCHOOL INTEGRATION; A COMPREHENSIVE CLASSIFIED
      BIBLIOGRAPHY OF 3,100 REFERENCES.* By Meyer
      Weinburg. Chicago, Integrated Education Assoc-
      iates, 1967, 137p.
This bibliography was compiled from references in the
journal *INTEGRATED EDUCATION.* Included are 3,100
references (journal articles, monographs and government reports), classified under 16 subject categories,
such as: effects on children, new approaches, law and
government, strategy and tactics, historical, role of
the church, Spanish Americans, and American Indians.

There is an author index.

442. *SPECIAL CATALOG OF FEDERAL ASSISTANCE PROGRAMS
FOR MINORITY BUSINESS ENTERPRISES.* Prepared by
the Office of Minority Business Enterprise.
Washington, D.C., G.P.O., 1970- . Irregular.
Each program description includes a section which
focuses on a series of references designed to aid the
reader in exploring other data relative to that program. For a complete description of the publication,
see Entry No. 290.

443. *TEACHING ETHNIC STUDIES: CONCEPTS AND STRATEGIES.*
Edited by James A. Banks. Washington, D.C.,
National Council for the Social Studies, 1973,
299p. (43rd Yearbook of the National Council
for the Social Studies).
For annotation, see Entry No. 14.

Chapter 7

AMERICAN INDIANS

(Indexes, Abstracts, Bibliographies, etc.)

444.   *AMERICAN INDIAN AND ESKIMO AUTHORS; A COMPRE-*
       HENSIVE BIBLIOGRAPHY. Compiled by Arlene B.
       Hirschfelder. New York, Association of American
       Indian Affairs, 1973, 99p. Dist. by Interbook,
       Inc.
Biographies, autobiographies, anthologies and other
writings by Indians on Indian affairs, culture, art,
and literature are cited in this briefly annotated bibliography. Tribal affiliation is indicated for each
of the authors. An attempt is made to provide comprehensive coverage. Indian periodicals are listed in a
separate section. An earlier and shorter edition of
this work was put out in 1970 under the title *AMERICAN
INDIAN AUTHORS: A REPRESENTATIVE BIBLIOGRAPHY* (New
York, Association of American Indian Affairs, 1970,
45p.).

445.   *AMERICAN INDIAN AND WHITE RELATIONS TO 1830;*
       NEEDS AND OPPORTUNITIES FOR STUDY; AN ESSAY.
       By William Nelson Fenton, Chapel Hill, University
       of North Carolina Press, 1957, 138p. (Institute
       of Early American History and Culture. Needs
       and Opportunities for Study Series).
The major section of this publication is a topically
arranged annotated bibliography of materials related to
American Indians. Only items issued prior to 1957 are
included. The annotations vary from thumbnail descriptions to short criticisms. The listing was compiled
to assist graduate students in identifying relevant
publications in the humanities and the social sciences.
There is a separate section which identifies locations
of useful manuscript collections in the United States
and Canada. In addition, the publication includes a
subject-author index and an essay on Indian and white
relations in Eastern North America. The publication
was reprinted without modification by Russell in 1971.

446.   *AMERICAN INDIAN EDUCATION, A SELECTED BIBLIO-*
       GRAPHY. Prepared by James E. Heathman and Cecilia
       J. Martinez. Las Cruces, New Mexico, ERIC Clear-
       inghouse on Rural Education and Small Schools,
       New Mexico State University, 1969, 98p. Annual

SUPPLEMENTS, 1970-   .

These bibliographies are prepared to provide access to research findings and documents relating to American Indian education. Entries cover such topics as American Indian culture, bilingual education, Eskimos, Federal legislation, etc. The citations include a wide variety of resource materials (reports, guides, books, articles, etc.). All items listed in these volumes were originally cited in either *RESOURCES IN EDUCATION* or *CURRENT INDEX TO JOURNALS IN EDUCATION*. Abstracts follow each citation. Order information is provided for all entries. Each volume has its own subject index.

447.   *THE AMERICAN INDIAN 1492-1970: A CHRONOLOGY AND FACT BOOK*. Compiled and edited by Henry C. Dennis. Foreword by Robert L. Bennett. Dobbs Ferry, New York, Oceana Publications, 1971, 137p. (Ethnic Chronology Series no. 1).

Several sections of this publication list books, articles, reports, and audio-visual materials relating to American Indian affairs. For a more detailed description, see Entry No. 20.

448.   *THE AMERICAN INDIAN IN GRADUATE STUDIES; A BIBLIOGRAPHY OF THESES, DISSERTATIONS AND CONTRIBUTIONS*. By F. J. Dockstader. New York, Museum of the American Indian, Heye Foundation, 1957, 399p. (Contributions from the Museum of the American Indian, Heye Foundation, v. 15). *SUPPLEMENT*, 1971, 250p.

Over 3,500 theses and dissertations dealing with Indians/Eskimos in North, Central and South America completed in the United States, Canada and Mexico between 1890 and 1955 are listed by author in this bibliography. The dissertations "extend beyond anthropology to include all academic fields...such as history, sociology, education, music, art and literature." Each entry contains complete publication information, including degree, date, institution, title and pages. Notes and comments are provided only for those titles which are not self-explanatory. There is a 35 page index by topic, tribe, archaeological site, geographic location, etc. A

supplement listing theses and dissertations published
from 1955 through 1970 was issued in 1971. These two
volumes were reissued as a set in 1973-4 by the Museum.

449. *AMERICAN INDIAN INDEX, 1953-1968*. By Russell L.
     Knor. River Grove, Illinois, Russell L. Knor,
     1953-1968, Irregular.
Irregularly issued, these indexes provide subject access to books, articles and government documents dealing with American Indians. Although intended to
identify all materials "relating to the American
Indians of North, Central and South America, including
the West Indies," coverage is not comprehensive. In
addition, because truncation is employed, many citations
are incomplete. The publisher of the set varied.
Huebner, in Chicago, issued some of the volumes.

450. *AMERICAN INDIAN PERIODICALS IN THE PRINCETON
     UNIVERSITY LIBRARY: A GUIDE TO THE COLLECTION*.
     Edited by Alfred L. Bush. New York, Clearwater
     Pub., 1976, 148p.
According to the preface, Princeton has made a "con-
scious effort" to collect American Indian periodicals
since the middle 1960s. This bibliography lists all
those subscribed to by the Library in 1975. The
collection includes only those periodicals produced
by or for American Indians (newspapers are included).
Archaeological publications -- even those which focus
exclusively on Indian prehistory -- and scholarly
journals "whose appeal is exclusively to the academic
community" are not noted here. The citations are
arranged by title. Bibliographic and holdings information is provided.

451. *AMERICAN INDIANS: A STUDY GUIDE AND SOURCE BOOK*.
     By Lynn P. Dunn. San Francisco, R & E Research
     Associates, 1975, 119p.
Appropriate study materials are identified for each
topic relating to American Indians covered in this
source book. For a complete annotation, see Entry
No. 21.

452. *AMERICAN INDIANS (U.S. & CANADA); A BIBLIOGRAPHY*
      OF CONTEMPORARY STUDIES AND URBAN RESEARCH. By
      James N. Kerri. Monticello, Illinois, Council
      of Planning Librarians, 1973, 165p. (Exchange
      Bibliographies, nos. 376-7).
Studies, publications, organizations, and agencies
concerned with the contemporary affairs of people of
American Indian ancestry are identified in this bibliography. The work is divided into seven parts
(contemporary studies and research, theoretical studies, organizations in Canada, U.S. research centers,
etc.). There is no index.

453. *AN ANNOTATED BIBLIOGRAPHY OF DISSERTATIONS ON*
      AMERICAN INDIAN, MEXICAN AMERICAN, MIGRANT AND
      RURAL EDUCATION. Prepared by Howard K. Conley.
      Las Cruces, New Mexico, ERIC Clearinghouse on
      Rural Education and Small Schools, New Mexico
      State University, 1973, 50p.
This bibliography lists doctoral dissertations written
between 1964-1972 covering American Indian, Mexican
American, migrant, and rural education. There are 62
dissertations for American Indians, 26 for Mexican
Americans, 7 for migrants, and 8 for rural and small
schools. Each dissertation is briefly annotated.
There is a subject index.

454. *AN ANTHROPOLOGICAL BIBLIOGRAPHY OF THE EASTERN*
      SEABOARD. Edited by Irving Rouse and John M.
      Goggin. New Haven, Connecticut, Eastern States
      Archaeological Federation, 1947-63, 2v. (Re-
      search Publication nos. 1-2).
This bibliography contains material on archaeology,
ethnology, and American Indian history. All types of
material (including bibliographies, reviews of publications, and research) are included. Unpublished
material (e.g., manuscripts, theses, and dissertations)
are excluded. The source is arranged in three sections:
archaeology, ethnology, and history. Each of these
categories contains a general section and is further
subdivided by geographic location: Eastern Canada,
New England, Middle Atlantic States and Southeast.

455. *A BIBLIOGRAPHICAL CHECK LIST OF NORTH AND MIDDLE
AMERICAN INDIAN LINGUISTICS IN THE E.E. AYER
COLLECTION.* Chicago, Newberry Library, 1941, 2v.
Over 5,000 items dealing with North and Middle American
Indian linguistics stored in the Edward E. Ayer Collection of the Newberry Library are listed here. Citations
include journal articles, serial publications, books,
and reports. The source is arranged by language (subdivided by 328 separate dialects or subdialects) and
indexed by author. This collection was begun by James
Pilling (whose linguistic bibliographies are described
in Entry No. 456), and enlarged by Edward Ayer (who
purchased Pilling's library). A catalog of all materials
in the Ayer collection is available and is described in
Entry No. 475.

456. *BIBLIOGRAPHIES OF THE LANGUAGES OF THE NORTH
AMERICAN INDIANS.* By James Pilling. Washington,
D.C., G.P.O., 1887-94, 9v. (U.S. Bureau of
American Ethnology Bulletins). Reprinted by
AMS Press, 1973, 3v.
The goal of this series is to "include in each bibliography everything printed or in manuscript relating to
the family of languages to which it is devoted: books,
pamphlets, articles, tracts, serials, etc., and such
reviews and announcements of publications as seemed
worthy of notice." While compiling this bibliography,
Pilling was in correspondence with nearly all writers
on American Indian languages living at the time. He
visited most of the important libraries and private
collections in this country and sought further material
in the British Museum and in France. The following
volumes make up Pilling's bibliographic series: *BIBLIO-
GRAPHY OF THE ALGONQUIN LANGUAGES* (1891); *BIBLIOGRAPHY
OF THE ATHPASCAN LANGUAGES* (1892); *BIBLIOGRAPHY OF THE
CHINOOKAN LANGUAGES* (1893); *BIBLIOGRAPHY OF THE ESKIMO
LANGUAGES* (1887); *BIBLIOGRAPHY OF THE IROQUOIAN LANGUA-
GES* (1888); *BIBLIOGRAPHY OF THE MUSKHOGEAN LANGUAGES*
(1889); *BIBLIOGRAPHY OF THE SALISHAN LANGUAGES* (1893);
BIBLIOGRAPHY OF THE SIOUAN LANGUAGES (1887); and *BIBLIO-
GRAPHY OF THE WAKASHAN LANGUAGES* (1894). Each biblio-
graphy is arranged by author and indexed chronologically.

457. *BIBLIOGRAPHY OF ARTICLES AND PAPERS ON NORTH AMERICAN INDIAN ART.* Compiled by Anne D. Harding and Patricia Billing. Washington, D.C., Indian Arts and Crafts Board, Department of the Interior, 1939, 265p. Reprinted by Kraus, 1969.

The bibliography, which consists mainly of citations to periodical publications of museums and universities, is divided into four parts. Part 1 consists of the complete list of articles and papers, the contents of which are indicated in each case. "The succeeding portions of the bibliography represent subdivisions of this material and are to be used with reference to the original list." Part 2 consists of two short lists: citations to materials on American Indian art in general and citations to materials on specific Indian arts and crafts. Part 3 lists the articles and papers which deal with regional arts and crafts; the arrangement is by tribal names. Part 4 lists all articles and papers by specific crafts. The cited articles may be located by author and date.

458. *A BIBLIOGRAPHY OF CALIFORNIA ARCHAEOLOGY.* Compiled by Robert F. Heizer and Albert B. Elasser, with the assistance of C. William Clewlow, Jr. Berkeley, Department of Anthropology, University of California, 1970, 78p. (Contributions of the University of California Archaeological Research Facility No. 6).

Articles, books, reports, and documents dealing with California Indians and other topics related to California archaeology are cited in this bibliography. The arrangement is by topic (techniques of stone working, California Indian flint chipping, trade and trails, caves and rockshelters, Santa Barbara coast and islands, etc.). There are no annotations. The bibliography revises a 1949 publication with the same title (No. 4 of the California Archaeological Survey).

459. *A BIBLIOGRAPHY OF CONTEMPORARY NORTH AMERICAN INDIANS: SELECTED AND PARTIALLY ANNOTATED WITH STUDY GUIDES.* By William H. Hodge. Introduction by Paul Prucha. New York, Interland Publishing Inc., 1976, 296p.

This bibliography is intended for use by the specialist and also the undergraduate and high school student.
Citations to over 2,600 articles, essays, monographs
and books are arranged according to 27 subject categories: history, linguistics, music, religion, health,
current newspapers, city living, migration patterns,
formal education, reference materials, etc. The
entries are briefly annotated. Two study guides are
included: "Indian Life Prior to 1875" and "Contemporary
American Indians;" these guides outline 25,000 years of
Indian life and include references to background readings. There is a tribe, state and geographic index to
the entire work.

460. *BIBLIOGRAPHY OF NONPRINT INSTRUCTIONAL MATERIALS
      ON THE AMERICAN INDIAN.* Prepared by the Insti-
      tute of Indian Services and Research, Brigham
      Young University. Provo, Utah, Brigham Young
      University Printing Service, 1972, 221p. Dist.
      by Brigham Young University Press.
Filmstrips, slides, 16mm films, 8mm film loops, transparencies, maps, charts, study prints, audio recordings,
and kits on the American Indian are listed in this
bibliography. The items are arranged alphabetically by
title. For each entry, a descriptive annotation is
given plus grade ranges and subject headings. A directory of distributors, a subject heading list and a
subject index are appended.

461. *A BIBLIOGRAPHY OF NORTH AMERICAN FOLKLORE AND
      FOLKSONG.* By Charles Haywood. 2nd rev. ed.
      New York, Dover Publications, Inc., 1961, 2v.
The purpose of this reference work is to provide "a
thorough bibliography of American folklore and folk-
song." It consists of two volumes; the first volume
surveys the folklore and folksongs of all people
living north of Mexico and the second volume concentrates on American Indians and Eskimos. This second
volume (*AMERICAN INDIANS NORTH OF MEXICO, INCLUDING
THE ESKIMOS*) is arranged by culture area and alphabetically subdivided by tribe. The citations (articles, books and recordings) are listed under the

following headings: bibliographies, serial publications, general studies and collections, myths and mythologies, belief, folktales, customs, folk poetry, folk medicine, proverbs, etc. Only publications written before 1961 are included. Author and subject access are provided in the index. For additional information about Haywood's bibliography, see Entry No. 415.

462. *A BIBLIOGRAPHY OF THE CONSTITUTIONS AND LAWS OF THE AMERICAN INDIANS*. By Lester Hargrett. Cambridge, Massachusetts, Harvard University Press, 1947, 124p.

This volume contains a descriptive list of the printed constitutions, statutes, session acts and resolutions passed "by properly authorized bodies, of once semi-independent and self-governing Indian tribes and nations of the present United States." Of the 225 publications described, over one-third of them are not recorded elsewhere. Each entry is annotated with biographical or historical notes. The location of the listed constitutions and laws in major libraries is identified. The source is arranged alphabetically by names of tribes. In addition to the bibliography, there is a chronology of important relevant events and a reprint of a "talk" by President Jefferson to a Cherokee delegation visiting Washington in 1809 which illustrates Federal encouragement accorded to Indian attempts to establish self-government. A general index completes the work. Each of the items cited in this bibliography has been reproduced on microfilm by KTO Microform (the U.S. Division of Kraus-Thomson Organisation Ltd.).

463. *BIBLIOGRAPHY OF THE DIEGUEÑO INDIANS*. By Ruth Farrell Almstedt. Ramona, California, Ballena Press, 1974, 52p.

The Diegueño Indians lived in what is now San Diego and Imperial Counties in California and in Baja California. Almstedt's bibliography cites both published and unpublished materials of an ethnographic, ethnohistorical, archaeological, linguistic or other anthropological nature which deal with this group of Indians.

Included are articles, books, manuscripts, reports, dissertations, field notes, etc. Newspaper articles on the Diegueño Indians are generally excluded. The work is arranged in alphabetical order by author's last name. There is no index.

464. *A·BIBLIOGRAPHY OF THE ENGLISH COLONIAL TREATIES WITH THE AMERICAN INDIANS INCLUDING A SYNOPSIS OF EACH TREATY.* By Henry F. De Puy. New York, AMS Press, 1972, 50p.

Many of the records of various treaties with the Indians between 1677 and 1768 exist only in manuscript. Some have been printed in the *JOURNALS* of the Governors and Councils or in the "Votes and Proceedings" of the legislative bodies. The purpose of this monograph is "to locate and describe such as were separately printed." The treaties are listed chronologically. Their contents are briefly noted. An identification is made of the location of copies of each in major libraries and private collections. Numerous facsimilies of the treaties' title pages are included. Originally published in 1917, the bibliography was reprinted by AMS Press in 1972.

465. *A BIBLIOGRAPHY OF THE NAVAHO INDIANS.* By Clyde Kluckhohn and Katharine Spencer. New York, Augustin, 1940, 93p. Reprinted by AMS Press, 1972.

Kluckhohn's bibliography covers the history and culture of the Navaho Indians from the 16th century to 1939. Brief notes accompany most of the serially numbered entries. The cited books, periodical articles, government documents and annuals are arranged alphabetically by author within six sections: 1) bibliographies, reference works, catalogs, collections of documents; 2) historical (primary and secondary) sources arranged chronologically; 3) environmental; 4) anthropological (archaeology, physical anthropology, linguistics, ethnology); 5) Navaho relations with whites; and 6) popular. An author index is provided.

466. *A BIBLIOGRAPHY ON THE AGRICULTURE OF THE AMERICAN*

INDIANS. Compiled by Everett Eugene Edwards and
Wayne D. Rosmussen. Washington, D.C., U.S.
Department of Agriculture, 1942, 107p.
Citations to materials dealing with Indian agriculture
are listed and described in this annotated bibliography.
Topics covered range from pre-Columbian activity to
agriculture on Indian reservations in the 1940s. One
section focuses on uncultivated plants used by American
Indians.

467. *A BIBLIOGRAPHY RELATIVE TO INDIANS OF THE STATE
OF LOUISIANA*. By Robert W. Neuman and Lanier A.
Simmons. Baton Rouge, Louisiana Geological Survey, 1969, 72p. (Anthropological Study No. 4).
Nearly 500 citations to published and unpublished
works dealing with Indians in the State of Louisiana
are cited in this bibliography. These references
date from 1752 to 1969 and relate to the prehistoric
as well as to the historic record. Many of the entries
are briefly annotated. The work is arranged by author
(whose publications are listed chronologically). There
is no subject access.

468. *BIOGRAPHICAL AND HISTORICAL INDEX OF AMERICAN
INDIANS AND PERSONS INVOLVED IN INDIAN AFFAIRS*.
Prepared by the U.S. Department of the Interior.
Boston, G.K. Hall, 1966, 8v.
This publication is a photo-reproduction of over
200,000 cards found in the catalog of the Bureau of
Indian Affair's Library. It was prepared to help
"anyone interested in Indian biography, history, and
social conditions during the latter half of the nineteenth and the first part of the twentieth century."
The arrangement is by subject, i.e., Indian tribes,
individuals (Indian agents, Indian chiefs, historically prominent Indians, and personnel of the Bureau
of Indian Affairs), events, and other historical items.
For each of these entries, citations are made to relevant articles, pamphlets, and portions of books which
were published between 1850 and 1920.

469. *CALIFORNIA INDIAN HISTORY, A CLASSIFIED AND ANNOTATED GUIDE TO SOURCE MATERIALS.* By Robert F. Heizer, Karen M. Nissen and Edward D. Castillo. Ramona, California, Ballena Press, 1975, 90p. (Ballena Press Publications in Archaeology, Ethnology and History No. 4).

"This bibliography is an attempt to provide a guide to the basic data available on California Indian history." The authors have listed works that "one might reasonably hope to find in a large library" or that "can be secured without undue difficulty." The 685 annotated references are arranged under the following headings: period of native history (?B.C. - 1542 A.D.); period of Spanish and Mexican contact (1542 - 1846); period of Anglo conquest (1846 - 1873); the aftermath of conquest (1873 - 1920); period of Indian nationalism (1920 - 1974); and works written by Indians. Each of these major topics is subdivided into specific subjects. The citations include monographs, journal articles, documents, reports, archival collections, a limited number of dissertations, and source materials (museum collections, documentary archives, films, pictorial archives, and bibliographies). The citations are indexes by tribe and by author.

470. *CATALOG TO MANUSCRIPTS AT THE NATIONAL ANTHROPOLOGICAL ARCHIVES, NATIONAL MUSEUM OF HISTORY, SMITHSONIAN INSTITUTION.* Boston, G.K. Hall, 1975, 4v.

The Smithsonian Institution National Anthropological Archives, a part of the Department of Anthropology of the National Museum of Natural History, contains the largest single collection of manuscripts covering the history and life of North American Indians. The *CATALOG TO MANUSCRIPTS* describes approximately 40,000 items under 5,000 main entries. The manuscripts concentrate on the languages, ethnology, and history of the Indians and include the following types: vocabularies, texts, grammatical notes and comparative linguistic data, ethnological and archaeological field notes and drafts of reports, originals and copies of correspondence, transcripts of oral history and music, ethnological extracts from published sources, drawings,

and maps with manuscript annotations. The manuscripts
cover the period 1848 to the present. The *CATALOG* is
arranged by tribe or geographic area and the documents
are listed in a single numerical order.

471. *CATALOGUE: AN INDEX TO INDIAN LEGAL MATERIALS*
      AND RESOURCES IN THE NATIONAL INDIAN LAW LIBRARY.
      Boulder, Colorado, Native American Rights Fund,
      1973/4- . Biennial.
The National Indian Law Library acts as a clearinghouse
--collecting, cataloging and making available to tribes,
legal services programs and lawyers, information on
Indian litigation and related issues. This publication
is an index to the Library's holdings. It is divided
into three major parts. "Part I of the catalogue
contains the Library's current holdings arranged by
subject matter. Each holding has an acquisition
number. Where the holding is a case, a brief description of the litigation is provided. Part II of the
catalogue lists the holdings numerically by individual
acquisition number, and indicates the specific holdings
in each file. Part III contains a plaintiff-defendant
listing and an author-title listing which is keyed to
the National Indian Law Library acquisition number for
easy referral to Part II." Most of the materials cited
in the catalog are available upon request from the
National Indian Law Library for a nominal per page
charge.

472. *CATALOGUE OF THE LIBRARY OF THE PEABODY MUSEUM*
      OF ARCHAEOLOGY AND ETHNOLOGY AT HARVARD UNIVER-
      SITY. Boston, G.K. Hall, 1963, 53v. *SUPPLEMENT*
      1, 1970, 12v. *SUPPLEMENT 2*, 1971, 5v.
The Peabody Museum of Archaeology and Ethnology is the
oldest museum of anthropology in the United States.
When the author and subject *CATALOGUES* of the Museum
Library were first published by G.K. Hall in 1963, the
Library contained over 80,000 books, serials and pamphlets; the catalog cards for these items are reproduced
in the original 53 volume set. Since that time, over
20,000 items have been added to the collection; these
acquisitions are reflected in the two additional *SUPPLE-*

MENTS which were issued in 1970 and 1971. Prehistoric and historic (but not Greek and Roman) archaeology, ethnography, and biological anthropology are the subjects represented in the collection. Substantial emphasis is placed on American Indian tribes (and, to a lesser extent, other ethnic groups in America). Publications treating several American Indian tribes together are listed under "North America" or under individual states. Materials on racial and tribal groups are found under linguistic stock (e.g., "Athabascan - Navaho").

473. *CHIPPEWA AND DAKOTA INDIANS: A SUBJECT CATALOG OF BOOKS, PAMPHLETS, PERIODICAL ARTICLES AND MANUSCRIPTS IN THE MINNESOTA HISTORICAL SOCIETY.* St. Paul, Minnesota Historical Society, 1969, 131p.

This subject catalog reproduces all the entries found in the public catalogs of the Minnesota Historical Society's Library under the subject headings "Chippewa Indians" and "Dakota Indians." The catalog is divided into two sections. The first part lists 1,400 printed materials (books, pamphlets, periodical articles); the second part identifies approximately 700 manuscripts.

474. *DICTIONARY CATALOG OF THE DEPARTMENT OF THE INTERIOR LIBRARY.* Boston, G.K. Hall, 1967, 37v. *SUPPLEMENTS* 1-4, 1969-75, 15v.

Although the U.S. Department of the Interior Library collected materials on many other topics, a substantial portion of their holdings focuses on American Indian affairs. These items are listed in the *DICTIONARY CATALOG* under the names of various Indian tribes, Indians of North America, etc. The *CATALOG* consists of reproductions of the author, title and subject cards in the Library's card catalog. Periodical articles, books, reports, documents, manuscripts, Indian constitutions, and Indian tribal laws are identified. According to the preface, "most of these are not indexed elsewhere." The *CATALOG* is particularly useful for citations to materials on government relations with Indian tribes.

475. *DICTIONARY CATALOG OF THE EDWARD E. AYER COL-
LECTION OF AMERICANA AND AMERICAN INDIANS IN
THE NEWBERRY LIBRARY, CHICAGO.* Boston, G.K.
Hall, 1961, 16v. *SUPPLEMENT*, 1970, 3v.
This publication is a subject, author and title arranged
photoreproduction of the 170,000 cards in the catalog of
the Edward E. Ayer collection of Americana and American
Indians located in the Newberry Library. The Ayer collection contains over 90,000 publications which focus
on North and South American Indians, prehistory, archaeology, ethnology and anthropology, etc. A three volume
supplement was issued in 1970.

476. *ECONOMIC DEVELOPMENT OF AMERICAN INDIANS AND
ESKIMOS, 1930 THROUGH 1967: A BIBLIOGRAPHY.*
Compiled by Marjorie P. Snodgrass for the U.S.
Bureau of Indian Affairs. Washington, D.C.,
G.P.O., 1969, 263p. (Interior Department Library
Bibliography Series, No. 10).
This bibliography is "a unique attempt to bring together in one place as much valuable information as
possible on the economic development of the American
Indians and Eskimos." Economic development is considered to mean individual and collective efforts on
and off the reservations that are directed to the production of tangible income. Almost 1,600 materials
published between 1930 and 1967 and many unpublished
materials are arranged alphabetically by author under
15 categories (e.g., arts, crafts, farming, irrigation,
minerals, tourism, etc.). Each entry identifies the
author, title, publisher, place, date, pages and,
occasionally, a library location; no annotations are
given. A reservation index and a list of Bureau of
Indian Affairs field offices complete the work.

477. *EDUCATION OF AMERICAN INDIANS: A SURVEY OF THE
LITERATURE.* Prepared by Brewton Berry for the
Special Subcommittee on Indian Education of the
U.S. Senate Committee on Labor and Public Welfare.
Washington, D.C., G.P.O., 1969, 121p.
During the initial hearings of the Special Subcommittee
on Indian Education, several witnesses stressed the

point that there was a serious lack of bibliographical
control of research findings on Indian education. This
bibliography was prepared to provide a comprehensive
list of materials on the topic. It identifies in the
literature specific problem areas which have contributed to the apparent failure of formal education
systems used with Indians. Over 700 books, articles,
theses, and dissertations published between 1899 and
1968 are discussed (in the first 78 pages) and cited on
pages 79-121. Unpublished materials (committee reports,
term papers, speeches, working papers, etc.) are generally omitted.

478. *ENCYCLOPEDIA OF INDIANS OF THE AMERICAS.* Edited
      by Keith Irvine. St. Clair Shores, Michigan,
      Scholarly Press, 1974- . To be published in
      20 volumes.
One volume of this planned 20 volume encyclopedic set
will contain a 25,000 item bibliography of materials
relating to Indians of the Americas. For a more complete annotation, see Entry No. 30.

479. *AN ESSAY TOWARDS AN INDIAN BIBLIOGRAPHY. BEING
      A CATALOGUE OF BOOKS RELATING TO THE HISTORY,
      ANTIQUITIES, LANGUAGES, CUSTOMS, RELIGION, WARS,
      LITERATURE, AND ORIGIN OF THE AMERICAN INDIANS,
      IN THE LIBRARY OF THOMAS W. FIELD. WITH BIBLIO-
      GRAPHICAL AND HISTORICAL NOTES, AND SYNOPSIS OF
      THE CONTENTS OF SOME OF THE WORKS LEAST KNOWN.*
      Compiled by T. W. Field. New York, Scribners,
      1873, 430p. Reprinted by Long's College Book
      Co., 1951; Gale Research Co., 1967.
This bibliography began as a catalog of Thomas W.
Field's personal collection, but expanded to include
other sources. Over 1,700 citations to historic,
narrative, literary, or poetic materials on American
Indian life are arranged alphabetically by author.
Titles in foreign languages are translated into English. Many of the listed items are annotated. Only
books written before 1873 are included. The catalog
has been reprinted several times (e.g., Long's College
Book Co. in 1951; Gale Research Co. in 1967).

480. *ETHNOGRAPHIC BIBLIOGRAPHY OF NORTH AMERICA.* By
     George Peter Murdock and Timothy J. O'Leary.
     4th ed. New Haven, Human Relations Area Files
     Press, 1975, 5v.
Approximately 44,000 items are cited in this classified
bibliography covering all of the area north of Mexico.
The publication is organized into 16 cultural areas
and, within each area, by tribal group. Included are
regional studies, geographical and historical sources,
travel accounts, etc. It is the purpose of the compilers to make the bibliography as complete as possible
on all ethnographic subjects.

481. *ETHNOHISTORICAL BIBLIOGRAPHY OF THE UTE INDIANS
     OF COLORADO.* By Omer C. Stewart. Boulder, Univ-
     ersity of Colorado Press, 1971, 91p. (University
     of Colorado, Series in Anthropology No. 18).
Arranged alphabetically by author, the materials on the
Ute Indians listed in this bibliography were written
between the early Spanish period and 1970. They range
from government documents to ultra popular sources;
historical materials are emphasized. There are two
appendices: the first lists the records of the Southern
Ute Agency from 1877 through 1952 that are located at
the Federal Center in Denver; the second lists titles
of articles about the Ute from Colorado and out-of-state
newspapers.

482. *FOLKLORE OF THE NORTH AMERICAN INDIANS; AN
     ANNOTATED BIBLIOGRAPHY.* Compiled by Judith
     C. Ullom for the Library of Congress. Washing-
     ton, D.C., G.P.O., 1969, 126p.
This is a selective bibliography of the recorded
folklore of North American Indians, including the
Eskimos. According to the author, "The tales with
which we are concerned here were gathered from widespread locations across North America from Alaska to
the Northeast, the Southeast, and the Southwest." The
entries are arranged by 11 culture areas (Eskimo, Pla-
teau, Central Woodland, Iroquois, etc.). In a general
background information section, relevant anthologies,
children's anthologies, folklore studies, bibliographies

and indexes are described. Detailed annotations are provided. The publication is indexed by subject, author and title.

483. *THE FORGOTTEN AMERICAN--AMERICAN INDIANS RE-
      MEMBERED: A SELECTED BIBLIOGRAPHY FOR USE IN
      SOCIAL WORK EDUCATION.* By Jere L. Brennan.
      New York, Council on Social Work Education,
      1972, 83p.
The purpose of this work is to provide background
reading for social workers interested in the American
Indian. It is a partially annotated bibliography of
books, articles and reference sources arranged under
the following categories: tribal history, government-
Indian relations, the missionaries and the Indian,
the military and the Indian, American Indians in
fiction, biographies, general reference, etc. Unpublished government reports, master's theses and
doctoral dissertations are omitted. Separate sections list American Indian newspapers and the area
offices of the Bureau of Indian Affairs.

484. *THE GILCREASE-HARGRETT CATALOGUE OF IMPRINTS.*
      Compiled by Lester Hargrett. Norman, Univer-
      sity of Oklahoma Press, 1972, 400p.
The purpose of *THE GILCREASE-HARGRETT CATALOGUE OF
IMPRINTS* is "to make known to historians and to the
general public some of the resources of the Gilcrease
Institute of American History and Art Library." The
catalog is an annotated bibliography of 2,500 rare
imprints (including maps, newspapers, and government
documents) pertaining to Indian affairs. A majority
of the entries focus on five tribes from Oklahoma,
but 40 other tribes of Western America are also represented. The publication is arranged by tribe and then
chronologically by imprint. There is a subject/author
index.

485. *GREAT BASIN ANTHROPOLOGY...A BIBLIOGRAPHY.* Com-
      piled by Catherine S. Fowler. Reno, Western
      Studies Center, University of Nevada System,

1970, 418p.
This is a subject arranged annotated listing of books,
periodicals, manuscripts, documents, unpublished records and other writings issued before 1968 on the
Great Basin Indians. "The Bibliography in its present
form is certainly not exhaustive, although it probably
includes a substantial percentage of the available
literature..." Sections include: archaeology, ethno-
history, anthropology (by tribes) and Federal and
State documents. Five maps show linguistic distribution, reservations, principal archaeological sites,
principal trails to California, and tribal distribution.
An annotated listing of unpublished manuscripts on
Great Basin Indians in the Bureau of American Ethnology
Collection, Smithsonian National Anthropology Archives,
is included as an appendix. There is an author index.

486. *GUIDE TO AMERICAN INDIAN DOCUMENTS IN THE CON-
GRESSIONAL SERIAL SET: 1817 - 1899.* By Steven
L. Johnson. New York, Clearwater Publishing Co.,
1976, 400p.
This guide, prepared under the sponsorship of The
Institute for the Development of Indian Law, is the
result of a page-by-page search of every volume in
the *CONGRESSIONAL SERIAL SET* from the end of the
AMERICAN STATE PAPERS to the end of the 19th Century.
Every document in *SERIAL SET* pertaining to American
Indians is identified, cataloged, and listed in chrono-
logical sequence. Nearly 10,000 documents are cited.
Each entry includes *SERIAL SET* number, date, source,
title, and subjects covered. Subject, tribal and
geographical indexes are included.

487. *A GUIDE TO ARTICLES ON THE AMERICAN INDIANS IN
SERIAL PUBLICATIONS.* Compiled by Frederick H.
Douglas. Denver, Department of Indian Art,
Denver Art Museum, 1934, 332p. Reprinted by
Xerox University Microfilms, 1968.
Articles on American Indians in 119 different serials
issued by 80 American, Canadian and English organiza-
tions are analyzed in this bibliography. Included are
publications by museums, government agencies, anthro-

pology departments, scientific organizations, and historical societies. The book is arranged by issuing
agency or title of the serial. Entries under each
title are arranged by date. There is no subject
access. The 1934 monograph was reprinted in its
entirety by Xerox University Microfilms in 1968.

488. *GUIDE TO LIFE AND LITERATURE OF THE SOUTHWEST*.
By James Frank Dobie. Rev. ed. Dallas, Southern Methodist University Press, 1952, 222p.
The author has written a bibliographic essay which
focuses on the works he feels best represent life
in the Southwest. The sources are grouped by subjects,
such as Indian Culture; Apaches, Comanches, and other
Plains Indians; women pioneers; Spanish and Mexican
Americans; pony express, and range life. Fiction,
including folk tales, is covered. Annotations are
provided. There is an author/title index.

489. *A GUIDE TO MANUSCRIPTS RELATING TO THE AMERICAN
INDIAN IN THE LIBRARY OF THE AMERICAN PHILOSO-
PHICAL SOCIETY*. Compiled by John F. Freeman and
Murphy D. Smith. Philadelphia, The American
Philosophical Society, 1966, 491p. (Memoirs
Series, v. 65).
The purpose of this publication is to provide "a complete listing of the data at hand on each language and
tribe together with a brief evaluation of the relia-
bility and significance of such data." The listing
encompasses linguistic, ethnological and historical
sources, both published and unpublished. At least 350
tribes and languages are represented, some in great
depth. The *GUIDE* is divided into four parts: 1) an
alphabetical list of 294 manuscript, microfilm, and
record collections containing materials related to
the American Indian; 2) a classified list of items and
groups of items within the collections arranged by
tribe; 3) a bibliography of printed materials referred
to in the first two lists; 4) and an alphabetical index.
All entries in the bibliography are annotated. Only
items available in the American Philosophical Society
Library are listed.

490. *A GUIDE TO MATERIALS BEARING ON CULTURAL RELA-
TIONS IN NEW MEXICO.* Compiled by Lyle Saunders.
Albuquerque, University of New Mexico Press,
1944, 528p.
This guide identifies published and manuscript materials relating to the cultural relations of the three
main ethnic groups in New Mexico: the Indians, Spanish speaking residents, and descendants of the early
American pioneers. For a more detailed annotation,
see Entry No. 646.

491. *HANDBOOK OF AMERICAN INDIANS: NORTH OF MEXICO.*
Edited by Frederick W. Hodge. Washington, D.C.,
G.P.O., 1907-10, 2v. (Bureau of American Ethnology Bulletin no. 30).
Over 40 pages of citations to materials pertaining
to various Indian tribes north of Mexico are presented
in volume 2 of Hodges' work. For a more complete
annotation, see Entry No. 34.

492. *HEALTH AND DISEASE OF AMERICAN INDIANS NORTH OF
MEXICO; A BIBLIOGRAPHY, 1800-1969.* By Mark V.
Barrow, Jerry D. Niswander and Robert Fortuine.
Gainesville, University of Florida Press, 1972,
147p.
"This bibliography has been compiled and arranged with
the aim of providing public health personnel, clini-
cians, nurses, and medical scientists ready access to
the medical literature on Indian health. Purposely
omitted are publications about Indian beliefs regarding
disease, the Indian medicine man, and various folk
remedies and medicines." The emphasis is on Indians
who lived north of Mexico; it includes Canadian and
Arctic Indians, but it excludes Eskimos and Aleuts.
There are 1,483 entries in the bibliography, classified
by topic and indexed by author, subject and tribe.

493. *THE HEALTH OF THE ESKIMOS: A BIBLIOGRAPHY, 1857-
1967.* Compiled by Robert Fortuine. Hanover,
New Hampshire, Dartmouth College Libraries, 1968,
87p.

Articles, monographs and books relating to the health
of the North American Eskimos are cited in this bibliography. Studies on the Aleuts of Alaska (who are
ethnically related to the Eskimos) are included, but
Arctic Indian material is not. Only writings by
nurses, doctors, medical scientists and anthropologists are listed. The publication is arranged by
topic: Eskimo folk medicine and anthropology; general
environmental health, housing, and sanitation; adap-
tation to cold; general health programs; diseases
transmitted from animals to man; etc. There is an
author index.

494. *HUMAN RELATIONS AREA FILES*. Prepared by George
    P. Murdock and others. New Haven, Connecticut,
    Human Relations Area Files, 1949- .
The *HUMAN RELATIONS AREA FILES* were developed under
the direction of George P. Murdock at the Institute
of Human Relations at Yale University to bring together and to organize "in readily accessible form the
available data on a statistically representative sample of all known cultures--primitive, historical, and
contemporary--for the purpose of testing cross-cultural
generalizations, revealing deficiencies in the descriptive literature and directing corrective field work."
A large proportion of the culture groups included
within the scope of the *FILES* is made up of American
Indian tribes. Thousands of books, articles, reports
and documents relating to selected societies and cultures of the world form the information base which is
analyzed by the *FILES*. The *FILES* are received by only
a few libraries in the United States, including the
University of Chicago, University of Colorado, Cornell
University, Harvard University, University of Illinois,
Indiana University, University of Michigan, University
of Pennsylvania, Princeton University, University of
Southern California, University of Utah, University
of Washington, and Yale University. The *FILES* received
by these participating institutions are housed in filing
cabinets with drawers to accommodate the paper or microfiche copies of the materials in the collection. There
is a separate file for each distinctive culture or sub-
culture, arranged according to the classification

scheme established in the *OUTLINE OF WORLD CULTURES*
(see below). Within each file, the materials are
arranged topically according to the categories presented in the *OUTLINE OF CULTURAL MATERIALS* (see below).
Full bibliographic information for each of the materials
included in the files is given through the *HUMAN RELA-
TIONS AREA FILES SOURCE BIBLIOGRAPHY* (see below).

All the source materials (books, journals, articles,
government publications, reports, etc.) which make up
the *HUMAN RELATIONS AREA FILES* are listed in the *HUMAN
RELATIONS AREA FILES SOURCE BIBLIOGRAPHY* (New Haven,
Connecticut, Human Relations Area Files Press, 1969,
unpaged). Complete bibliographic information is given
for each source material. The items are arranged alpha-
numerically according to the classification scheme used
in the *OUTLINE OF WORLD CULTURES* (see below). An area
index, an alphabetical culture unit index, and an author
index complete the bibliography.

All tribes represented by materials in the *SOURCE BIBLI-
OGRAPHY* are listed in the *OUTLINE OF WORLD CULTURES* (By
George P. Murdock and others. 3rd ed. rev. New Haven,
Connecticut, Human Relations Area Files Press, 1963,
227p.). The societies and cultures of the world listed
in this source are classified according to a flexible
system under which each society or group of culturally
related societies is designated by a code. Indians of
North America have been assigned the designation: N3.

The subject headings which can be used to access information contained in the documents which make up the
HUMAN RELATIONS AREA FILES are listed in the *OUTLINE OF
CULTURAL MATERIALS* (By George P. Murdock and others.
4th rev. ed. New Haven, Connecticut, Human Relations
Area Files Press, 1961, 164p.). Over 600 subject terms
are classified into 79 major divisions. Each of the
terms is annotated to indicate the range of information
to be filed or sought under that particular heading.
Closely related concepts are normally grouped in the
same section and, wherever possible, adjacent to one
another. Cross references are made liberally and there
is a subject index at the end of the publication.

495. *INDEX TO BULLETINS 1-100 OF THE BUREAU OF AMER-
ICAN ETHNOLOGY, WITH INDEX TO CONTRIBUTIONS TO
NORTH AMERICAN ETHNOLOGY, INTRODUCTIONS, AND
MISCELLANEOUS PUBLICATIONS*. By Biren Bonnerja.
Washington, D.C., G.P.O., 1963, 726p. (Smith-
sonian Institution, Bureau of American Ethnology
Bulletin, no. 178).
The Bureau of American Ethnology was organized in 1879
and was placed by Congress under the supervision of
the Smithsonian Institution. By 1963, its publications
consisted of *CONTRIBUTIONS TO NORTH AMERICAN ETHNOLOGY,
ANNUAL REPORTS, BULLETINS, INTRODUCTIONS,* and *MISCEL-
LANEOUS PUBLICATIONS*. Bonnerja's work contains indexes
to *BULLETINS* 1 through 100 (subject, author, title and
illustrations) and to *CONTRIBUTIONS TO NORTH AMERICAN
ETHNOLOGY, INTRODUCTIONS,* and *MISCELLANEOUS PUBLICA-
TIONS* (author, title, and subject). For an author-
title updating, see *LIST OF PUBLICATIONS OF THE BUREAU
OF AMERICAN ETHNOLOGY* (Entry No. 506).

496. *INDEX TO LITERATURE ON THE AMERICAN INDIAN,
1970-* . Edited by Jeannette Henry and others.
San Francisco, Indian Historical Press, 1970-
Annual.
Compiled and published by American Indian scholars and
through the American Indian Historical Society, the
INDEX TO LITERATURE ON THE AMERICAN INDIAN is an annual
bibliographic guide to current literature about American Indians. Over 700 popular and scholarly periodicals and books are indexed annually. The material is
arranged by subject (e.g., acculturation, alcoholism
culture change, environment, land, peyote, tribal
governments, women, etc.) and then by author. For
each item, illustrations and bibliographic references,
when appropriate, are identified in the books and
articles listed. A list of over 500 Indian periodicals
published by Native American organizations and tribes
is included in each annual. The latest annual issued
covers the literature of 1973.

497. *INDEX TO THE DECISIONS OF THE INDIAN CLAIMS
COMMISSION*. Edited by Norman A. Ross. New

York, Clearwater Publishing Co., 1973, 158p.
(The Library of American Indian Affairs).
The Indian Claims Commission was established in 1946
to operate as a tribunal for the hearing and determi-
nation of claims by Indian tribes against the United
States. All the claims and decisions of the Indian
Claims Commission as heard by the Commission between
1946 and 1973 are indexed in this publication by
tribe, docket number and case name. The tribal index
and the docket index cite docket numbers. The table
of cases gives the record of each claim, including
tribe, docket number, volume, page, decision and date.
All of the claims and decisions listed here are reproduced in the microfiche publication *DECISIONS OF THE
INDIAN CLAIMS COMMISSION* (see Entry No. 224).

498. *INDEX TO THE EXPERT TESTIMONY BEFORE THE INDIAN
     CLAIMS COMMISSION: THE WRITTEN REPORTS*. Compiled
     by Norman A. Ross. New York, Clearwater Publish-
     ing Co., 1973, 102p. (The Library of American
     Indian Affairs).
This volume "indexes the written expert reports submitted before the Indian Claims Commission in the course
of litigation over the past 25 years." They are listed
in docket number sequence and described in the following
way: report title, number of pages, author and party
affiliations, and whether illustrations, maps or bibliographies are contained in the report. The entries are
indexed by author, tribe, state, Royce area and docket
number. All of the reports indexed in this publication
are included in the microfiche publication *EXPERT TESTI-
MONY BEFORE THE INDIAN CLAIMS COMMISSION* (see Entry No.
227).

499. *INDIAN LAND TENURE: BIBLIOGRAPHICAL ESSAYS AND A
     GUIDE TO THE LITERATURE*. By Imre Sutton. New
     York, Clearwater Publishing Co., 1975, 290p.
     (The Library of American Indian Affairs).
More than 1,000 entries with full bibliographic data
on Indian land tenure are listed in this bibliography.
They are arranged in seven major topics (which were
selected to facilitate research in Indian land tenure):

aboriginal occupancy and territoriality; land cessions
and the establishment of reservations; land administration and land utilization; aboriginal title and land
claims; title clarification and change; tenure and
jurisdiction; and, land tenure and culture change.
Also included are eight maps and other illustrations,
nine analytical essays (each followed by a brief bibliography of relevant works), and a foreword by Dr.
Wilcomb E. Washburn. The citations are indexed by
subject, tribe/authors, and geography/authors.

500. *THE INDIANS AND ESKIMOS OF NORTH AMERICA: A
BIBLIOGRAPHY OF BOOKS IN PRINT THROUGH 1972.*
By Jack W. Marken. Vermillion, University of
South Dakota Press, 1973, 200p.
Marken has attempted to list all books by and about
American and Canadian Indians and Eskimos in print
as of 1972 in this bibliography. Citations to nearly
4,000 publications are listed. Juvenile works with
grade levels indicated and a select number of 20th
century novels are included. Arrangement is by author
within six sections: bibliographies, handbooks, autobiographies, myths and legends, all other books, and
reprints in American archaeology and ethnology. Each
citation indicates author, title, place and publisher,
year, pages and price and whether it is available in
paperback. Indian authors are identified. There is
a subject index.

501. *INDIANS OF MAINE: A BIBLIOGRAPHICAL GUIDE; BEING
LARGELY A SELECTED INVENTORY OF MATERIAL ON THE
SUBJECT IN THE SOCIETY'S LIBRARY.* Compiled by
Roger B. Ray. Portland, Maine Historical Society,
1972, 45p. (Bibliographical Guides, No. 2).
Updating and expanding the Maine Historical Society's
1969 preliminary inventory, this bibliography cites
the Society's holdings of material on Maine Indians
in 1972. The work is arranged by subject (e.g., ceremonies and ceremonial dress, history, languages,
missions and missionaries, population estimates, etc.)
and indexed by author. Brief descriptions are provided
for many items. Books, articles, reports, and documents

are cited. This bibliographical guide is the second
in a uniform series sponsored by the Maine Historical
Society (other volumes feature lumbering in Maine,
colonial activities, and shipbuilding).

502. *INDIANS OF OREGON: A BIBLIOGRAPHY OF MATERIALS
     IN THE OREGON STATE LIBRARY*. By Leroy Hewlett.
     Salem, Oregon State Library, 1971, 125p.
The emphasis of this bibliography is on Indians of
Oregon. Originally, the source was intended to include only this group. However, tribal, geographic
and historical bounderies overlap in such a way that
it became impractical to place this restriction on
the publication. Consequently, citations are also
made to materials on Indians of California, Washington, Idaho, Montana, and British Columbia if they
contain information pertinent to the study of Indians
in Oregon. All types of materials are identified:
books, periodical articles, newspaper accounts, pamphlets, government publications, etc. The source is
arranged by main entry and indexed by subject (agriculture, Bannock Indians, Columbia County, games,
plants, etc.).

503. *INDIANS OF THE UNITED STATES AND CANADA: A
     BIBLIOGRAPHY*. Edited by Dwight L. Smith.
     Santa Barbara, California, ABC-CLIO Press,
     1974, 453p. (Clio Bibliography Series No. 3).
This bibliography consists of nearly 1,700 abstracts
of scholarly periodical articles published between
1954 and 1972 in the United States and abroad on the
history and culture of North American Indians. The
abstracts were originally published in the quarterly
index *AMERICA: HISTORY AND LIFE* (Santa Barbara, ABC-
Clio, 1964-) and are reprinted here. They are
arranged in four sections (Pre-Columbian Indian History; Tribal History 1492-1900; General Indian History
1492-1900; The Indian in the Twentieth Century). These
sections are subdivided by geographic area and by tribe.
Each abstract contains full bibliographic information.
The entries are indexed by subject, author, name and
geographic area. To update this listing, check *AMERICA:*

504. *KNOWING AND EDUCATING THE DISADVANTAGED: AN
     ANNOTATED BIBLIOGRAPHY*. Alamosa, Colorado,
     Center for Cultural Studies, Adams State Col-
     lege, 1965, 460p.
For annotation, see Entry No. 435.

505. *THE LAKE MOHONK CONFERENCE OF FRIENDS OF THE
     INDIAN. GUIDE TO ANNUAL REPORTS*. By Larry
     E. Burgess. New York, Clearwater Publishing
     Co., 1975, 164p. (The Library of American
     Indian Affairs).
The Lake Mohonk Conferences of Friends of the Indian
were held annually from 1883 to 1916 (and again in
1929). This guide contains subject indexes and indexes
to speakers and writers which access the papers presented at the Conferences.

506. *LIST OF PUBLICATIONS OF THE BUREAU OF AMERICAN
     ETHNOLOGY WITH INDEX TO AUTHORS AND TITLES
     1894-1971*. Washington, D.C., G.P.O., 1971,
     134p. (Smithsonian Institution, Bureau of
     American Ethnology Bulletin no. 200).
The publications analyzed in this source include:
NORTH AMERICAN ETHNOLOGY (1877-1895), the *BULLETIN
SERIES* (1886-1971), 16 titles issued by the Institute
of Social Anthropology (1944-1953), and miscellaneous
volumes put out by the Bureau of American Ethnology
between 1894 and 1971. Author and title indexes are
provided. For a subject index to many of these materials, see the Bureau's *INDEX TO BULLETINS* (Entry No.
495). With the issuance of the *LIST* (*BULLETIN* 200),
the Bureau of American Ethnology's series ceased. The
BULLETIN series is superseded by *SMITHSONIAN CONTRIBU-
TIONS TO ANTHROPOLOGY* (1965-). "The new series
provides not only for publication of scholarly studies
of the American Indian but is worldwide in scope, re-
flecting the broadening activities of the Smithsonian
Institution's anthropologists over the past few decades."

507. *LITERATURE BY AND ABOUT THE AMERICAN INDIAN: AN ANNOTATED BIBLIOGRAPHY FOR JUNIOR AND SENIOR HIGH SCHOOL STUDENTS*. By Anna Lee Stensland. Urbana, Illinois, National Council of Teachers of English, 1973, 208p.

Over 400 books focusing on American Indians and written on a high school level are listed and described in this selective bibliography. The entries are arranged by broad subject headings (history, modern life and problems, aids for the teacher, myths, etc.) and indexed by author and title. Introductory essays discuss the suppression of Indian cultures in the United States, dominant themes in Native American literature, Indians as literary stereotypes and the problems of selecting materials "true to the Indian way." Also included in the publication are 25 biographies of American Indian authors, a bibliography of "Basic Books for a Collection by and about the American Indian for Junior and Senior High School," a list of "Sources of Additional Materials," and study guides to selected books. The National Council of Teachers of English has also issued a similar bibliography focusing on Blacks (see Entry No. 617).

508. *THE LITERATURE OF AMERICAN ABORIGINAL LANGUAGES*. By Hermann E. Ludewig. London, Trubner and Co., 1858, 258p. Reprinted by Kraus, 1971.

Books which illustrate the history of native languages in America are cited in this bibliography. The source is arranged alphabetically by languages, within geographic areas. There is an index.

509. *NARRATIVES OF CAPTIVITY AMONG THE INDIANS OF NORTH AMERICA: A LIST OF BOOKS AND MANUSCRIPTS ON THIS SUBJECT IN THE EDWARD E. AYER COLLECTION OF THE NEWBERRY LIBRARY*. Chicago, Newberry Library, 1912; reprinted by Gryphon Books and dist. by Gale, 1971, 120p. *SUPPLEMENT 1*, Chicago, Newberry Library, 1928; reprinted by Gryphon Books and dist. by Gale, 1971, 49p.

"Chiefly as an aid to research, therefore, and to some extent an account of the inadequacy of existing biblio-

graphic descriptions of this class of Americana, the
present list of narratives of Indian captivity has
been compiled." The captivity narratives listed here
are from the Edward E. Ayer Collection of Americana
and American Indians located in the Newberry Library.
The bibliography, originally issued in 1912, lists
over 300 of these narratives of white men who had
been captured by various Indian tribes. The 1928
supplement lists over 140 items and includes 78 additional narratives not named in the earlier work as
well as different editions of some of the narratives
already listed in the first publication. Full bibliographic information is given for each entry, plus a
detailed annotation which describes the content,
value and veracity of the works. Arrangement is by
author and there is a "captive" name index. A complete list of materials in the Edward E. Ayer Collection has also been published (see Entry No. 475).

510. *NATIVE AMERICANS OF NORTH AMERICA: A BIBLIO-
      GRAPHY*. Prepared by David Perkins and Norman
      Tanis. Northridge, California State Univer-
      sity, 1975, 558p. (Bibliography Series).
The 3,500 books on North American Indians in the
Library at California State University, Northridge
are cited in the bibliography. The bibliography
"is intended principally for academic and public
libraries serving undergraduate and advanced high
school students who want to know what the best books
are from among the many that have been published."
The book is arranged in 21 subject categories (tribes,
biography, etc.), with several topics subdivided by
geographic region. An author-title index is provided.

511. *NAVAJO BIBLIOGRAPHY*. By David M. Brugge, et.
      al. Window Rock, Arizona, Navajoland Publica-
      tions, 1967, 291p.
This bibliography was up-dated and revised by the
1969 publication, *NAVAJO BIBLIOGRAPHY WITH SUBJECT
INDEX* (For annotation, see Entry No. 512).

512. *NAVAJO BIBLIOGRAPHY WITH SUBJECT INDEX.* By J.
Lee Correll, Editha Watson and David M. Brugge.
Rev. ed. Window Rock, Arizona, Navajo Tribe,
1969, 394p. (Navajo Tribe. Navajo Parks and
Recreation, Research Section. Research Report
No. 2).

Revising a 1967 publication (see Entry No. 511), this
bibliography contains "all available references to
Navajo-people, their land and environment, regardless
of source..." Included are over 2,500 historical,
ethnographic, biographic, technical, popular, and
fictional works, archival and congressional materials,
newspaper accounts, articles from journals, maps,
books, pamphlets, manuscripts, and technical papers
from government and Navajo Tribal files. The citations are arranged by author and indexed by such
subjects as acculturation, death, Federal relations,
legends and myths, marriage, and sex. There are no
annotations.

513. *THE NORTH AMERICAN INDIAN: A BIBLIOGRAPHY OF
COMMUNITY DEVELOPMENT.* Washington, D.C., Lib-
rary, U.S. Department of Housing and Urban
Renewal, 1975, 65p.

Developed by the HUD Library at the request of the
Assistant Secretary for Equal Opportunity, this
bibliography lists books, articles, reports, and documents on American Indian affairs. A selection of items
detailing Native American history and relations with
Federal/state governments precedes sections on social,
economic, health, educational, and community development. Specialized bibliographies are listed at the
end of each of these sections. The materials are
indexed by geographic location and subject areas. A
separate section is devoted to the listing of "Comprehensive Planning (701) Reports of Indian Tribal
Bodies."

514. *REFERENCE ENCYCLOPEDIA OF THE AMERICAN INDIAN.*
By Barry T. Klein and Dan Icolari. 2nd. ed.
Rye, New York, Todd Publications, 1973-4, 2v.

Newspapers, magazines, periodicals, visual and instructional aids (films, picture sets, songbooks, maps, charts, recordings), government publications, and 2,500 in-print books dealing with American Indians are cited in this reference work. For a more complete annotation, see Entry No. 50.

515. *A REFERENCE RESOURCE GUIDE OF THE AMERICAN IN-DIAN.* By George A. Gill. Tempe, Center for Indian Education, Arizona State University, 1974, 187p.

Audio-visual and other materials "concerning all aspects of our First American" are included in this "reference resource guide." For a more detailed annotation, see Entry No. 296.

516. *SELECT CATALOG OF NATIONAL ARCHIVES MICROFILM PUBLICATIONS: AMERICAN INDIAN.* Washington, D.C., U.S. National Archives and Records Service, 1972, 50p.

All records published on microfilm by the National Archives and Records Service "that relate directly to Indians, to the formation and enforcement of Federal Indian policy, and to the personnel that created or enforced that policy" are listed in this catalog by subject. The main chapters are: records of the Bureau of Indian Affairs; records of the Indian Division, Office of the Secretary of the Interior; records of the War Department; records relating to Indian treaties; records relating to territories; records relating to appointments; and miscellaneous (including consular dispatches and treasury records). Positive prints of all items cited in the *CATALOG* can be purchased from the National Archives; negative prints of all the microfilms are housed in the National Archives.

517. *A SELECTED BIBLIOGRAPHY OF MISSOURI ARCHEOLOGY.* By Randy L. Cottier, Susan B. Traub, and Don C. Traub. Columbia, University of Missouri, 1973, 340p.

Each section in this bibliography (specific geographic

areas) is preceded by a map of the area covered. Citations give author, title, place, publisher, date, and pages. There is an alphabetical index of authors.

518. *SOCIAL AND ECONOMIC DIMENSIONS OF HEALTH AND ILLNESS BEHAVIOR IN NEW MEXICO; AN ANNOTATED BIBLIOGRAPHY*. By Helen Rose Potter. Albuquerque, University of New Mexico Press, 1969, 220p.
The bibliography "attempts to facilitate access to social and economic information pertinent to health and illness behavior" among Mexican Americans and Indians living in New Mexico. For a more complete annotation, see Entry No. 671.

519. *THIS COUNTRY WAS OURS: A DOCUMENTARY HISTORY OF THE AMERICAN INDIAN*. By Virgil J. Vogel. New York, Harper and Row, 1972, 473p.
In addition to documents, an extensive bibliography of books pertaining to Indian history and culture is included. For a more detailed annotation, see Entry No. 233.

520. *THREE ATLANTIC BIBLIOGRAPHIES*. Compiled by Harold Franklin McGee, Stephen A. Davis and Michael Taft. Halifax, Canada, Department of Anthropology, Saint Mary's University, 1975, 201p. (Occasional Papers in Anthropology No. 1).
The first issue of the newly established *OCCASIONAL PAPERS IN ANTHROPOLOGY*, this publication contains compilations of references concerning the archaeology and ethnography of the native peoples of Maine, Nova Scotia and Atlantic Canada. The first of the three bibliographies, "Ethnographic Bibliography of Northeastern North America," consists of over 700 references to the culture, history and social anthropology of the Abenaki, Micmac, Malecite-Passamaquoddy, Renobscot, and Beothuk. The second, "Preliminary Archaeology Bibliography of Atlantic Canada and Maine," is the first published bibliography pertaining to the pre-historic archaeology of the region. The last, "A Bibliography for Folklore Studies in Nova Scotia," cites nearly 500 authors who

have written works relevant to the study of folklife
and folklore of the Province of Nova Scotia.

521. *UNITED STATES CODE ANNOTATED. TITLE 25: INDIANS.*
St. Paul, Minnesota, West Publishing Co., 1963;
1976 pocket supplement, 253p.
References are made throughout the work to statutes
and court decisions. For a more detailed annotation,
see Entry No. 234.

522. *THE UTE PEOPLE; A BIBLIOGRAPHICAL CHECKLIST.* By
S. Lyman Tyler. Provo, Utah, Brigham Young University, 1964, 120p.
Materials "pertinent to research on the history of the
Ute Indians and their linguistic relatives" are cited
in this bibliography. The publication begins with
the Spanish period in the early 1600s. The citations
are arranged by format: bibliographies and guides,
manuscript material, government documents, newspapers
and periodicals.

Chapter 8

ASIAN AMERICANS

(Indexes, Abstracts, Bibliographies, etc.)

523. *AMERICANS AND CHINESE; A HISTORICAL ESSAY AND BIBLIOGRAPHY*. Edited by Kwang-Ching Liu. Cambridge, Harvard University Press, 1963, 211p.

The first part of this source is an essay which examines the problems arising from early American-Chinese relations. The rest of the publication is devoted to a 150 page bibliography of little known archival and published sources (biographies, memoirs, newspapers, periodicals and reference books) in the United States relating to Chinese-American relations at the non-governmental level. The citations are to materials in Western languages (mostly of American authorship). There is an author index.

524. *ANTI-FILIPINO MOVEMENTS IN CALIFORNIA: A HISTORY, BIBLIOGRAPHY AND STUDY GUIDE*. By Howard A. De Witt. San Francisco, R & E Research Associates, 1976, 180p.

The major themes developed in this work are the origins of Filipino migration into California during the 1920s, the inducements provided by the agribusiness community to migrate, and the early reaction to this phase of Oriental labor. The themes are covered in the history, bibliography and study guide included in the publication. Heavy use is made of primary source materials, particularly the personal papers of United States Senators and Representatives, California State Legislators, and the contemporary Filipino press.

525. *ASIAN AMERICANS: A STUDY GUIDE AND SOURCE BOOK*. By Lynn P. Dunn. San Francisco, R & E Research Associates, 1975, 111p.

"Notes and Sources" (appropriate study materials) accompany the chronological study outline. For a complete annotation, see Entry No. 53.

526. *ASIAN AMERICANS: AN ANNOTATED BIBLIOGRAPHY*. Compiled by Harry H. L. Kitano. Los Angeles, Asian American Studies Center, University of California, 1971, 76p.

This publication is very similar to *ASIANS IN AMERICA: A SELECTED BIBLIOGRAPHY FOR USE IN SOCIAL WORK EDUCA- TION* (see Entry No. 530).

527. *ASIANS IN AMERICA; A BIBLIOGRAPHY.* By William
Wong Lum. Davis, Asian American Research Project, University of California, 1969. 48p.
SUPPLEMENT, 1970, 22p.
Books, periodical articles, and theses covering all
facets of Asian American life are cited in this bibliography. A major section of the publication focuses
on anti-Asian legislation, with each Asian nationality
treated separately. Social organization, economic
status, and acculturation are covered in other chapters. Unlike the subject arranged 1969 volume, the
1970 supplement is divided by form of material (reference materials, books, and periodicals).

528. *ASIANS IN AMERICA, A BIBLIOGRAPHY OF MASTER'S
THESES AND DOCTORAL DISSERTATIONS.* Compiled
by William Wong Lum. Davis, Asian American
Studies, Department of Applied Behavioral
Sciences, University of California, 1970, 78p.
(Working Publication No. 2).
For annotation, see Entry No. 549.

529. *ASIANS IN AMERICA: A SELECTED ANNOTATED BIBLIO-
GRAPHY.* By Isao Fujimoto, Michiyo Yamaguchi
Swift and Rosalie Zucker. Davis, Asian American
Studies, Department of Applied Behavioral
Sciences, University of California, 1971, 295p.
(Working Publication No. 5).
The purpose of this bibliography is "to provide an
overview of the variety of materials available in
English language sources concerning the Asian exper-
ience in America." Over 800 items (monographs, books,
master's theses, doctoral dissertations, articles, and
government documents) are chronologically listed in
such chapters as: Chinese Experience in America;
Japanese Experience in America; Bibliographies and
Sources of Information; etc. Each entry is annotated.

Asian community and movement newspapers are listed in the appendix. There are author and geographic indexes. An earlier and more selective bibliography, *ASIANS IN AMERICA; A BIBLIOGRAPHY* was done by the Asian American Research Project, University of California, Davis, in 1969 (see Entry No. 527).

530. *ASIANS IN AMERICA: A SELECTED BIBLIOGRAPHY FOR USE IN SOCIAL WORK EDUCATION.* Compiled by Harry H. L. Kitano. New York, Council on Social Work Education, 1971, 79p.

Publications dealing with American-born Chinese, Japanese, Koreans and Filipinos are listed in this annotated bibliography. Arranged by nationality, the citations are further subdivided by such subject headings as psychology-personality, sociology-social work, race and ethnic relations, economics, immigration, and Japanese evacuation-relocation. There is a separate listing of recent master's theses and doctoral dissertations on the subject. For a more extensive bibliography of materials on Asians in America, see Isao Fujimoto's publication (Entry No. 529). Kitano also compiled a similar bibliography issued by the Asian American Studies Center at U.C.L.A. entitled *ASIAN AMERICANS: AN ANNOTATED BIBLIOGRAPHY* (1971, 76p.).

531. *BIBLIOGRAPHY OF THE CHINESE QUESTION IN THE UNITED STATES.* By Robert Ernest Cowan and Boutwell Dunlap. San Francisco, A. M. Robertson, 1909, 68p.

Books, pamphlets, reports, manuscripts and unpublished papers on Chinese immigration in its various phases are cited and briefly described in this bibliography. Government documents and articles in newspapers or journals are not included. The arrangement is by author (or main entry). There is no index. A facsimile of the 1909 publication was issued without change by R & E Research Associates in 1970.

532. *A BURIED PAST: AN ANNOTATED BIBLIOGRAPHY OF THE JAPANESE AMERICAN RESEARCH PROJECT COLLECTION.*

Compiled by Yuji Ichioka and others. Berkeley,
University of California Press, 1974, 227p.
This is a listing of 1,500 Japanese American materials
in UCLA's Research Library. The citations are arranged
under 18 subject categories (education, literature,
history, etc.). Each of these categories is preceded
by a brief summary which places the citations in
historical perspective. The general introduction to
this work discusses the current status of publications
of Japanese Americans.

533. *THE CHINESE IN AMERICA 1820-1973: A CHRONOLOGY
      AND FACT BOOK.* By William L. Tung. Dobbs Ferry,
      New York, Oceana Publications, 1974, 150p. (Ethnic
      Chronology Series no. 14).
The final section of the source is a selective, unannotated bibliography of primary and secondary source
materials (government documents, books, pamphlets,
articles, etc.) arranged alphabetically. For a complete
annotation, see Entry No. 54.

534. *THE CHINESE IN CALIFORNIA: A BRIEF BIBLIOGRAPHIC
      HISTORY.* Edited by Gladys C. Hansen and William
      F. Heintz. Portland, Oregon, Richard Abel and
      Company, 1970, 140p. (Abel Bibliographic Series,
      Volume 1).
This "systematic bibliographic" work lists over 400
19th century primary sources and 20th century secondary
sources dealing with Chinese immigrant life in California. Books, chapters of books, even single pages
are cited. Only those materials found in the California
Room of the San Francisco Public Library are listed.
Included are citations to pro- and anti-Chinese propa-
ganda tracts, personal narratives, and California local
histories. The entries are arranged alphabetically by
author and include descriptive annotations. Author and
subject indexes are included at the end of the source.
A lengthy introduction to the history of the Chinese
in California is included.

535. *THE CHINESE IN HAWAII: A BIBLIOGRAPHIC SURVEY.*

By Chuan-hua Lowe. Taipei, Taiwan, China Printing Ltd., 1972, 148p.
There are three main sections in *THE CHINESE IN HAWAII:*
1) a historical sketch which highlights "what the
Chinese have done in Hawaii and what Hawaii has done
for them;" 2) a chronology of events of interest and
significance to the Chinese in Hawaii; and 3) a selected, annotated bibliography of 400 Chinese and English
writings (articles, books, dissertations, manuscripts,
monographs, reports, studies, etc.) dealing with the
affairs, conditions, problems and progress of Hawaii's
Chinese. "Designed to be selective rather than exhaustive, this bibliography is almost entirely limited to
Chinese and English writings..." The citations are
indexed by author and subject.

536. *THE CHINESE IN HAWAII: AN ANNOTATED BIBLIOGRAPHY.*
      By Nancy Foon Young. Honolulu, Social Science
      Research Institute, University of Hawaii; distri-
      buted by University Press of Hawaii, 1973, 149p.
      (Hawaii Series No. 4).
Nearly 700 books, articles, pamphlets, government
documents, theses, dissertations and trade publications which concentrate on the Chinese experience in
Hawaii are listed in this annotated bibliography.
Newspaper articles are excluded. "While emphasis is
on the Chinese in the Hawaiian Islands, selected
references on the homeland are included to provide
background on emigration and the home country." The
list is limited to materials found in public libraries
in Honolulu; the library location is given in each
entry. Arrangement is by author, or by title if there
is no author. Chinese language sources are included
in alphabetical order according to the English trans-
lation of the author or title of the publication.
There is a glossary of Chinese character titles and
a 10 page subject index. The *HAWAII SERIES* includes
bibliographies on the Japanese (Entry No. 542-3),
Koreans (Entry No. 545), Filipinos (Entry No. 538),
and their culture and behavior in Hawaii (Entry No. 537).

537. *CULTURE AND BEHAVIOR IN HAWAII: AN ANNOTATED*

BIBLIOGRAPHY. By Judith Rubano. Honolulu, Social Science Research Institute, University of Hawaii; distributed by University Press of Hawaii, 1971, 147p. (Hawaii Series No. 3).
"This bibliography is an effort to...[bring] together materials which relate to the attitudes and behavior of the people of Hawaii, particularly those attitudes and behaviors which have some ethnic relevance." The work includes citations to over 600 materials: books, pamphlets, journal articles, documents, theses and dissertations. Newspaper and popular magazine articles are excluded. Each entry is annotated. The arrangement is by author. There is a subject index. The *HAWAII SERIES* includes bibliographies on the Chinese (Entry No. 536), Japanese (Entry No. 542-3), Filipinos (Entry No. 538), and Koreans (Entry No. 545) in Hawaii.

538. *THE FILIPINOS IN HAWAII: AN ANNOTATED BIBLIOGRAPHY*. By Ruiz Alcantara. Honolulu, Social Science Research Institute, University of Hawaii; distributed by University Press of Hawaii, 1972, 52p. (Hawaii Series No. 4).
This annotated bibliography includes relevant books and articles on the Filipinos in Hawaii. The bibliography contains the materials available at the Hawaii State Library Hawaii collection, the University of Hawaii's Hawaiian and Pacific collection, and the University of Hawaii's Hamilton Library collection. A chronology of events related to Filipino immigration to Hawaii is included plus a suggested reading list. The *HAWAII SERIES* includes bibliographies on the Chinese (Entry No. 536), Koreans (Entry No. 545), Japanese (Entry No. 542-543) and their behavior and culture in Hawaii (Entry No. 537).

539. *A GUIDE TO DOCTORAL DISSERTATIONS BY CHINESE STUDENTS IN AMERICA 1905-1960*. Compiled by T'ung-Li Yüan. Washington, D.C., published under the auspices of the Sino-American Cultural Society, Inc., 1961, 248p.
The purpose of this compilation is "to provide a com-

plete record of the doctoral dissertations submitted
by Chinese students and accepted by American universities between the years 1905 and 1960." Nearly
2,800 dissertations are listed alphabetically by
author within three parts: 1) humanities, social and
behavioral sciences; 2) physical, biological and
engineering sciences; and 3) Canadian dissertations,
1926-1960. For each entry, the following information
is provided: author's name, Chinese name, birth year,
title of degree, institution awarding degree, date of
degree, and title of dissertation. Identification is
made of those papers listed in *DISSERTATION ABSTRACTS
INTERNATIONAL* (Ann Arbor, Michigan, University Microfilms, 1952-) or *MICROFILM ABSTRACTS* (Ann Arbor,
Michigan, University Microfilms, 1938-1952). Two
appendices contain 1) a listing of the recipients of
honorary degrees conferred by Chinese and foreign
institutions of higher learning and 2) statistical
tables of degrees granted by institution and topic.
There is an index of fields of study. The listing is
continued by *A LIST OF DOCTORAL DISSERTATIONS BY
CHINESE STUDENTS IN THE UNITED STATES, 1961-1964*
(see Entry No. 546).

540. *JAPANESE AMERICAN EVACUATION AND RESETTLEMENT:
      CATALOGUE OF MATERIALS IN THE GENERAL LIBRARY.*
      Berkeley, University of California Library, 1958,
      177p.
Materials dealing with the Japanese-American evacuation,
internment, and resettlement during World War II held
at U.C. Berkeley's Main Library (Documents Department)
and Bancroft Library are listed in this bibliography.
Books, diaries, journals, pamphlets, leaflets, phono-
graphic records, press releases, reports, slides,
surveys, and public opinion polls are included. The
citations are listed in chronological order, divided
into five main parts: 1) Exclusion and Internment of
Japanese in Assembly Centers; Pearl Harbor to December,
1942; 2) Internment in Relocation Centers and Condition-
al Freedom; December, 1942 - December, 1944; 3) Freedom
and Individual Exclusion; December 1944 - March, 1946;
4) Vital Statistics; 5) Japanese-American Evacuation
and Resettlement Study. There is a detailed table of

contents in outline form which serves as a subject
index to the citations and outlines the scheme used
to organize the materials in the catalog.

541. *THE JAPANESE IN AMERICA 1843-1973: A CHRONOLOGY
      AND FACT BOOK.* Compiled and edited by Masako
      Herman. Dobbs Ferry, New York, Oceana Publica-
      tions, 1974, 152p. (Ethnic Chronology Series
      no. 15).
One section contains an annotated bibliography of
pertinent books. For a complete annotation, see
Entry No. 57.

542. *THE JAPANESE IN HAWAII; AN ANNOTATED BIBLIOGRAPHY
      OF JAPANESE AMERICANS.* By Mitsugu Matsuda. Re-
      vised by Dennis M. Ogawa with Jerry Y. Fujioka,
      Honolulu, Social Science and Linguistics Insti-
      tute, University of Hawaii; distributed by Univer-
      sity Press of Hawaii, 1974, 304p. (Hawaii Series
      No. 5).
This bibliography is a revision of Matsuda's *JAPANESE
IN HAWAII, 1868-1967: AN ANNOTATED BIBLIOGRAPHY OF THE
FIRST HUNDRED YEARS* (see Entry No. 543). "The primary
purpose of this bibliography is to provide a reference
guide for the undergraduate, English-speaking student
who is attempting to understand the Japanese-American
experience in Hawaii." Over 700 English and Japanese
materials (books, articles, reports, etc.) are cited.
The publication is arranged by author and indexed by
subject. There is a separate listing of Japanese
newspapers and periodicals in Hawaii. The *HAWAII
SERIES* includes bibliographies on the Chinese (Entry
No. 536), Koreans (Entry No. 545), Filipinos (Entry
No. 538), and their behavior and culture (Entry No.
537) in Hawaii.

543. *THE JAPANESE IN HAWAII, 1868-1967: AN ANNOTATED
      BIBLIOGRAPHY OF THE FIRST HUNDRED YEARS.* By
      Mitsugu Matsuda. Honolulu, Social Science Re-
      search Institute, University of Hawaii; distri-
      buted by University Press of Hawaii, 1968, 222p.

(Hawaii Series No. 1).
This bibliography is the first in a series of annotated
bibliographies on Hawaii's people of Asian ancestry.
In it, citations are made to Japanese and English
language materials presently available in Hawaii, which
relate to all aspects of the life of Japanese immigrants
and their descendants in Hawaii. Annotations are provided for each entry. The titles of Japanese language
materials are translated into English. There is a
title index. The bibliography was revised in 1975 and
issued as the fifth publication in the *HAWAII SERIES;*
for others in the series, see Entry Nos. 536-8, 542,
545.

544. *THE KOREANS IN AMERICA 1882-1974: A CHRONOLOGY
      AND FACT BOOK.* Compiled and edited by Hyung-
      Chan Kim and Wayne Patterson. Dobbs Ferry,
      New York, Oceana Publications, 1974, 147p.
      (Ethnic Chronology Series no. 16).
One section presents a selective, unannotated bibliography of materials on Koreans in America between
1882 and 1974. For a complete description, see Entry
No. 58.

545. *THE KOREANS IN HAWAII: AN ANNOTATED BIBLIOGRAPHY.*
      By Arthur L. Gardner. Honolulu, Social Sciences
      Research Institute, distributed by University
      Press of Hawaii, 1970, 83p. (Hawaii Series No.
      2).
Over 200 items (books, articles, newspaper accounts,
diaries, theses, etc.) dealing with the Koreans in
Hawaii are arranged by main entry in this annotated
bibliography. Materials are included irrespective of
publication date or specific subject orientation.
"This bibliography attempts to include all of the
materials presently available in Hawaii in either the
English or the Korean language that would be helpful
to anyone attempting such research." Organizations
oriented toward the Korean community in Hawaii are
described in the appendix. A seven page introduction
provides a short history of the Koreans in Hawaii and
a commentary on sources of information. Most of the

items listed can be found in libraries in Hawaii.
Locational symbols are provided. There is an index
to co-authors and titles of cited materials. This
volume represents the second of a series designed to
identify bibliographic source materials on Hawaii's
people of Asian ancestry; for others in the series,
see Entry Nos. 536-8, 542-3.

546. *A LIST OF DOCTORAL DISSERTATIONS BY CHINESE
      STUDENTS IN THE UNITED STATES, 1961-1964.* Com-
      piled by Tze-Chung Li. Chicago, Chinese American
      Educational Foundation, 1967, 84p.
Over 800 dissertations are listed in this bibliography.
Most of the studies were completed between 1961 and
1964; some items date earlier than 1961 if they were
not included in the Yüan bibliography (see Entry No.
539). The dissertations are arranged by subject and
are indexed by author.

547. *LITERATURE OF THE FILIPINO-AMERICAN IN THE UNITED
      STATES: A SELECTIVE AND ANNOTATED BIBLIOGRAPHY.*
      By Irene P. Norell. San Francisco, California,
      R & E Research Associates, 1976, 178p.
Annotated in this bibliography are general works and
works on Asian Americans containing works on Filipino
Americans, Filipino Americans in the United States
with special reference to California and Hawaii, Filipino immigration and exclusion (including legal aspects,
aspects of race and racism), social and economic conditions of Filipino-Americans (with special reference to
labor), and Filipinos in the Armed Forces and educational institutions.

548. *THE RELOCATION OF JAPANESE AMERICANS DURING WORLD
      WAR II: A GUIDE TO RESEARCH MATERIALS IN THE
      HOOVER INSTITUTION ARCHIVES.* Stanford, California,
      SWOPSI, Stanford University, 1970, 178p.
Letters, newspaper articles, bulletins, reports, and
newsletters dealing with the relocation of Japanese
Americans during World War II in the Hoover Institution
Archives are cited in this publication. The bibliogra-

phy is annotated. It was prepared by members of a
Stanford undergraduate course under the direction of
Franz Lassner (Hoover Institution) and Ann Waswo
(History Department).

549. *THESES AND DISSERTATIONS ON ASIANS IN THE U.S.;*
     WITH SELECTED REFERENCES TO OTHER OVERSEAS
     ASIANS. Compiled by Paul M. Ong and William
     Wong Lum. Davis, Asian American Studies, De-
     partment of Applied Behavioral Sciences, Univ-
     ersity of California, 1974, 113p.
THESES AND DISSERTATIONS is a revision and expansion
of *ASIANS IN AMERICA: A BIBLIOGRAPHY OF MASTER'S*
THESES AND DOCTORAL DISSERTATIONS (Compiled by William
Wong Lum, University of California, Davis, 1970, 78p.).
More than 1,400 dissertations and theses on subjects
relating to the Asian experience in America are included. Listing is by ethnic group and sub-topics (e.g.,
origins, immigration, discrimination, social organization, etc.). There are author and keyword subject
indexes.

550. *WRITINGS ON THE CHINESE IN CALIFORNIA.* By Pearl
     Ng. San Francisco, R & E Research Associates,
     1972, 118p.
Written originally as a thesis in 1939 at the University
of California, the bibliographic compilation is divided
into two sections. The first section investigates "why
the Chinese were welcomed in the early days of California
...what the underlying factors were which caused the
change of attitude, and resulted in organized agitation
and subsequent legislation and what effect this attitude
had on the Chinese..." The second section lists books,
pamphlets, theses, newspapers, articles, pamphlets, and
reference books. The entries are listed either under
form (bibliographies, general works, Federal documents,
newspapers, etc.) or subject (Chinese question, exclusion, sociological data, San Francisco's Chinatown,
etc.). Although the bibliography does not attempt to
be exhaustive, "it comprises all material found, to
date, available on the subject; especially in the phase
of articles in periodical literature..." The material

in the Bancroft Library and the University of California Library forms the nucleus of the bibliography. There is an author index.

Chapter 9

BLACK AMERICANS

(Indexes, Abstracts, Bibliographies, etc.)

551. *AFRICAN AND BLACK AMERICAN STUDIES*. Compiled
by Alexander S. Birkos and Lewis A. Tambs. Littleton, Colorado, Libraries Unlimited, 1975,
205p. (Academic Writer's Guide to Periodicals
Series, Vol. 3).
This guide to African and Black American studies
focuses on "serial publications with either a primary
or an occasional interest in any of the areas of
Africa (North Central, South, East, or West), the
African nations of the Middle East, or the nations
or colonies on the African continent. Included also
are publications that deal with Black American interests in Canada, Latin America and the United States."
Over 200 journals (all of which deal with the humanities and the social sciences) are listed by title.
The information provided for each entry includes:
editors, address, sponsor, frequency of publication,
price, subscribers, editorial interest, editorial
policies, indexing sources, and special features.
The data were gathered through questionnaires sent
to the journal editors. Suggestions for manuscript
preparation and submission are included. There are
four sections to the index: general, chronological,
geographical, topical. The *GUIDE* is the third volume
in the *ACADEMIC WRITER'S GUIDE TO PERIODICALS* series,
which describes periodicals devoted to disciplines
within the humanities and social sciences. The first
2 volumes of the series covered Latin America and
Soviet/East European studies. In all, seven volumes
are projected for the series.

552. *THE AFRICAN SLAVE TRADE AND ITS SUPPRESSION: A
CLASSIFIED AND ANNOTATED BIBLIOGRAPHY OF BOOKS,
PAMPHLETS AND PERIODICAL ARTICLES*. By Peter C.
Hogg. London, Cass; dist. by International
Scholarly Book Services, 1974, 409p. (Slavery
Series).
This is a bibliography of books, pamphlets, periodical
articles, and theses dealing with the African slave
trade (participated in not only by America, but also
by Spain, Portugal, Britain, France, Denmark, etc.).
Manuscripts, many government documents, and Slavic,
African and Arabic materials are excluded. The over

4,000 entries are arranged in two main sections. The
first section contains citations to contemporary
accounts of slavery, histories of slavery, biographies of slaves, etc. The second part is divided
into sections: sermons, legislative speeches, debates,
publications of abolition societies, conferences, etc.
Each of the entries contains a short annotation. The
cut off date for slave trade as a subject is 1900; for
publication date, it is 1972. An introduction lists
guides to documents and manuscript materials. An
appendix cites relevant master's theses and dissertations. The volume concludes with author, personal
name, geographical name, and anonymous title indexes.

553. *AFRO-AMERICAN HISTORY: A BIBLIOGRAPHY*. Edited
     by Dwight L. Smith. Santa Barbara, California,
     ABC-Clio Press, 1974, 856p. (Clio Bibliography
     Series no. 2).
The abstracts included in this bibliography were
taken from the data base *AMERICA: HISTORY AND LIFE*
(1964-1972) and *HISTORICAL ABSTRACTS* (1953-1964).
Over 2,000 abstracts of articles provide information
on and citations to materials dealing with the social,
political, and economic characteristics of Blacks in
America (Black nationalism, separatism, civil rights,
Black power, etc.). The publication is divided into
the following chapters: 1) traditions in Afro-American
culture; 2) the Black experience in colonial America;
3) slavery and freedom (1783-1865); 4) Reconstruction
and its aftermath (1865-1900); 5) Afro-American society
in the twentieth century; 6) the contemporary scene
(since 1945). The volume is intended for "the scholar
in compiling his bibliography, the professor in preparing his lecture, the advanced student in seeking a
term topic, and the serious reader in general." An
integrated index provides subject, author, biographical
and geographical access. Updating is provided through
continuing issues of *AMERICA: HISTORY AND LIFE*.

554. *AFRO-AMERICANA 1553-1906; AUTHOR CATALOG OF THE
     LIBRARY COMPANY OF PHILADELPHIA AND THE HISTORICAL
     SOCIETY OF PENNSYLVANIA*. Boston, G.K. Hall, 1973,

714p. (Seventy Series).
This author catalog represents the Afro-American
holdings of the Library Company of Philadelphia and
the Historical Society of Pennsylvania. The collections contain important and rare material on Black
history in America and Africa. Explorations and
travel, biographies, anti-slavery pamphlets and
tracts, reports of abolition societies, and the
papers of the Pennsylvania Abolition Society and
the American Negro Historical Society are a sample
of the subjects included in the collection. The
17,000 entries are divided into three sections:
books and pamphlets (including newspapers and periodicals); manuscripts; and broadsides. Each entry
gives the following information: author, title,
place published, publisher, date of publication,
pagination, and library. The catalog is alphabetically arranged by author with a subject index to
the "books and pamphlets" section.

555. *AFRO-AMERICANS IN THE FAR WEST: A HANDBOOK
     FOR EDUCATORS.* By Jack D. Forbes. Berkeley,
     California, Far West Laboratory for Educational
     Research and Development, 1970, 106p.
Citations are provided for readings on Afro-American
history, contemporary issues, education of culturally
different and low-income groups, audio-visual sources,
etc. For a complete annotation, see Entry No. 61.

556. *AMERICAN BLACK WOMEN IN THE ARTS AND SOCIAL
     SCIENCES: A BIBLIOGRAPHIC SURVEY.* By Ora
     Williams. Metuchen, New Jersey, Scarecrow
     Press, 1973, 141p.
For annotation, see Entry No. 680.

557. *ANALYTICAL GUIDES AND INDEXES TO: ALEXANDER'S
     MAGAZINE, 1905-1909; THE COLORED AMERICAN
     MAGAZINE, 1900-1909; THE CRISIS: 1910-1960;
     THE VOICE OF THE NEGRO, 1904-1907.* Westport,
     Connecticut, Greenwood Press, 1974-75, 7v.
These analytical guides and indexes to *ALEXANDER'S*

MAGAZINE, THE COLORED AMERICAN MAGAZINE, THE CRISIS, and THE VOICE OF THE NEGRO, prepared retrospectively by Greenwood Press, provide chronological abstracts to articles, the names of authors, article titles, and subject information on the contents of these important Black journals of the early twentieth century.

558. *ANNOTATED BIBLIOGRAPHY OF THE PUBLISHED WRITINGS OF W.E.B. DUBOIS*. By Herbert Aptheker. New York, Kraus, 1973, 626p.
Nearly 2,000 citations to the writings of W.E.B. DuBois, scholar-activist in the Black liberation movement, are listed and abstracted in this publication. Included are writings by DuBois in magazines and newspapers edited by others; writings in magazines edited by DuBois; newspaper columns, government publications and proceedings; writings in works edited by others; works edited by DuBois; pamphlets, leaflets and books noted by DuBois, etc. There are three indexes: books noted by DuBois, proper names and subjects.

559. *AN ANNOTATED GUIDE TO BASIC REFERENCE BOOKS ON THE BLACK AMERICAN EXPERIENCE*. Compiled by Guy T. Westmoreland, Jr. Wilmington, Delaware, Scholarly Resources, 1974, 98p.
"The primary purpose of this guide is to organize and describe reference books which deal primarily with the black American experience." Part One covers general reference sources, including bibliographic guides and catalogs of special library collections, biographical sources, dictionaries, encyclopedias, handbooks, yearbooks, indexes and multi-subject bibliographies. Part Two deals with subject area reference sources, covering civil rights and Black America, fine arts, economic life, education, history, literature, media, slavery, society and culture. Over 100 sources are described. Author, title and subject indexes are appended.

560. *BIBLIOGRAPHIC GUIDE TO BLACK STUDIES: 1975*. Boston, G.K. Hall, 1975, 318p.

BIBLIOGRAPHIC GUIDE TO BLACK STUDIES: 1975 is an
annual supplement to the *DICTIONARY CATALOG OF THE
SCHOMBURG COLLECTION OF NEGRO LITERATURE AND HISTORY*
(see Entry No. 599). The supplement includes publications cataloged during the year by the Schomburg
Center for Research in Black Culture. Complete cataloging information is given: main entry, added entries,
titles and series, and subject. Headings are in one
alphabetical arrangement. The material is classified
by the Dewey Decimal system with LC subject headings
supplemented by special headings developed for the
Schomburg Collection.

561. *BIBLIOGRAPHIC SURVEY: THE NEGRO IN PRINT.* Wash-
     ington, D.C., Negro Bibliographic and Research
     Center, 1965-   , Bi-monthly.
BIBLIOGRAPHIC SURVEY: THE NEGRO IN PRINT is an annotated bibliographical periodical listing fiction, non-
fiction, poetry, paperbacks, children's books, pamphlets, and periodical articles that would be of interest to Black Americans. Special topics are included
from time to time, for example: Black studies'
programs, Black literary magazines, books for young
readers, etc. The bibliography is published six times
a year with annual author and title indexes. A five
year subject index (1965-1970) by Dolores C. Leffal
was published in 1971. From 1965 to 1971, the publication was issued under the title *THE NEGRO IN PRINT*.

562. *A BIBLIOGRAPHY OF AFRO-AMERICAN AND OTHER AMER-
     ICAN MINORITIES REPRESENTED IN LIBRARY AND
     LIBRARY LISTINGS*. By Clara O. Jackson. New
     York, The American Institute for Marxist Stud-
     ies, 1970, 32p. (Bibliographical Series No. 7);
     SUPPLEMENT, 1972, 51p. (Bibliographical Series
     No. 9).
Of interest primarily to librarians, this bibliography
cites lists of Black (and some other ethnic) studies'
materials prepared by libraries across the country.
The cited lists cover all types of materials (including audio-visuals) and vary from a single mimeographed
sheet to 165 pages. Jackson provides annotations for

most of the items. The bibliography was issued first in 1970 and updated in 1972.

563. *A BIBLIOGRAPHY OF AFRO-AMERICAN (BLACK) STUDIES.*
By James N. Kerri and Anthony Layng. Monticello, Illinois, Council of Planning Librarians, 1974, 82p. (Exchange Bibliographies Nos. 657-8).
The bibliography is designed "to serve as a research guide for students with a scholarly interest in the past and present behavior of Black Americans." Basically, a subject arrangement is followed (African heritage, segregation, economic behavior, civil rights movement, etc.). There are also separate chapters listing newspapers and periodicals, bibliographies, and Afro-American studies programs. There are no annotations or indexes.

564. *A BIBLIOGRAPHY OF ANTISLAVERY IN AMERICA.* By
Dwight L. Dumond. Ann Arbor, University of Michigan Press, 1961, 119p.
This bibliography, prepared to accompany Dumond's book *ANTISLAVERY; THE CRUSADE FOR FREEDOM IN AMERICA,* lists "the literature written and circulated by those active in the antislavery movement and used by the author." In the preface, Dumond states that "no item of major importance has been overlooked." Works published up to the time of the Civil War are included. The entries are arranged by author. There are no annotations or indexes.

565. *A BIBLIOGRAPHY OF DOCTORAL RESEARCH ON THE NEGRO,*
1933-66. Edited by Earle H. West. Ann Arbor, University Microfilms, 1969, 134p.
Over 1,400 dissertations dealing with Afro-Americans have been extracted from the listings in *AMERICAN DOC-TORAL DISSERTATIONS* and *DISSERTATION ABSTRACTS INTER-NATIONAL* between 1933 and 1966. These dissertations are arranged in seven major categories: social institutions, individual characteristics, economic status and problems, education, history, political and civil rights, and humanities. Information given for each

dissertation includes: author, title, name of accepting university, date of completion, description of contents, and University Microfilms' order number (if listed in *DISSERTATION ABSTRACTS*). Dissertations concerned primarily with Blacks outside the United States are excluded. There is an author index. A supplement covering 1967-1969 updates the original work.

566. *A BIBLIOGRAPHY OF NEGRO HISTORY AND CULTURE FOR YOUNG READERS*. Edited by Miles M. Jackson, Jr. Pittsburgh, University of Pittsburgh Press, 1969, 160p.

Audio-visual aids and books concerned with Afro-American life, culture, heritage and contributions to American life are described in this annotated bibliography. Included are fiction materials, non-fiction (by subject area), biographies (under field in which person is known), audio-visual materials, magazines, and reference books. The materials listed are appropriate for students in grades 7 and up. The bibliography has author and title-subject indexes.

567. *BIBLIOGRAPHY OF NEGRO HISTORY: SELECTED AND ANNOTATED ENTRIES, GENERAL AND MINNESOTA*. By Earl Spangler. Minneapolis, Ross and Haines, 1963, 101p.

In the first section of this source, citations are included for materials on the Afro-American experience in the United States, in selected states and in certain localities. The second (and larger) section cites books, articles, clippings, etc., which describe the Black experience in Minnesota. There is also a list of Black newspapers published between 1885 and 1963 in Minnesota.

568. *A BIBLIOGRAPHY OF NEGRO MIGRATION*. By Frank Alexander Ross and Louise Venable Kennedy. New York, Burt Franklin, 1969, 251p. (Burt Franklin Bibliography and Reference Series No. 370).

Critical notes, mimeographs, manuscripts, and bibliographies comprise the 200 titles of this annotated
bibliography, which is the fifth volume (and only
reference work) produced under Columbia University's
Negro Migration project. The bibliography covers the
migration of Afro-Americans from rural to urban areas
and from the South to the North from 1865 to 1932.
The titles are also indexed in separate sections by
geographical locations and topical categories. The
1969 issue is a reprint of the original 1934 edition.

569. *A BIBLIOGRAPHY OF NORTH AMERICAN FOLKLORE AND
      FOLKSONG.* By Charles Haywood. 2nd rev. ed.
      New York, Dover Publications, 1961, 2v.
Part three of the first volume focuses on Blacks. For
a complete annotation, see Entry No. 461.

570. *A BIBLIOGRAPHY OF THE NEGRO IN AFRICA AND AMER-
      ICA.* Compiled by Monroe N. Work. New York,
      Wilson, 1928, 698p.
Work, long time editor of the *NEGRO YEAR BOOK* (see
Entry No. 94), prepared this bibliography as a
comprehensive, classified listing of 17,000 books,
pamphlets, public documents and periodical articles
in various languages published before 1928 covering
Black life in Africa and America. The publication
is divided into two parts: The Negro in Africa; The
Negro in America. The entries are further subdivided
into 74 classified chapters. A few of the chapters
included are: African civilization, education of
Afro-Americans, and Black suffrage. Some of the
entries are annotated. There is no subject index.
In 1965 the bibliography was reprinted by Octagon
Books.

571. *BIBLIOGRAPHY ON THE URBAN CRISIS; THE BEHAVIORAL,
      PSYCHOLOGICAL AND SOCIOLOGICAL ASPECTS OF THE
      URBAN CRISIS.* Prepared by the National Institute
      of Mental Health. Washington, D.C., G.P.O., 1969,
      452p. (Public Health Service Publication No.
      1948).

For annotation, see Entry No. 437.

572. *THE BLACK ALMANAC.* By Alton Hornsby, Jr. Rev.
     ed. Woodbury, New York, Barron's Educational
     Service, 1975, 212p.
Bibliographies, general surveys, books and articles
covering 1619 to the present are cited and described.
For a complete annotation, see Entry No. 65.

573. *BLACK AMERICANS: A STUDY GUIDE AND SOURCE BOOK.*
     By Lynn P. Dunn. San Francisco, R & E Research
     Associates, 1975, 112p.
Each page is arranged in two columns: one column
presents a study outline and the other lists publications to accompany the outline. For a complete
annotation, see Entry No. 68.

574. *BLACK AMERICANS IN AUTOBIOGRAPHY: AN ANNOTATED*
     BIBLIOGRAPHY OF AUTOBIOGRAPHIES AND AUTOBIOGRA-
     PHICAL BOOKS WRITTEN SINCE THE CIVIL WAR. By
     Russell C. Brignano. Durham, North Carolina,
     Duke University Press, 1974, 118p.
This bibliography lists and annotates over 400 autobiographies and autobiographical books written by
Black Americans from the end of the Civil War to
early 1973. The first section of the source, "Autobiographies," identifies volumes describing apprecia-
ble spans of the authors' lives. In Section II,
"Autobiographical Books," diaries, travelogs, collections of letters, collections of essays, eyewitness
reports and narrations of relatively brief periods of
time in the authors' lives are included. The third
section is an unannotated checklist of autobiographies
and autobiographical books written before the end of
the Civil War and reprinted, or published for the first
time, since 1945. Each section is arranged alphabetically by author. Each entry contains the following
information: the author and, if applicable, the co-
author; the author's year of birth and, if applicable,
the author's year of death; the title, the volume
number, information about forewords, introductions,

illustrations, afterwords, notes, bibliographies,
indexes; the place of publication, the publisher;
the year of publication; pages, reprint information;
symbols for up to 10 known library locations, a
description of the contents; and a cross reference to
other autobiographical volumes by the author or by a
member of the family. There are three indexes: experiences, occupations and professions; geographical
locations and educational institutions; and titles.

575. *BLACK BIBLIOGRAPHY*. Salt Lake City, Utah,
      Marriott Library, University of Utah, 1974,
      825p. (Bibliographic Series, v. 2).
This is the second volume of the University of Utah
Marriott Library Bibliographic Series (the first,
CHICANO BIBLIOGRAPHY, is described in Entry No. 637).
It contains a listing, generally by subject, of the
Black materials available in the University of Utah
Libraries; ERIC materials, government documents,
periodicals and nonprint items are listed in separate
sections. In general, only those items published
since the 1954 case of Brown v. Board of Education of
Topeka are included. Citations within each section
are arranged alphabetically by main entry. Author
and biography indexes are provided. The Library's
holdings in Black history have not been listed in
this bibliography; they will be published later in
a supplementary volume.

576. *BLACK BOOKS BULLETIN*. Chicago, Institute of
      Positive Education, 1971- , Quarterly.
BLACK BOOKS BULLETIN is an annotated quarterly listing
of significant books by and about Blacks. "No subject
area is excluded as long as the material deals with
issues that affect Black People wherever they may be."
Social and political commentary sections accompany the
critical reviews. Although intended as a quarterly
publication, it is somewhat irregular.

577. *BLACK CHILDREN AND THEIR FAMILIES: A BIBLIOGRAPHY*.
      By Charlotte J. Dunmore. San Francisco, Califor-

nia, R & E Research Associates, to be published
in 1976.
This bibliography is an attempt to pull together the
literature written on American children of African
descent.

578. *THE BLACK FAMILY AND THE BLACK WOMAN, A BIBLIO-*
      GRAPHY. Bloomington, Indiana, Indiana Univer-
      sity, 1972, 107p.
For annotation, see Entry No. 690.

579. *BLACK HISTORY VIEWPOINTS: A SELECTED BIBLIOGRA-*
      PHICAL GUIDE TO RESOURCES FOR AFRO-AMERICAN AND
      AFRICAN HISTORY: 1968. Prepared by the African
      Bibliographic Center. Washington, D.C., Negro
      Universities Press, 1969, 71p. (Special Biblio-
      graphic Series, Vol. 7, No. 1).
The focus on this bibliographical guide is on sources
which emphasize the historical role of Blacks in America and Africa. The citations are selected from the
literature issued between 1967 and early 1969. Short
annotations are provided for each item. Pertinent periodicals are listed. There is an author-title index.

580. *BLACK INFORMATION INDEX.* Herndon, Virginia,
      Infonetics, 1970- . Bi-monthly.
BLACK INFORMATION INDEX is a bi-monthly subject index
to current sources of information by and about Blacks.
Over 80 periodicals, newspapers and monographs are
scanned regularly. The majority of topics covered
are in the social sciences (history, economics, education, law, race relations, etc.). Other topics
covered include entertainment, sports, science, and
technology. Survey essays and subject-geographical
indexes complete each issue.

581. *BLACK RHETORIC: A GUIDE TO AFRO-AMERICAN COM-*
      MUNICATION. By Robert W. Glenn. Metuchen,
      New Jersey, Scarecrow Press, 1976, 376p.
This book "began in 1969 as a survey of primary and

secondary materials that might be useful in a course
on Afro-American oratory at Dartmouth College." It
is a bibliography of nearly 4,000 items arranged by
format of materials cited: bibliographies; anthologies; books and essays; speeches and essays. There
are numerous cross listings. The books and essays
are arranged topically and identified in the table
of contents; the other three sections are arranged
alphabetically by author. There is a separate chronology by year for the speeches listed. The source
can answer such questions as: Where can one find
good texts by Delany and Garnet? What speeches and
essays are available from 1808?

582.   *THE BLACK SEPARATISM CONTROVERSY: AN ANNOTATED
       BIBLIOGRAPHY*. Compiled by Betty Jenkins and
       Susan Phillis. Prepared under the auspices of
       the Metropolitan Applied Research Center. West-
       port, Connecticut, Greenwood Press, 1976, 163p.
Focusing on the numerous writings advocating various
forms of separatism and self-segregation, this bibliography cites books, pamphlets, chapters from books,
articles, speeches and letters written in the 1960s
and 1970s. Some earlier works are included if they
illustrate Blacks' reactions to racism in the United
States. The entries are arranged in two sections
(Part 1: The Separation-Integration Controversy; Part
2: Institutional and Psychological Dimensions) and are
annotated. An introductory survey on the ideological
disagreement between integrationists and racial separa-
tists (written by Kenneth B. Clark, Ralph Ellison,
Adelaide Cromwell Gulliver, Robert C. Weaver, etc.)
is included. The work is indexed. The occasion for
the preparation of this publication was a series of
meetings attended by the Hastie Group (a group of
Black scholars) who were invited by the Metropolitan
Applied Research Center to discuss the trend toward
separatism in the post-civil rights era.

583.   *BLACK STUDIES: A BIBLIOGRAPHY FOR THE USE OF
       SCHOOLS, LIBRARIES, AND THE GENERAL READER*.
       Compiled by Leonard B. Irwin. Brooklawn, New

Jersey, McKinley, 1973, 122p. (McKinley Bibliographies).
Nearly 900 titles of books on Black studies are
briefly annotated and coded to indicate reading level:
adult, young adult, grades 6 to 10. Fiction books
and textbooks are excluded. The titles are arranged
in six sections: history of Blacks in America; biographies and memoirs; general essays and anthologies
on current problems; African history; literature of
the arts; and miscellaneous. Author and title indexes are provided.

584. *BLACK-WHITE RACIAL ATTITUDES: AN ANNOTATED
       BIBLIOGRAPHY.* By Constance E. Obudho. Westport,
       Connecticut, Greenwood Press, 1976, 180p.
Covering Black-white race relations in the United
States between 1950 and 1974, this annotated bibliography lists research articles, essays and books on the
following topics: racial attitude formation and
change in children; racial attitudes in young people;
racial attitude change in adults; and concomitants of
racial attitudes. The entries are indexed by author
and by subject.

585. *THE BLACK WOMAN IN AMERICAN SOCIETY: A SELECTED,
       ANNOTATED BIBLIOGRAPHY.* By Lenwood G. Davis.
       Boston, G.K. Hall, 1975, 159p.
For annotation, see Entry No. 691.

586. *BLACKS AND THEIR CONTRIBUTIONS TO THE AMERICAN
       WEST: A BIBLIOGRAPHY AND UNION LIST OF LIBRARY
       HOLDINGS THROUGH 1970.* Compiled by James de T.
       Abajian. Boston, G.K. Hall, 1974, 487p. (Seventy
       Series).
This bibliography provides citations to materials on
the Black experience in 13 Western states of the United
States. Population, employment, housing, education,
politics, race relations, religion, sports, and entertainment are examples of the categories of entries
included. The over 4,300 books, pamphlets, periodical
articles, archival holdings, manuscript collections

and museum artifacts are arranged in classified order. Descriptive annotations of the holdings of area libraries are provided. Considerable material relates to California because of its long history and large Black population. A detailed author and subject index (with many entries for business and social organizations) completes the source. The bibliography was compiled for the Friends of the San Francisco Public Library, in cooperation with the American Library Association.

587. *BLACKS IN AMERICA: BIBLIOGRAPHICAL ESSAYS*. By James M. McPherson and others. Garden City, New York, Doubleday, 1971, 430p.
Utilizing an interdisciplinary approach, five Princeton professors have written 100 bibliographic essays on the Afro-American experience (ranging from Africa and the slave trade to life styles in urban ghettos) from 1500 A.D. to the present. Each topic is introduced by one or more paragraphs which summarize the factual data and problems involved in a study of the subject. Next, the major books, articles and primary sources relevant to the topic are described. In this way, over 4,000 titles are organized into several hundred paragraphs, each paragraph dealing with a specific facet of Black culture or history. There is an author and title index. The cited materials are appropriate for Black studies' readings in high school and up.

588. *BLACKS IN AMERICA 1492-1970: A CHRONOLOGY AND FACT BOOK*. Compiled by Irving J. Sloan. 3rd rev. ed. Dobbs Ferry, New York, Oceana Publications, 1971, 149p. (Ethnic Chronology Series no. 2).
One section contains a bibliography. For a complete annotation, see Entry No. 72.

589. *BLACKS IN AMERICAN MOVIES: A SELECTED BIBLIOGRAPHY*. Compiled and edited by Anne Powers. Metuchen, New Jersey, Scarecrow Press, 1974, 167p.
This annotated bibliography is a listing of various

types of materials which deal with Blacks in films
and in the film industry. Books, indexes, bibliographies, general reference works, excerpts and dissertations are arranged by form. Periodical articles are
listed by subject. A listing of feature films from
1904 to 1930 (identifying producers), is included.
There is an author and subject index.

590. *BLACKS IN SELECTED NEWSPAPERS, CENSUSES AND OTHER
     SOURCES; AN INDEX TO NAMES AND SUBJECTS.* Compiled
     by James de T. Abajian. Boston, G.K. Hall, to be
     published in 1977, 3v.
Planned for publication in 1977, this reference work
will index the coverage of Blacks in Black newspapers
and periodicals; U.S. and state census records (especially in the 11 Western States); city directories before
1880; and hundreds of books, pamphlets and monographs.
The index will be arranged alphabetically, with names
and subjects interfiled. Subject coverage will be given
to Black activities in such areas as medicine, dentistry,
law, art, architecture, journalism, printing, biography,
women's liberation, education, photography, social and
religious institutions, and the labor movement.

591. *BLACKS IN THE CITIES: 1900-1974: A BIBLIOGRAPHY.*
     By Lenwood G. Davis. 2nd ed. Monticello, Illi-
     nois, Council of Planning Librarians, 1975, 82p.
     (Exchange Bibliographies Nos. 787-8).
Designed as a "reference for those who wish to learn
more about the life of Blacks in urban areas from 1900-
1974," this bibliography lists relevant articles, books,
government documents, reports, Black newspapers, etc.
It is arranged by form of material. There are no
annotations. The bibliography is a revision of a 1972
edition published under the same title by the Council
of Planning Librarians.

592. *BLACKS IN THE PACIFIC NORTHWEST: 1788-1974; A
     BIBLIOGRAPHY OF PUBLISHED WORKS AND OF UNPUB-
     LISHED SOURCE MATERIALS ON THE LIFE AND CONTRI-
     BUTIONS OF BLACK PEOPLE IN THE PACIFIC NORTHWEST.*

245

By Lenwood G. Davis. 2nd. ed. Monticello, Illinois, Council of Planning Librarians, 1975, 93p.
(Exchange Bibliographies Nos. 767-8).
The purpose of this bibliography is to serve "as a
reference for those who wish to learn more about Blacks
in the Pacific Northwest. The materials listed cover
every period of that section's history from the earliest
records of Blacks' arrival to the present." Oregon,
Washington, Idaho, Montana and British Columbia are
covered. The work is arranged by form of material;
separate sections list manuscripts, letters and clippings, public documents, unpublished works, Black
newspapers, articles, and books. This bibliography
is a revision of the first edition which was issued
in 1972.

593. *BLACKS IN THE STATE OF OREGON: 1788-1974.* By
Lenwood G. Davis. 2nd. ed. Monticello, Illinois, Council of Planning Librarians, 1974,
85p. (Exchange Bibliographies No. 616).
The materials cited in this bibliography cover "every
period of the State's history from the earliest records
of Blacks' arrival to the present. Since the majority
of Blacks live in the greater Portland area most of
the contemporary materials cited pertain to that area."
Newspaper articles, periodical articles, official
documents, books, and unpublished materials are
identified. The bibliography is arranged by form of
material and is indexed by subject and author. An
earlier edition of Davis' bibliography was issued in
1971.

594. *THE CHICAGO AFRO-AMERICAN UNION ANALYTIC CATALOG:
AN INDEX TO MATERIALS ON THE AFRO-AMERICAN IN THE
PRINCIPAL LIBRARIES OF CHICAGO, 1972.* Boston,
G.K. Hall, 1972, 5v.
In five volumes, this union catalog contains over 75,000
entries covering every phase of Afro-American history
and literature up to 1940. The catalog provides a comprehensive index to the material available in the five
major Chicago research libraries. Books, periodicals,
agency reports, theses, conference proceedings, year-

books, art exhibit catalogs, and many unpublished
works (excluding newspapers) are annotated and organized by author, title and subject. A special feature
of the catalog is its analytic index of articles found
in over 1,000 foreign and domestic journals from the
late 1800s to 1940.

595. *A CLASSIFIED CATALOGUE OF THE NEGRO COLLECTION
IN THE COLLIS P. HUNTINGTON LIBRARY, HAMPTON
INSTITUTE.* Compiled by Mentar A. Howe and
Roscoe E. Lewis. St. Clair Shores, Michigan,
Scholarly Press, 1971, 341p.
This source was originally compiled by workers in the
Writers Program of the Works Projects Administration
in the State of Virginia and published in 1940. The
1971 edition is simply a reprint. "This bibliography
covers the holdings of this collection up to 1940...
The collection is made up of manuscripts, documents,
clippings, periodicals, pamphlets, and other forms of
printed materials by and about the Black man." The
emphasis is on Civil War and Reconstruction materials.
A substantial newspaper clipping file on slavery, Reconstruction and lynching is also represented. The
140,000 monographs and 1,300 documents listed are
arranged alphabetically within specific subject classifications. The subject classifications cover the
Negro in Africa and in the United States, with sub-
sections for such topics as education, Black women,
crime, race problems, and race relations. Each citation provides the following information: author,
title, date and place of publication, pagination, and
a very brief annotation of the work. Author and specific subject indexes are also included.

596. *DICTIONARY CATALOG OF THE ARTHUR B. SPINGARN
COLLECTION OF NEGRO AUTHORS, HOWARD UNIVERSITY
LIBRARIES.* Boston, G.K. Hall, 1970, 2v.
This two volume catalog consists of an alphabetical
list by author, title, and subject of books written
by Black authors throughout the world, in all languages and all time periods. Also included are works
translated, illustrated, or edited by Blacks. Slave

narratives and autobiographies, early Afro-American writings, and Afro-Brazilian literature are special areas emphasized in this catalog. An index of Black composers and their music is provided.

597. *DICTIONARY CATALOG OF THE JESSE E. MOORLAND COLLECTION OF NEGRO LIFE AND HISTORY, HOWARD UNIVERSITY LIBRARIES*. Boston, G.K. Hall, 1970, 9v.
This catalog represents the Jesse Edward Moorland Collection which today contains over 100,000 cataloged and indexed books and pamphlets, periodicals, theses, manuscripts, music newspaper clippings and pictures. The collection contains extensive antislavery holdings (about 2,000 printed items), as well as materials on the African slave trade, and many important titles donated by founders of the University interested in foreign missions, African history, and travel. The *CATALOG* contains subject, title, and author cards as well as an index to African and American periodicals.

598. *DICTIONARY CATALOG OF THE NEGRO COLLECTION OF THE FISK UNIVERSITY LIBRARY*. Boston, G.K. Hall, 1974, 6v.
The Fisk University Library Negro Collection is one of the oldest and most distinguished collections of Negroana in the United States. It contains material dating from the 18th century; the bulk of the collection, however, covers the 19th century to the present. The holdings include books and pamphlets, sheet music, microfilm, recordings, clippings, photographs and reports. These items are cited in the six volume *CATALOG* by author, title, and subject.

599. *DICTIONARY CATALOG OF THE SCHOMBURG COLLECTION OF NEGRO LITERATURE AND HISTORY*. Boston, G.K. Hall, 1962, 9v. *SUPPLEMENTS*, 1967, 1972.
The Schomburg collection of the New York Public Library is one of the world's largest and most important resources for the study of Black life and history. International in scope, it includes works by and about

Blacks on all subjects, in all languages, from all parts of the world where Blacks have lived in significant numbers. All types of materials have been collected: books, magazines, pamphlets, newspaper clippings, playbills, programs, and broadsides, etc. The *CATALOG* (in 9 volumes) lists references to these items by author, title, and subject. Updates were issued in 1967 (2 volumes) and 1972 (4 volumes), following the same format used in the main set. *BIBLIOGRAPHIC GUIDE TO BLACK STUDIES* will appear annually, beginning in 1975, as a supplement to the *CATALOG* (for annotation, see Entry No. 560).

600. *ECOLOGY OF BLACKS IN THE INNER CITY: AN EXPLORA-
     TORY BIBLIOGRAPHY.* By Lenwood G. Davis. Monti-
     cello, Illinois, Council of Planning Librarians,
     1975, 80p. (Exchange Bibliographies Nos. 785-6).
Materials dealing with the effects of the physical environment on Blacks in cities and elsewhere are cited in this unannotated bibliography. The bibliography is arranged by format: general reference books, selected Black periodicals, bibliographies, government documents, books, articles, etc. There is no index.

601. *EIGHT NEGRO BIBLIOGRAPHIES.* Compiled by Daniel
     T. Williams. Tuskegee Institute, Alabama,
     Tuskegee Institute, 1961-1969, various pagings.
     Reprinted by Kraus, 1970.
The bibliographies reprinted here were compiled for use by the Tuskegee Institute between 1961 and 1969. The titles of these bibliographies are: The Freedom Rides: A Bibliography; The Southern Students' Protest Movement: A Bibliography; The University of Mississippi and James H. Meredith: A Bibliography; The Black Muslims in the United States: A Selected Bibliography; Martin Luther King, Jr., 1929-1968: A Bibliography; The Awesome Thunder of Booker T. Washington: A Bio-bibliographical Listing; The Lynching Records at Tuskegee Institute with Lynching in America: A Bibliography; The Perilous Road of Marcus Garvey: A Bibliography; and Some Correspondence with Booker T. Washington, Emmet J. Scott, and Robert

Russa Moton. Earlier bibliographies prepared for the
Tuskegee Institute (between 1949 and 1961) were reprin-
ted by Kraus in 1970 under the title *RECORDS AND RE-
SEARCH PAMPHLETS* (see Entry No. 621).

602. *ENCYCLOPEDIA OF THE NEGRO, PREPARATORY VOLUME
     WITH REFERENCE LISTS AND REPORTS*. By W.E.B.
     DuBois, Guy B. Johnson, and others. New York,
     The Phelps-Stokes Fund, 1945, 207p.
Only one volume of this planned four volume encyclopedia was ever issued. It lists proposed subject
headings of topics to be covered in the other volumes
and bibliographies for each of these subjects. For a
complete annotation, see Entry No. 85.

603. *GUIDE TO FILMS ABOUT NEGROES*. Edited by Daniel
     Sprecher. Alexandria, Virginia, Serina Press,
     1970, 86p.
Information on over 750 films covering the lives, culture, history and problems of Blacks in America and
Africa is contained in this guide. Also included are
a directory of sources for renting or purchasing the
listed films and an index.

604. *IN BLACK AND WHITE: AFRO-AMERICANS IN PRINT: A
     GUIDE TO AFRO-AMERICANS WHO HAVE MADE CONTRIBU-
     TIONS TO THE UNITED STATES OF AMERICA FROM 1619
     TO 1975*. Edited by Mary Mace Spradling. Kala-
     mazoo, Michigan, Kalamazoo Library System, 1976,
     505p.
The *GUIDE* lists materials (books, magazines, newspapers)
where information on important Black Americans can be
found. For a complete description of this item, see
Entry No. 161.

605. *INDEX TO BLACK HISTORY AND STUDIES--MULTIMEDIA*.
     2nd. ed. Los Angeles, National Information
     Center for Educational Media (NICEM), 1971, 260p.
Intended to "provide media staff, library personnel
and educators with a bibliographical guide to non-book

media in this important curriculum area," this index
is divided into three sections: subject guide to
Black history and studies; alphabetical guide to Black
history and studies; and a directory for producers and
distributors. Over 6,000 filmstrips, 8mm motion cartrid-
ges, 16mm films, videotapes, records, audio tapes and
transparencies are listed and their contents described.
Recommended audience level or grade level is indicated
for each entry. This reference source was produced by
searching the NICEM data base using selected key words
for retrieval. In addition to this index, the following volumes have been issued by NICEM: *INDEX TO 16MM
EDUCATIONAL FILMS; INDEX TO 35MM FILMSTRIPS; INDEX TO
EDUCATIONAL AUDIO TAPES; INDEX TO EDUCATIONAL RECORDS;
INDEX TO PRODUCERS AND DISTRIBUTORS; INDEX TO ECOLOGY--
MULTIMEDIA*; etc.

606. *INDEX TO PERIODICAL ARTICLES BY AND ABOUT NEGROES*.
      Boston, G.K. Hall, 1950- . Annual.
The librarians at Central State University (Wilber-
force, Ohio) began this index as a continuation of A.P.
Marshall's *GUIDE TO NEGRO PERIODICAL LITERATURE* (1941-
1946). Originally entitled the *INDEX TO SELECTED
PERIODICALS* (from 1950-1954), it changed its name to
the *INDEX TO SELECTED PERIODICAL ARTICLES BY AND ABOUT
NEGROES* in the 1960's. Since 1960, approximately 4,000
articles from popular and scholarly journals have been
listed each year. The index is divided into two parts:
part one is an index to the articles in periodicals
received by the Hallie Q. Brown Library and part two
is an index to the periodical articles in the Schomburg
collection (N.Y. Public Library). Both sections provide
specific subject-author access to the articles cited.
Decennial cumulations have been prepared for 1950-1959
and 1960-1969.

607. *MULTIMEDIA MATERIALS FOR AFRO-AMERICAN STUDIES:
      A CURRICULUM ORIENTATION AND ANNOTATED BIBLIO-
      GRAPHY OF RESOURCES*. Edited by Harry Alleyn
      Johnson. New York, Bowker, 1971, 353p.
This resource tool for Black studies programs, which
lists 1,400 instructional items (with an emphasis on

audio-visual materials), consists of three parts. Part
I contains four position papers authored by noted Black
scholars which identify problems encountered in teaching ghetto youth. Some bibliographies are cited in
this section. Part II is an annotated bibliography
of various media dealing with Afro-Americans. All
types of materials are included here: films, audio
tapes, filmstrips, multimedia kits, records, slides,
study prints, transparencies, video tapes and a list
of 100 paperback books. Part III follows the same
format, but annotates items concentrating on people in
Africa. The following information is provided for
each audio-visual entry: producer/distributor, grade
range, running time, price, and a description of
contents. Directories of producers, distributors and
publishers of paperback books, as well as an index to
authors and broad subjects, are included at the end of
the source.

608. *NEGRO HISTORY 1553-1903: AN EXHIBITION OF BOOKS,
     PRINTS, AND MANUSCRIPTS FROM THE SHELVES OF THE
     LIBRARY COMPANY OF PHILADELPHIA AND THE HISTORI-
     CAL SOCIETY OF PENNSYLVANIA.* Philadelphia, The
     Library Company of Philadelphia, 1969, 83p.
The contributions of Blacks to their own history in
America are emphasized in this bibliography, which is
a catalog of an exhibit put on by The Library Company
of Philadelphia and The Historical Society of Pennsylvania in 1969. Each of the 238 items selected for this
bibliography is extensively annotated. Several plates
reproduced from the cited materials are included. A
chronological arrangement is used for the bibliography.
A much more extensive listing of the holdings of the
two libraries is presented in Entry No. 554.

609. *THE NEGRO IN AMERICA; A BIBLIOGRAPHY.* By Eliza-
     beth W. Miller. 2d. ed. rev. and enl. by Mary
     L. Fisher. Cambridge, Massachusetts, Harvard
     University Press, 1970, 351p.
This selective bibliography is a listing of over 6,500
books, serials, articles, pamphlets, and government
documents, published in the United States from 1954 to

February, 1970. Brief annotations are provided for
most of the entries. Excluded are reprints, dissertations, and newspaper articles. The bibliography
is arranged under 20 topics, such as history, civil
rights, Black power movements, biography, economics,
education, social institutions, and politics. The
source concludes with a guide to further research and
an author index. This edition (1970) is nearly twice
as inclusive as the original publication which came
out in 1956 under the editorship of Elizabeth Miller.

610. *THE NEGRO IN PRINT.* Washington, D.C., Negro
      Bibliographic and Research Center, 1965-1971,
      7v. in 4.
In 1971, the publication changed its name to *BIB-
LIOGRAPHIC SURVEY: THE NEGRO IN PRINT.* For an anno-
tation, see Entry No. 561.

611. *THE NEGRO IN THE CONGRESSIONAL RECORD, 1789- .*
      Compiled and annotated by Peter M. Bergman and
      Jean McCarroll. New York, Bergman Publishers,
      1969- . (The Negro in the Congressional Record,
      v. 2-).
THE NEGRO IN THE CONGRESSIONAL RECORD is a reproduction of extracts from the *ANNALS OF THE CONGRESS OF
THE UNITED STATES* (published by Gales and Seaton under
the title *THE DEBATE AND PROCEEDINGS IN THE CONGRESS
OF THE UNITED STATES*) and the *CONGRESSIONAL RECORD*
which contain discussions about Blacks and slavery.
Thus, this series acts as a subject index to these
congressional publications. The series will contain
approximately 23 volumes. The first volume, which
analyzes entries in the *JOURNALS OF THE CONTINENTAL
CONGRESS* is described in Entry No. 612.

612. *THE NEGRO IN THE CONTINENTAL CONGRESS.* Com-
      piled and annotated by Peter M. Bergman and Jean
      McCarroll. New York, Bergman Publishers, 1969,
      153p. (Negro in the Congressional Record, v. 1).
THE NEGRO IN THE CONTINENTAL CONGRESS is a reproduction of those pages from the *JOURNALS OF THE CONTIN-*

ENTAL CONGRESS (1774-1789) which contain references
to discussions about Blacks and slavery. Thus, this
source acts in part as a subject index to the *JOURNALS*.
Notes in the margin are included to clarify the material. This volume is the first of a series which will
contain approximately 23 volumes on the subject of
Blacks in America as it appears in the *CONGRESSIONAL
RECORD* (for a description of other volumes in the
series, see Entry No. 611).

613.   *THE NEGRO IN THE FIELD OF BUSINESS (AN ANNOTATED
        BIBLIOGRAPHY)*. Compiled by Thelma Y. Halliday.
        2nd ed. Washington, D.C., Institute for Minority
        Business Education, Howard University, 1972, 86p.
Over 200 books, articles, government documents and other
materials which deal with Black involvement in business
are included in the second edition of this annotated
bibliography. The entries are arranged by topic: Black
capitalism; Black economic development; Blacks as
consumers; Blacks in higher education; etc. There is
no index.

614.   *THE NEGRO IN THE UNITED STATES; A RESEARCH GUIDE*.
        By Erwin K. Welsch. Bloomington, Indiana Univ-
        ersity Press, 1965, 142p.
Welsch's book serves as an introduction to the literature describing the history and life of Blacks in
America. Nearly 500 books, periodicals and essays
(chosen because they are the "best or the most important") are listed and annotated in four chapters covering science, history, the arts and major contemporary
issues (e.g., housing). The three appendices list
bibliographies, periodicals, and organizations publishing pertinent reports. There are author and subject
indexes.

615.   *THE NEGRO IN THE UNITED STATES; A SELECTED BIB-
        LIOGRAPHY*. Compiled by Dorothy B. Porter. Wash-
        ington, D.C., G.P.O., 1970, 313p.
The emphasis of this selective bibliography is on
recent monographs covering all aspects of Black life

and culture found in the Library of Congress collection. It is "designed to meet the current needs of students, teachers, librarians, researchers and the general public for introductory guidance to the study of the Negro in the United States." The entries are arranged under broad subject headings, such as biography and autobiography, civil rights, history, economic conditions, education, politics, social conditions, and reference sources. Brief annotations are included when the title is not self-explanatory. There are author and subject indexes to the nearly 800 items included in the bibliography.

616. *THE NEGRO IN THE UNITED STATES; A WORKING BIBLIOGRAPHY.* Compiled by Dorothy B. Porter. Ann Arbor, Michigan, University Microfilms, 1969, 202p.

This working bibliography is intended as a guide to be used in developing collections of Afro-Americana. Prices for many titles are cited. English language monographs are emphasized; there are a few periodical articles also included. The items are arranged under broad subject categories, such as reference tools, economic conditions, education, history, law, politics, racial dissent, social conditions, sports and recreation. No annotations are included, but a name index is provided.

617. *NEGRO LITERATURE FOR HIGH SCHOOL STUDENTS.* By Barbara Dodds. Champaign, Illinois, National Council of Teachers of English, 1968, 157p.

This selective bibliography reviews 150 books by and about Blacks appropriate for high school readers. The materials are arranged by broad subject headings. Also included are an historical/biographical survey of Negro writers pre-Civil War to the present, a bibliography of books reviewed, the Detroit Curriculum supplement on Negro literature for grade 9 and guidelines for collections, and a combined author and title index. The National Council of Teachers of English has also issued a similar bibliography covering American Indians (see Entry No. 507) and Blacks on the elementary and high school level (see Entry No. 626).

618. *NEGRO PROGRESS IN ATLANTA, GEOGRIA, 1961-1970:*
      A SELECTIVE BIBLIOGRAPHY ON RACE AND HUMAN RE-
      LATIONS FROM FOUR ATLANTA NEWSPAPERS. Compiled
      by Annie McPheeters. Atlanta, The author, 1972,
      225p.
News stories, features and editorials on individual
Blacks or the Atlanta Black community (between 1961
and 1970) in four Atlanta newspapers--the *CONSTITU-*
TION, JOURNAL, DAILY WORLD and *INQUIRER*--are indexed
in this bibliography. The citations are arranged by
subject and identify the headline, newspaper, date,
page and author (if known).

619. *NEW JERSEY AND THE NEGRO: A BIBLIOGRAPHY, 1715-*
      1966. Compiled by the Bibliography Committee of
      the New Jersey Library Association. Trenton,
      New Jersey Library Association, 1967, 196p.
The purpose of this bibliography is to identify "all
published works which bear with reasonable significance on the subject of New Jersey and the Negro."
It covers publications issued between 1715 and 1966.
Three principal types of subject matter are emphasized
throughout the volume: 1) the life of Blacks in New
Jersey; 2) New Jersey's role in Black American history;
3) and the attitudes and behaviors of white Jerseyites
toward Blacks. All forms of materials are cited: newspaper articles, journals, books, pamphlets, reports,
mimeographed items, doctoral dissertations, government
documents, etc. The location of cited materials in
New Jersey libraries is identified. The source is
arranged by subject chapters (colonization, underground
railroad, education, slavery, etc.) and indexed by
author and subject.

620. *RACE AND REGION; A DESCRIPTIVE BIBLIOGRAPHY COM-*
      PILED WITH SPECIAL REFERENCE TO RELATIONS BETWEEN
      WHITES AND NEGROES IN THE UNITED STATES. By
      Edgar T. Thompson and Alma M. Thompson. Chapel
      Hill, University of North Carolina Press, 1949,

194p.

This extensive, annotated bibliography of Negro-white
relations in the United States is arranged by subject
and covers such topics as the Negro in America, Blacks
in the city, Black families, etc. One chapter contains bibliographies, fact books and study outlines.
Every title listed in this bibliography was, in 1948,
located in one of three libraries in the Durham-
Chapel Hill area (Duke University, University of North
Carolina and North Carolina College). There is an
author index.

621. *RECORDS AND RESEARCH PAMPHLETS*. Prepared under
     the direction of Jessie P. Gugman for the Tuske-
     gee Institute. Tuskegee Institute, Alabama,
     Tuskegee Institute, 1949-1961, various pagings.
     Reprinted by Kraus, 1970.

Ten bibliographies were compiled for use within the
Tuskegee Institute between 1949 and 1961 and were
reprinted in one publication by Kraus in 1970. The
titles of these bibliographies are: Some Achievements
of the Negro through Education; Civil Rights and the
Negro: A List of References Relating to Present Day
Discussions; George Washington Carver: A Classified
Bibliography; A Selected List of References Relating
to Desegregation and Integration in Education, 1949
to June, 1955; A Selected List of References Relating
to the Elementary, Secondary and Higher Education of
Negroes, 1949 to June, 1955; A Selected List of Refer-
ences Relating to Discrimination and Segregation in
Education, 1949 to June, 1955; A Selected List of
References Relating to the Negro Teacher, 1949 to
June, 1955; A Bibliography of The Tuskegee Gerryman-
der Protest; A Bibliography of the Student Movement
Protesting Segregation and Discrimination, 1960; A
Selected List of References on the Race Problems.
Bibliographies prepared for the Tuskegee Institute
between 1961 and 1970 were reprinted collectively by
Kraus in 1970 under the title *EIGHT NEGRO BIBLIOGRA-
PHIES* (see Entry No. 601).

622. *THE SOUTHERN BLACK: SLAVE AND FREE; A BIBLIO-*

GRAPHY OF ANTI- AND PRO-SLAVERY BOOKS AND PAM-
PHLETS; AND OF SOCIAL AND ECONOMIC CONDITIONS
IN THE SOUTHERN STATES FROM THE BEGINNINGS TO
1950. Compiled by Lawrence S. Thompson. Troy,
New York, Whitston Pub., 1970, 576p.
Over 4,000 books and pamphlets describing the pro-
and anti-slavery movement in the United States between
the 17th century and the 19th century are listed in
this bibliography. The sources cited emphasize social
and economic conditions. The work is alphabetically
arranged by main entry. There is no subject approach
to the entries listed. All the titles cited here are
available in microcard edition from Lost Cause Press
(Louisville, Kentucky). The listed entries are taken
from T.D. Clark's *TRAVELS IN THE OLD AND NEW SOUTH*,
E. Coulter's *TRAVELS IN THE CONFEDERATE STATE*, the
Hubbard catalog of the Oberlin slavery collection and
Lyle Wright's bibliography of American fiction before
1900.

623. *THE STUDY AND ANALYSIS OF BLACK POLITICS: A*
     BIBLIOGRAPHY. By Hanes Walton, Jr. Metuchen,
     New Jersey, Scarecrow Press, 1973, 179p.
Designed to cover the literature dealing with Black
political activities in the United States, this
bibliography lists over 1,000 relevant books, theses,
pamphlets, conference papers, and articles from
scholarly and popular journals and newspapers. No
annotations are included. The bibliography is
arranged into 13 broad subject chapters, each containing a brief introduction. Subjects covered include
Black political socialization, Blacks and the Supreme
Court, and Blacks in international politics. Articles from the *NEW YORK TIMES* on presidential elections
between 1900 and 1956 and on Black Republicans are
placed in separate appendices. There is an author
index, but no specific subject or title approach.

624. *SURVEY OF BIBLIOGRAPHIC ACTIVITIES OF U.S.*
     COLLEGES AND UNIVERSITIES ON BLACK STUDIES.
     By Gail Juris and others. St. Louis, Pius
     XII Library, St. Louis University, 1971, 60p.

(Bibliographic Series, no. 7).
The "bibliographic efforts in regard to Black Studies
completed or in progress" are identified in this survey. Information is presented on 200 colleges and
universities doing bibliographic work in the area of
Black studies. Pamphlets, guides, and books prepared
by these institutions are listed. There is an index.

625. *TEACHERS' GUIDE TO AMERICAN NEGRO HISTORY*. By
     William Loren Katz. Chicago, Quadrangle Books,
     1971, 192p.
The purpose of this source is to offer "a framework
for the full-scale integration of Negro contributions
into the existing American history course of study."
The work is arranged in four sections. The first
section discusses the integration of Black history
into high school curricula. The second part presents
suggestions for a teacher's reference library, teaching goals and objectives, and evaluation procedures.
The third section, the largest in the book, consists
of an annotated bibliography for 26 major units in
Black American history. Sources of free and inexpen-
sive materials are listed in the last part of the
book. In the appendices are: a reading list on race,
a directory of libraries with Black history collections, and a directory of museums and places of interest to Black history. The work is indexed by name,
author and title. This 1971 publication is a revision
of the original 1968 edition.

626. *WE BUILD TOGETHER: A READER'S GUIDE TO NEGRO
     LIFE AND LITERATURE FOR ELEMENTARY AND HIGH
     SCHOOL USE*. Edited by Charlemae Rollins.
     Champaign, Illinois, National Council of
     Teachers of English, 1967, 71p.
Issued first in 1941, this bibliography "was intended to fill the need, often expressed by teachers,
librarians, and parents, for a list of really good
books for children and young people that would present Negroes as human beings and not as stereotypes."
The citations are divided into the following chapters:
picture-books and easy-to-read books, fiction, his-

tory, biography, poetry, science, and sports. Each entry is annotated. A directory of publishers is included. The source is indexed by biographees, authors and titles. A later list put out by the National Council of Teachers of English focuses on materials only at the high school level (see Entry No. 617).

627. *WORLD ENCYCLOPEDIA OF BLACK PEOPLES*. St. Clair
    Shores, Michigan, Scholarly Press, 1974, 18v.
One of the volumes is devoted entirely to citations of materials dealing with Black studies. For a complete annotation, see Entry No. 102.

Chapter 10

SPANISH
AMERICANS

(Indexes, Abstracts, Bibliographies, etc.)

628. *AN ANNOTATED BIBLIOGRAPHY OF DISSERTATIONS ON*
AMERICAN INDIAN, MEXICAN AMERICAN, MIGRANT AND
RURAL EDUCATION. Prepared by Howard K. Conley.
Las Cruces, New Mexico, ERIC Clearinghouse on
Rural Education and Small Schools, New Mexico
State University, 1973, 50p.
For annotation, see Entry No. 453.

629. *ANNOTATED BIBLIOGRAPHY OF MATERIALS ON THE*
MEXICAN AMERICAN. By Eliseo Navarro. Austin,
Graduate School of Social Work, University of
Texas, 1969, 53p.
This bibliography was revised and published under the
title *THE CHICANO COMMUNITY: A SELECTED BIBLIOGRAPHY*
FOR USE IN SOCIAL WORK EDUCATION (For annotation,
see Entry No. 638).

630. *AN ANNOTATED BIBLIOGRAPHY OF SPANISH FOLKLORE*
IN NEW MEXICO AND SOUTHERN COLORADO. Compiled
by Marjorie F. Tully and Juan B. Rael. Albuquerque, University of New Mexico Press, 1950, 124p.
Designed to serve as a guide to the literature of
Spanish folklore in New Mexico and Southern Colorado,
this bibliography lists relevant books, articles and
book reviews by author. Each entry is briefly annotated. The publication, which began as Tully's
master's thesis, supplements the coverage provided
by Lyle Saunders' *A GUIDE TO MATERIALS BEARING ON*
CULTURAL RELATIONS IN NEW MEXICO (see Entry No. 645).

631. *BIBLIOGRAFIA CHICANA: A GUIDE TO INFORMATION*
SOURCES. By Arnulfo D. Trejo. Detroit, Gale
Research, 1975, 193p. (Ethnic Studies Information Guide Series, Vol. 1).
The purpose of Trejo's bibliography is "to bring
together titles of monographic works concerning the
Chicano life experience." The titles listed are intended to "qualify for a core collection in an academic
library" or a high school library and cover 1848 to
the present. The entries are arranged in five major
headings: general reference books, humanities, social

sciences, history, and applied sciences. For each
publication cited, Trejo gives the author, title,
imprint (place, publisher and date), collation (paging,
illustrations, tables, bibliographies, indexes, etc.),
and a critical or descriptive annotation. Supplementing the bibliography are an introductory essay, a
glossary, a directory of Chicano publishers, a listing
of Chicano newspapers and periodicals (which identify
title, address, date established, frequency, rate,
target reading population, language, publisher, circulation, editorial orientation, special features and
indexing source), and author-title indexes.

632. *BIBLIOGRAFIA DE AZTLAN: AN ANNOTATED CHICANO
     BIBLIOGRAPHY*. Edited by Ernie Barrios. San
     Diego, California, Centro de Estudios Chicanos
     Publications, San Diego State College, 1971,
     174p.
Arranged alphabetically by author under such topics
as history, education, literature, health, and sociology, this bibliography lists journal articles and books
on the history and culture of the Chicano. The annotations were written by specialists and present a Chicano
viewpoint. Separate sections listing serial publications, bibliographies, and Chicano newspapers complete
the source.

633. *A BIBLIOGRAPHY FOR CHICANO HISTORY*. By Matt S.
     Meier and Feliciano Rivera. San Francisco, R &
     E Research Associates, 1972, 96p.
This bibliography lists selected "items useful to understand each of the major historical periods from the
Mexican American's origin to the present day struggles
for justice." Books, government documents, pamphlets,
periodical articles, master's theses and doctoral
dissertations are cited in broad chronological categories. Additional sections cover labor and immigration, Chicano culture, civil rights, and Mexican American bibliographies. An earlier edition was issued
under the title *A SELECTIVE BIBLIOGRAPHY FOR THE STUDY
OF MEXICAN AMERICAN HISTORY* (San Jose, California,
Spartan Bookstore, San Jose State College, 1971, 79p.).

634. *A BIBLIOGRAPHY OF STUDIES CONCERNING THE SPANISH-SPEAKING POPULATION OF THE AMERICAN SOUTHWEST.* By Barbara H. Mickey. Greeley, Colorado, Museum of Anthropology, Colorado State College, 1969, 42p.

The purpose of this bibliography is "to gather together references useful to an anthropological study of the Spanish-speaking population of the American Southwest." Over 500 books, articles, travel accounts, doctoral dissertations and sociological studies published between 1930 and the 1960s are cited. The book is arranged alphabetically by author. There is no index.

635. *BILINGUAL EDUCATION, A SELECTED BIBLIOGRAPHY.* Compiled by David M. Altus. Las Cruces, New Mexico, ERIC Clearinghouse on Rural Education and Small Schools, New Mexico State University, 1970, 228p.

Access to current research findings and developments in the area of bilingualism and bilingual education is provided in this bibliography. The publication is divided into two sections: Part I consists of 176 citations with abstracts which have been extracted from *RESEARCH IN EDUCATION* through June 1970. Part II contains 28 citations listed in *CURRENT INDEX TO JOURNALS IN EDUCATION* through July 1970. Each section has a subject index based on terms used in the *THESAURUS OF ERIC DESCRIPTORS*. Ordering information for the cited documents is provided.

636. *CESAR CHAVEZ AND THE UNITED FARM WORKERS; A SELECTIVE BIBLIOGRAPHY.* By Beverly Fodell. Detroit, Wayne State University Press, 1974, 103p.

"This bibliography represents a revision and expansion of the bibliography *CESAR CHAVEZ AND THE UNITED FARM WORKERS*, privately printed by the Archives of Labor History and Urban Affairs of Wayne State University in January 1970...The primary emphasis is on the current organizing efforts of farm workers which began with the grape strike in Delano, California." Materials on California agriculture and Chicano subjects

are also included. The bibliography is divided into
separate sections listing bibliographies, government
documents, theses and dissertations, unpublished
materials, books, pamphlets, periodical and newspaper
articles, annual reports and proceedings, and articles
from labor union, grower and church publications. Each
item is briefly annotated.

637. *CHICANO BIBLIOGRAPHY 1973*. Salt Lake City, Mar-
      riott Library, University of Utah, 1973, 295p.
      (Bibliographic Series, v. 1).
CHICANO BIBLIOGRAPHY is the first of a series of
ethnic studies bibliographies to be published by the
University of Utah Marriott Library (for a description
of volume two in the series, see Entry No. 575). The
publication is divided into six sections, each one
covering a different format (books, periodical articles, juvenile and textbook material, etc.). The majority of the citations are to books. Arrangement is by
author.

638. *THE CHICANO COMMUNITY: A SELECTED BIBLIOGRAPHY
      FOR USE IN SOCIAL WORK EDUCATION*. Compiled by
      Eliseo Navarro. New York, Council on Social
      Work Education, 1971, 57p.
Sponsored by the Council on Social Work Education,
this bibliography "is presented with the purpose of
providing the resource material for social work students and faculty to understand the quality of life of
this minority group." The publication lists and critically annotates both books and articles. The citations
are arranged alphabetically by author. Each entry is
given a code letter indicating the subject matter of
the material (e.g., reference, historical background,
acculturation, education, religion, economics, literature, Chicano organizations, etc.). A list of eight
Chicano periodicals is appended. The work is a revision of Navarro's *ANNOTATED BIBLIOGRAPHY OF MATERIALS
ON THE MEXICAN AMERICAN* (Austin, Graduate School of
Social Work, University of Texas, 1969, 53p.). For
another bibliography which identifies minority materials useful in social work education, see Entry No. 483.

266

639. *CHICANOS: A STUDY GUIDE AND SOURCE BOOK.* By
      Lynn P. Dunn. San Francisco, R & E Research
      Associates, 1975, 122p.
The outline format of this publication is supplemented
by citations to appropriate study materials. For a
complete annotation, see Entry No. 104.

640. *A COMPREHENSIVE CHICANO BIBLIOGRAPHY, 1960-1972.*
      By Gilbert Cruz and Jane Talbot. Edited by
      Edward Simmen. Austin, Texas, Jenkins Publish-
      ing Company, 1973, 375p.
The purpose of this work is to compile a bibliography
"that will make available to any serious researcher a
list of publications by and about the Chicano." Over
2,000 titles written since 1960 are cited. These
materials (books, articles, government documents,
unpublished master's theses, and Ph.D. dissertations)
are arranged under such subject headings as history,
acculturation, statistics, politics and justice, economics, migrant labor, United Farm Workers, education,
health, religion, literature, and music. Other sections in the publication list Chicano bibliographies,
Chicano journals and newspapers, and audio-visual aids.
A few of the entries are annotated. A "cross index"
serves as a subject index. There is also an author
index.

641. *DISADVANTAGED MEXICAN AMERICAN CHILDREN AND
      EARLY EDUCATION EXPERIENCE.* By Charles B.
      Brussell. Austin, Texas, Southwest Educational
      Development Corporation, 1968, 105p.
Emphasizing early educational experiences described
in the literature since 1950, this publication serves
both as a synthesis of the literature and as a bibliography. The literature is summarized in six chapters
(e.g., history and demography, social characteristics,
education of young children, etc.) and followed by a
bibliography of relevant materials grouped by the subjects covered earlier in the monograph.

642. *FARM LABOR ORGANIZING: AN ANNOTATED BIBLIOGRAPHY*

INCLUDING A GLOSSARY WITH A SECTION ON THE GRAPE
BOYCOTT. Compiled by Colin Cameron and Joanne
Edilson. Madison, Institute for Research on
Poverty, University of Wisconsin, 1969, 62p.
The purpose of this bibliography is to "point the way
to sources on farm laborers and to record the crucial
events that have been occurring in farm labor organizing." The source is arranged by subject (employment
of the farm labor force, mechanization as it affects
the farm worker, early attempts to organize, legislation and public policy, etc.). Within these categories,
the materials are listed by main entry. Annotations
are provided for most items. All types of materials
are cited: government documents, articles, books, pamphlets, newspapers, etc. A glossary of terms is included.

643. *GUIDE FOR THE STUDY OF THE MEXICAN AMERICAN
     PEOPLE IN THE UNITED STATES*. By Feliciano
     Rivera. San Jose, California, Spartan Bookstore,
     1969, 226p.
The historical background of Mexican Americans is
traced in outline form and complemented by citations
to suggested reading sources. For a more complete
annotation, see Entry No. 106.

644. *GUIDE TO LIFE AND LITERATURE OF THE SOUTHWEST*.
     By James Frank Dobie. Rev. ed. Dallas, South-
     ern Methodist University Press, 1952, 222p.
For annotation, see Entry No. 488.

645. *A GUIDE TO MATERIALS BEARING ON CULTURAL RELA-
     TIONS IN NEW MEXICO*. Compiled by Lyle Saunders.
     Albuquerque, University of New Mexico Press,
     1944, 528p.
This guide identifies published and manuscript materials relating to the cultural relations of the three
main ethnic groups in New Mexico: the Indians, Spanish speaking residents, and descendants of the early
American pioneers. The materials cited concentrate
on Chicano folklore, history, education and economic

conditions. Short annotations are provided for each of the 263 titles listed in the source. Separate sections are included for historical periodicals, specific cultural groups and reference materials. There are author and subject indexes.

646. *GUIDE TO MATERIALS RELATING TO PERSONS OF MEXICAN HERITAGE IN THE UNITED STATES.* Prepared by the U.S. Inter-Agency Committee on Mexican American Affairs. Washington, D.C., G.P.O., 1969, 186p.
Citations are made to materials focusing on the sociological and economic aspects of the Mexican American. Materials are arranged by format: books; reports; hearings; proceedings; periodical literature; dissertations; audio-visual materials; and bibliographies. There is a separate list of Spanish language radio and television stations in the United States along the Mexican borders. The work is not indexed. It is updated in 1971 by *THE SPANISH SPEAKING IN THE UNITED STATES: A GUIDE TO MATERIALS* (see Entry No. 674).

647. *GUIDE TO THE LATIN AMERICAN MANUSCRIPTS IN THE UNIVERSITY OF TEXAS LIBRARY.* By Carlos E. Castaneda and Jack Autrey Dabbs. Cambridge, Massachusetts, Harvard University Press, 1939, 217p.
This is a listing of rare books and manuscripts relating to the history and culture of former Spanish possessions in what is now the United States (as well as of Latin American countries) in the University of Texas Library. They are arranged alphabetically by geographic areas. Complete bibliographic information (author, title, number of leaves or pages, size, illustrations, maps) is given for each item. Some manuscripts are briefly annotated.

648. *KNOWING AND EDUCATING THE DISADVANTAGED: AN ANNOTATED BIBLIOGRAPHY.* Alamosa, Colorado, Center for Cultural Studies, Adams State College, 1965, 460p.
For annotation, see Entry No. 435.

649. *LATINO MENTAL HEALTH: BIBLIOGRAPHY AND ABSTRACTS.*
      By Amado M. Padilla and Paul Arnada. Washington,
      D.C., National Institute of Mental Health, 1974,
      288p.
Over 490 abstracts on the psychological and mental
health of the Spanish surnamed, Spanish speaking, or
people of Spanish origin in the United States are
included in this bibliography. Several dissertation
citations are also provided. Material published
through 1972 is represented. There is a subject index.
This publication supplements *LATINO MENTAL HEALTH: A
REVIEW OF THE LITERATURE* (by Amado M. Padilla and Rene
A. Ruiz. Rockville, Md., National Institute of Mental
Health, 1973, 189p.).

650. *MATERIALS RELATING TO THE EDUCATION OF SPANISH-
      SPEAKING PEOPLE IN THE UNITED STATES: AN ANNOTATED
      BIBLIOGRAPHY.* By George I. Sánchez and Howard
      Putnam. Austin, The Institute of Latin American
      Studies, University of Texas, 1959, 76p. (Latin-
      American Studies, 17). Reprinted by Greenwood
      Press, 1971.
Although the primary emphasis of this bibliography
is on the education of Spanish speaking people in the
United States who are of Mexican descent, many other
aspects are covered. Over 880 annotated items published between 1929 and 1956 are arranged alphabetically by author under six headings: books; articles;
monographs, bulletins and pamphlets; courses of study;
bibliographies; and unpublished theses and dissertations. Each item is annotated. A subject index containing cross references is appended. This bibliography has been reprinted in the anthology, *MEXICAN
AMERICAN BIBLIOGRAPHIES* (see Entry No. 653).

651. *THE MEXICAN AMERICAN: A NEW FOCUS ON OPPORTUNITY,
      A GUIDE TO MATERIALS RELATING TO PERSONS OF
      MEXICAN HERITAGE IN THE UNITED STATES.* Washing-
      ton, D.C., Inter-Agency Committee on Mexican
      American Affairs, 1969, 186p.
This publication is generally cited as *A GUIDE TO
MATERIALS RELATING TO PERSONS OF MEXICAN HERITAGE*

IN THE UNITED STATES. For an annotation, see Entry
No. 646.

652. *THE MEXICAN AMERICAN: A SELECTED AND ANNOTATED
BIBLIOGRAPHY.* By Luis G. Nogales. 2nd ed. Palo
Alto, California, Stanford University Bookstore,
1971, 162p.
The purpose of Nogales' bibliography is to bring together material which discusses the contemporary interests, aspirations and concerns of the Mexican American.
This work is a revised and enlarged edition of his 1969
bibliography, *THE MEXICAN AMERICAN: A SELECTED AND
ANNOTATED BIBLIOGRAPHY* (Palo Alto, California, Stanford
University, 1969, 139p.). The 474 annotated items
include books, articles, government documents, papers
at conferences, and unpublished dissertations. Entries are arranged alphabetically by authors' last
names and give the following bibliographic information:
title, publisher, place, year, and pages. Very long,
informative annotations accompany each citation. A
subject and field index (anthropology, education,
history, literature, psychology, sociology, etc.)
provides access to the bibliography. A listing of
Chicano periodicals by state is appended.

653. *MEXICAN AMERICAN BIBLIOGRAPHIES.* Edited by
Carlos E. Cortés. New York, Arno Press, 1974,
various pagings.
This anthology gathers together and reproduces in
original format five early bibliographies of material
concerning Mexican Americans dating from 1929 to 1960.
The bibliographies included are: *THE MEXICAN IMMIGRANT:
AN ANNOTATED BIBLIOGRAPHY* by Emory S. Bogardus (Los
Angeles, Council on International Relations, 1929,
21p.); *MEXICANS IN THE UNITED STATES: A BIBLIOGRAPHY*
by Robert C. Jones (Washington, D.C., Pan American
Union, 1942, 14p.); *SPANISH-SPEAKING AMERICANS AND
MEXICAN-AMERICANS IN THE UNITED STATES: A SELECTED
BIBLIOGRAPHY* by Lyle Saunders (New York, Bureau for
Intercultural Education, 1944, 12p.); *MATERIALS RELA-
TING TO THE EDUCATION OF SPANISH-SPEAKING PEOPLE IN
THE UNITED STATES: AN ANNOTATED BIBLIOGRAPHY* by George

I. Sánchez and Howard Putnam (Austin, Institute of
Latin American Studies, University of Texas, (1959,
76p.); and *THE UNITED STATES-MEXICAN BORDER: A
SELECTIVE GUIDE TO THE LITERATURE OF THE REGION* by
Charles C. Cumberland (A supplement to *RURAL SOCIOLOGY*,
Vol. 25, June, 1960, 236p.).

THE MEXICAN IMMIGRANT cites books, reports, and articles "dealing with the culture backgrounds of Mexican
immigrants." It is arranged by subject and subdivided
by format. Each entry is annotated. Jones' bibliography is a "selected list intended to supplement the
bibliography published by Professor Emory S. Bogardus
in 1929." It is arranged by topics and subdivided by
author. Saunders' bibliography on *SPANISH-SPEAKING
AMERICANS AND MEXICAN-AMERICANS IN THE UNITED STATES*
is an unannotated list arranged by author within broad
subject headings (health and nutrition, architecture,
social and economic conditions, etc.). The bibliography prepared by Sánchez and Putnam is described in
Entry No. 650. Cumberland's *THE UNITED STATES-MEXICAN
BORDER* is annotated in Entry No. 676.

654. *MEXICAN AMERICAN EDUCATION, A SELECTED BIBLIOGRA-
     PHY.* Compiled by James E. Heathman and Cecilia
     Martinez. Las Cruces, New Mexico, Educational
     Resources Information Center (ERIC), Clearing-
     house on Rural Education and Small Schools
     (CRESS), New Mexico State University, 1969, 59p.
     SUPPLEMENT 1, compiled by David M. Altus, 1971,
     206p. *SUPPLEMENT 2,* compiled by Albert D. Link,
     1972, 350p.
This series of bibliographies contains citations which
originally appeared in *RESOURCES IN EDUCATION* (Washington, D.C., G.P.O., 1966- . Monthly) through 1972
and *CURRENT INDEX TO JOURNALS IN EDUCATION* (New York,
Macmillan Publishing Co., 1969- . Monthly) between
1970 and 1972. Cited are speeches, conference papers,
reports, pamphlets, theses, etc. concerned with the
education of Mexican American children and adults.
Some material is also included on Native Americans
and Blacks. Ordering information for microfiche and
hard copy reproductions is included for each entry.

Descriptive words and phrases are used to describe
the contents of the cited items. There are subject
indexes.

655. *MEXICAN AMERICANS: A RESEARCH BIBLIOGRAPHY.*
      By Frank Pino. East Lansing, Latin American
      Studies Center, Michigan State University,
      1974, 2v.
This is a computer-based bibliography concerning all
aspects of Mexican-American life and culture from the
earliest Spanish settlements to the present day.
Books, monographs, master's theses, doctoral dissertations, articles, government documents, personal
diaries and travel logs are cited. Newspaper articles
are excluded. Many international publications are
listed. The material is arranged into 35 subject
areas (e.g., anthropology, art, economics, education,
geography, law, Spanish American history). The bibliography is not annotated. There is an alphabetical
author index but no subject index.

656. *MEXICAN AMERICANS: AN ANNOTATED BIBLIOGRAPHY OF
      DOCTORAL DISSERTATIONS.* Compiled by Adelaide
      Jablonsky. Washington, D.C., ERIC, 1973, 88p.
      (ERIC-IRCD Doctoral Research Series, No. 1).
Over 700 doctoral dissertations on the Mexican Americans are listed in this publication. Abstracts in
DISSERTATION ABSTRACTS INTERNATIONAL were photocopied
and indexed. The dissertations are organized by
subject (bilingual, verbal, reading, comparisons with
other groups, cultural, parental influences, self
concept, and Jensen theory). There are subject, author, and institution indexes. The present document
is the first of several being prepared for a new
series of publications entitled *ERIC-IRCD DOCTORAL
RESEARCH SERIES.*

657. *MEXICAN-AMERICANS IN THE MIDWEST: AN ANNOTATED
      BIBLIOGRAPHY.* By Nancy Saldaña. East Lansing,
      Rural Manpower Center, Michigan State Univer-
      sity, 1969, 68p. (Special Paper No. 10).

This is a selected bibliography of sources dealing
with Mexican Americans living in Michigan and other
parts of the Midwest. Some sources from the Southwest (especially Texas) are also cited because many
Northern migrants originally came from that area.
Publications issued between 1920 and the 1960s are
cited. The source is arranged by topic (acculturation
and assimilation, education, employment and income,
marriage and family patterns, housing, political behavior, etc.). Within each of these sections, one
part lists the relevant sources and another part,
"Discussion," describes the theses and contributions
of the publications.

658. *MEXICAN AMERICANS; RESOURCES TO BUILD CULTURAL
     UNDERSTANDING.* By Lois B. Jordan. Littleton,
     Colorado, Libraries Unlimited, 1973, 265p.
This two-part bibliography identifies over 1,000
print and non-print materials considered by the com-
piler to be suitable for readers in junior high school,
senior high school, and college. The first section
describes 751 books related to Chicanos arranged by
subject (e.g., history, education, health, art, literature, etc.). The second section describes 277 audio-
visual materials (films, filmstrips, records, maps,
and transparencies). Each entry includes complete
bibliographic information and an evaluative annotation.
Appendices provide supplementary information about
distinguished Mexican American personalities, Mexican
American organizations, pertinent periodicals and
newspapers, and general reference sources related to
Mexican American studies. Author, title and subject
indexes are included.

659. *MIGRANT EDUCATION: A SELECTED BIBLIOGRAPHY.*
     Compiled by James E. Heathman. Las Cruces, New
     Mexico, ERIC Clearinghouse on Rural Education
     and Small Schools, New Mexico State University,
     1969, 66p. *SUPPLEMENT 1,* 1970, *SUPPLEMENT 2,*
     1971, *SUPPLEMENT 3,* 1973.
This bibliography was compiled "to provide access to
some of the latest developments in the education of

migrant children." The reports included in this bibliography were found in the citations which make up
the *ERIC CATALOG OF SELECTED DOCUMENTS ON THE DISAD-
VANTAGED*, the *OFFICE OF EDUCATION RESEARCH REPORTS,
1956-65*, and *RESEARCH IN EDUCATION*. Each entry includes a lengthy abstract. The source is arranged
by document ED number. There is a subject index.
Unless otherwise specified, all documents with ED
numbers are available for purchase from the ERIC
document reproduction service in either microfiche or
hardcopy. Three supplements have been issued to
date, in 1970, 1971, and 1973. They follow the same
arrangement as the main volume.

660. *PERSONS OF MEXICAN DESCENT IN THE UNITED STATES;
A SELECTED BIBLIOGRAPHY*. By William W. Winnie,
John F. Stegner and Joseph P. Kopachevsky. Fort
Collins, Colorado, Center for Latin American
Studies, Colorado State University, 1970, 78p.
Over 1,000 items published between 1891 and 1968 on
persons of Mexican descent in the United States are
included in this bibliography. The scope of the
publication is multidisciplinary, with an emphasis
on sociological and anthropological entries. Excluded are works on Mexico and Latin America in general.
There is a special section devoted to relevant bibliographies.

661. *PROYECTO LEER BULLETIN*. Washington, D.C.,
Organization of American States, 1968- .
Quarterly.
The purpose of this quarterly is to identify useful
print and non-print materials which deal with the
Spanish-speaking in the United States. The materials
are listed under broad subject categories, evaluated
according to reading levels (e.g., grades K-3, grades
7-10, etc.) and briefly described. A separate section
provides the addresses of publishers and distributors.

662. *THE PUERTO RICANS: AN ANNOTATED BIBLIOGRAPHY*.
Edited by Paquita Vivo. New York, Bowker, 1973,

299p.
Sponsored by the Puerto Rican Research and Resources
Center, Inc., this bibliography attempts "to present
a complete bibliographic overview of Puerto Ricans."
The bibliography is compiled from collections of
Puerto-Ricana in the Library of Congress, University
of Puerto Rico Library, New York Public Library and
others. Over 2,600 annotated entries of Spanish and
English language materials covering all aspects of
Puerto Rican life are contained in this work. The
entries are divided into four sections: 1) books,
pamphlets and dissertations; 2) commonwealth and U.S.
government documents; 3) periodical literature; and
4) audiovisual materials. The book and periodical
sections are further subdivided under 21 subject headings, such as: history, economics, education, juvenile
literature, migration and the Puerto Rican experience
on the U.S. mainland, arts, music, religion, philosophy,
description and travel, traditions, government and
politics, language and law. Rare and archival materials as well as current in-print works are included.
A list of publishers and distributors of Puerto Rican
materials is appended. There are separate author,
title and subject indexes.

663. *THE PUERTO RICANS 1493-1973: A CHRONOLOGY AND
      FACT BOOK.* Compiled and edited by Francesco
      Cordasco. Dobbs Ferry, New York, Oceana Publi-
      cations, 1973, 137p. (Chronology Series no. 11).
The last section of this publication is a classified,
annotated bibliography of pertinent Spanish and English
books and articles. For a more complete annotation,
see Entry No. 109.

664. *THE PUERTO RICANS: MIGRATION AND GENERAL BIBLIO-
      GRAPHY.* New York, Arno Press, 1975, various
      pagings. (The Puerto Rican Experience).
This publication consists of reprints of various
bibliographies published between 1901 and 1971 on
Puerto Rico and Puerto Ricans. Three of the biblio-
graphies included are: A.P. Griffin's *A LIST OF BOOKS
WITH REFERENCES TO PERIODICALS ON PUERTO RICO* (1901);

C. Senior and J. DeRoman's *A SELECTED BIBLIOGRAPHY ON
PUERTO RICO AND THE PUERTO RICANS* (1951); and J.
Dossick's *DOCTORAL RESEARCH ON PUERTO RICO AND PUERTO
RICANS* (1967). A special report, "The Impact of
Puerto Rican Migration on Governmental Services in
New York City" (1957) is also reprinted here. No
name or subject index is provided.

665. *PUERTO RICANS ON THE MAINLAND: A BIBLIOGRAPHY
     OF REPORTS, TEXTS, CRITICAL STUDIES AND RELATED
     MATERIALS.* By Francesco Cordasco, with Eugene
     Bucchioni and Diego Castellanos. Totowa, New
     Jersey, Rowman and Littlefield, 1972, 146p.
Over 750 items (bibliographies, articles, books,
government documents, and dissertations) describing
the Puerto Rican experience on the United States
mainland are arranged by subject in this bibliography.
For each entry, complete bibliographic information is
given; some entries are annotated. Occasionally,
additional references and source materials are indicated. Most of the publications listed in the bibliography were published in the 1950s and 1960s. The
introduction and preface constitute essays on the
social and cultural experience of Puerto Rican immigrants. There is an author index.

666. *LA RAZA IN FILMS: A LIST OF FILMS AND FILMSTRIPS.*
     Compiled by Cynthia Baird. Oakland, California,
     Latin American Library, Oakland Public Library,
     1972, 68p.
Approximately 270 English and Spanish language films
on all levels (children through adult) are listed in
this bibliography. The films are arranged in three
groups: 1) background on Mexico and Latin America;
2) Spanish-speaking in the United States; 3) Third
World in Latin America. The title, physical description, language, price and distributor are given for
each film cited in the bibliography. All film titles
are listed in the table of contents; there is no index.
A directory of distributors is appended.

667. *REFERENCE MATERIALS ON MEXICAN AMERICANS: AN ANNOTATED BIBLIOGRAPHY.* By Richard D. Woods. Metuchen, New Jersey, Scarecrow Press, 1976, 190p.

Nearly 400 publications (from cookbooks and children's literature to genealogical sources and government statistics) are listed and critically described in this bibliography on Chicano activities in the United States. Author, title and subject indexes are provided.

668. *REVISED BIBLIOGRAPHY.* Prepared by the Mexican American Study Project with a bibliographic essay by Ralph Guzman. Los Angeles, University of California, 1967, 99p. (Advance Report, No. 3).

The first section of this publication is a bibliographic essay by Ralph Guzman. The essay reviews the existing literature by and about Chicanos. The material listed in the bibliography emphasizes social and economic characteristics of urban Chicanos in the Southwest. Arrangement is by type of material: books, journal articles, unpublished doctoral and master's dissertations, government documents, other unpublished materials and bibliographies. Also included are citations to some speeches, newspaper articles, and court cases. Materials published after 1940 are annotated, but pre-1940 materials are not. No subject arrangement is provided.

669. *A SELECTIVE BIBLIOGRAPHY FOR THE STUDY OF MEXICAN AMERICAN HISTORY.* San Jose, California, Spartan Bookstore, San Jose State College, 1971, 79p.

For annotation, see Entry No. 633.

670. *SELECTIVE MEXICAN-AMERICAN BIBLIOGRAPHY.* Compiled by Philip D. Ortego. El Paso, Texas, Border Regional Library Association in cooperation with the Chicano Research Institute, 1972, 121p.

Intended to show "the varied literary interests of

Mexican Americans and their forefathers who settled in
the American Southwest," this bibliography lists books,
periodical articles, documents, reports, dissertations
and mimeographed publications by subject. A majority
of the entries are annotated.

671. *SOCIAL AND ECONOMIC DIMENSIONS OF HEALTH AND
      ILLNESS BEHAVIOR IN NEW MEXICO; AN ANNOTATED
      BIBLIOGRAPHY.* By Helen Rose Potter. Albuquer-
      que, University of New Mexico Press, 1969, 220p.
The bibliography "attempts to facilitate access to
social and economic information pertinent to health
and illness behavior" among Mexican Americans and
Indians living in New Mexico. References are taken
from the literature published between 1950 and 1967
(standard works are included if they were issued after
1940). Annotations accompany each bibliographic entry.
One library location for each citation is identified.
The source is arranged by author and indexed by subject.

672. *SPAIN AND SPANISH AMERICA IN THE LIBRARIES OF
      THE UNIVERSITY OF CALIFORNIA; A CATALOGUE OF
      BOOKS.* Berkeley, Library, University of Calif-
      ornia, 1928-30, 2v. Reprinted by Burt Franklin,
      1964. (Burt Franklin Bibliography and Reference
      Series, No. 115).
This two volume catalog lists books in the Bancroft,
General and departmental libraries of the University
of California at Berkeley as of January 1927 "in the
Spanish language or relating to Spain and Spanish
America, including those on Spanish exploration,
colonization, and rule in other countries." Over
15,000 titles are included. The catalog is arranged
alphabetically by main entry. A subject index that
follows the Library of Congress classification scheme
is included.

673. *THE SPANISH IN AMERICA 1513-1974: A CHRONOLOGY
      AND FACTBOOK.* Compiled and edited by Arthur A.
      Natella, Jr. Dobbs Ferry, New York, Oceana

Publications, 1975, 139p. (Ethnic Chronology
   Series no. 12).
One section of this source lists relevant books, arti-
cles, and doctoral dissertations in English and Spanish.
For a more complete annotation, see Entry No. 111.

674. *THE SPANISH SPEAKING IN THE UNITED STATES: A
      GUIDE TO MATERIALS.* Prepared by the U.S. Cabi-
      net Committee on Opportunities for Spanish
      Speaking People. Washington, D.C., G.P.O.,
      1971, 175p.
This guide to materials and information on Spanish-
speaking Americans (Cubans, Mexican Americans and
Puerto Ricans) is a revision and expansion of *A
GUIDE TO MATERIALS RELATING TO PERSONS OF MEXICAN
HERITAGE IN THE UNITED STATES* (see Entry No. 646),
a bibliography published in 1969 by the Committee's
predecessor, the Inter-Agency Committee on Mexican
American Affairs. It is arranged by form of material
cited (bibliographies, books, articles, reports,
speeches, government publications, dissertations,
newspapers, and audio-visual materials). Over 1,300
sources are identified. The emphasis is on items
published in the 1950s and 1960s. Some entries are
briefly annotated. The work also includes lists of
U.S. producers/distributors of Spanish-language A-V
materials, current periodicals, and Spanish-language
radio and TV stations and programs. A subject index
completes the source. The bibliography was reprinted
without changes in 1975 by Blaine Ethridge.

675. *SPANISH-SURNAMED POPULATIONS OF THE UNITED
      STATES: A CATALOG OF DISSERTATIONS.* By Richard
      V. Teschner, et. al. Ann Arbor, Michigan, Xerox
      University Microfilms, 1974, 43p.
This catalog attempts "to list all doctoral dissertations pertaining to the several Hispanic or Spanish-
surnamed populations of the United States and possessions." The 1,197 cited dissertations are arranged
under four major headings: social sciences, education,
humanities, and sciences. Each section is further
subdivided into various disciplines. The listing was

compiled from the *COMPREHENSIVE DISSERTATION INDEX 1861-1972* and *DISSERTATION ABSTRACTS INTERNATIONAL 1973-1974*. References to the *DISSERTATION ABSTRACTS INTERNATIONAL* entry and order number are provided for each dissertation. There is an author index.

676. *THE UNITED STATES-MEXICAN BORDER: A SELECTIVE GUIDE TO THE LITERATURE OF THE REGION.* By Charles C. Cumberland. A supplement to *RURAL SOCIOLOGY*, Vol. 25, June, 1960, 236p.

References to books, monographs, government publications, theses, manuscripts and articles dealing with the socioeconomic and political conditions of the Spanish borderlands and their people are arranged in 12 chapters: Spanish-speaking Americans; education, folklore; bibliographies and guides; etc. Omitted from the bibliography are "light readings" and materials describing the colonial period in the Southwest. The citations cover the period from Mexican independence to 1958. Although the bibliography includes literature describing conditions on both sides of the border, most of the publications were written by Americans. The bibliography was reprinted by Johnson in 1960 and is included as one of the selections in *MEXICAN AMERICAN BIBLIOGRAPHIES* (see Entry No. 653).

Chapter 11

WOMEN

(Indexes, Abstracts, Bibliographies, etc.)

677. *ABORTION BIBLIOGRAPHY*, v. 1- 1970- . Compiled
by Mary K. Floyd. Troy, New York, Whitston,
1972- . Annual.
ABORTION BIBLIOGRAPHY is issued each Fall and is an
annual, classified list of books and articles published
the preceding year. The topics covered include legal,
social, medical and psychological aspects of abortion.
Non-English language sources are included. The materials, international in scope, are listed by format.
The books are arranged alphabetically by author. The
articles are arranged by title and subject. There is
an author index.

678. *ABORTION IN CONTEXT: A SELECT BIBLIOGRAPHY*. Compiled by Charles Dollen. Metuchen, New Jersey,
Scarecrow Press, 1970, 150p.
This unannotated bibliography lists books and articles
in the English language on marriage, family, the sexual
revolution and abortion. The emphasis is on recent
materials, particularly those published during 1967-9.
Entries are listed by both author and title. Subject
and source indexes are appended.

679. *ADJUSTMENT TO WIDOWHOOD AND SOME RELATED PROBLEMS:
A SELECTIVE AND ANNOTATED BIBLIOGRAPHY*. By Cecile
Strugnell. New York, Health Sciences Publishing,
1974, 201p.
This selective bibliography is the first of three volumes based on research done in the Widow-to-Widow Program at Harvard Medical School's Laboratory of Community
Psychiatry. The over 600 English language books and
articles published before 1972 listed in this source
provide a review of the literature dealing with widowhood and bereavement. The book is divided into subject
areas (e.g., bereavement, widowhood, childhood bereavement, loneliness, role of women, mutual help groups and
non-professionals). Most entries are annotated. There
is no index, but cross referencing is provided.

680. *AMERICAN BLACK WOMEN IN THE ARTS AND SOCIAL SCI-
ENCES: A BIBLIOGRAPHIC SURVEY*. By Ora Williams.

Metuchen, New Jersey, Scarecrow Press, 1973, 141p.
The purpose of this bibliography is to acquaint "many
Americans with the names and talents of some American
Black women authors, composers, painters, and sculptors."
It is a revision and expansion of an article which appeared originally in the March 1972 issue of *CLA* (a
journal of the College Language Association). Over
1,000 entries written by and/or about Black women are
arranged in three basic sections. The first section
concentrates on the literary productions of Black women
in various genres, subdividing the sources cited by
format (e.g., bibliographies, encyclopedias, autobiographies, anthologies, etc.). The second part of the
source presents selected bibliographies for 15 Black
women artists and scholars, such as Gwendolyn Brooks,
Philippa Duke Schuyler, and Dorothy Porter. The final
section lists Black women painters, sculptors, composers, and lyricists. Four pages of audio-visual citations (films, cassettes, tapes, videotapes, etc.) are
included. In addition, the names and addresses of
Black periodicals and publishing houses are indicated.
The index is limited to names; no subject access is
provided.

681.   *THE AMERICAN WOMAN IN COLONIAL AND REVOLUTIONARY
        TIMES, 1565-1800; A SYLLABUS WITH BIBLIOGRAPHY.*
        By Eugenie A. Leonard and Sophie Drinker. Phil-
        adelphia, University of Pennsylvania Press,
        1962, 169p.
Intended as an outline for study of colonial women,
this bibliography is a listing of 765 books, 309 articles, and eight pictorial works on the subject. The
material is arranged by topic and each topic (not each
individual item) is annotated. Topics include: general
references on the period, women in the earliest settlements, heroic and patriotic activities, status and
rights, the home, etc. A list of 104 outstanding colonial women, with references on each, makes up a substantial part of the work; brief biographical information
is also provided for each of those women. The bibliography was reprinted in 1975 by Greenwood Press.

682. *AMERICAN WOMEN AND AMERICAN STUDIES*. By Betty
     E. Chmaj. Pittsburgh, Know, Inc., 1971, 258p.
An assortment of facts, research data, course outlines,
and articles are included in this reference source.
Part I contains the report of the American Studies
Association Commission on Women, which outlines patterns of discrimination taken from employment practices.
Part II is a listing of women's studies courses supplemented by 27 assigned reading lists. Part III is a
selection of book reviews, articles and speeches on
issues relating to women. While no index is provided,
there is a detailed table of contents.

683. *AN ANNOTATED BIBLIOGRAPHY OF HOMOSEXUALITY*. By
     Vern L. Bullough, W. Dorr Legg, and Barrett W.
     Elcano. New York, Garland Press, 1976, 1000p.
Using an interdisciplinary approach, this bibliography
attempts to cover all literature on the subject of
homosexuality. Over 14,000 entries that date from the
early sixteenth century through 1975 and works in
several foreign languages are listed. Only the most
important works have descriptive annotations. The
bibliography is arranged in broad subject categories:
Bibliographies; General Studies; Behavioral and Social
Sciences--Anthropology, History, Psychology, Sociology;
Education and Children; Law and Enforcement; Military;
Medicine and Biology; Religion and Ethics; Biography and
Autobiography; Literature; the Movement. Sections dealing with transsexualism and transvestism are also included. There is an author index.

684. *ARTHUR AND ELIZABETH SCHLESINGER LIBRARY ON THE*
     HISTORY OF WOMEN. THE MANUSCRIPT INVENTORIES
     AND THE CATALOGS OF MANUSCRIPTS, BOOKS AND
     PICTURES, RADCLIFFE COLLEGE, CAMBRIDGE, MASS-
     ACHUSETTS. Boston, G. K. Hall, 1973, 3v.
Located at Radcliffe College, the Schlesinger Library
has one of the largest collections of source material
on the history of American women from 1800 to the present. The three volumes are a reproduction of the
Library's card catalog. There are separate catalogs
for manuscripts, books, and pictures. The manuscript

and book catalogs contain subject, title and author
cards. The picture catalog is an alphabetical listing
by subject. Over 12,000 volumes, 200 major collections
and many smaller ones of the papers of individual American women, 31 archives of important women's organizations, periodicals both historical and current, and
pictures comprise the citations in this collection.
Women whose lives are documented in the collection
range from Susan B. Anthony to Betty Friedan. Areas
covered include women in medicine, women in business,
women in government, women and arts, the art of cooking, and Black history.

685. *BARRIERS TO WOMEN'S PARTICIPATION IN POST-SECON-
     DARY EDUCATION; A REVIEW OF RESEARCH AND COMMEN-
     TARY AS OF 1973-74.* By Esther M. Westervelt.
     Washington, D.C., G.P.O., 1975, 74p. (Sponsored
     Reports Series 1).
Over 300 items on sex discrimination in higher education are identified and described. The topics covered
in the bibliography include institutional barriers
(admissions practices, financial aid practices, faculty
and staff attitudes), social constraints (social class,
racial group, family circumstances), and psychological
factors.

686. *BIBLIOGRAPHY OF AMERICAN WOMEN.* By H. Carleton
     Marlow. New Haven, Connecticut, Research Publi-
     cations, 1975, microfilm.
Part I of this comprehensive bibliography of materials
written by and about women has been completed. It
covers the period to 1904 and contains approximately
50,000 books and other printed materials. The entries
are listed alphabetically, chronologically, and by
topic. There are no annotations. Fictional and scientific literature written by women supplements the
historical citations. The publication is unusually
expensive ($1,500) and, consequently, will generally
be available only at research libraries. Unlike most
other reference sets, this bibliography has been issued
on microfilm, rather than in bound copy.

687. *A BIBLIOGRAPHY ON DIVORCE*. Compiled and edited
        by Stanley Israel. New York, Bloch, 1974, 300p.
The legal, sociological and religious aspects of divorce
are emphasized in this annotated bibliography. Over 150
books published in the United States from the 1940s to
the 1970s are described. The arrangement is by author.
Occasionally, tables of contents from the publications
are reproduced. In addition, there is a list of over 70
other recent books and 300 older materials. The bibliography was first published in 1973 and then republished
in 1974.

688. *BIBLIOGRAPHY ON WOMEN WORKERS (1861-1965)*. By
        Suzanne Nicolas. Geneva, International Labour
        Office, 1970, 252p. (International Labour Office.
        Centeral Library and Documentation Branch. Bibli-
        ographical Contributions, No. 26).
References to 1,800 publications dealing with women
workers issued between the mid-nineteenth century and
1965 are listed in this bibliography. International
and historical in scope, the bibliography is broken
down into chapters, each dealing with a particular
subject (employment and unemployment, equal pay, older
workers, married women and maternity protection, women's
and professional organizations, etc.). The articles,
books, reports, monographs and government documents
listed here are indexed by author, country and subject.

689. *BIOGRAPHICAL ENCYCLOPEDIA OF WOMEN*. Chicago,
        World Biography, 1975, 14v.
Bibliographies accompany each of the 12,438 biographi-
cal sketches. For a complete annotation, see Entry
No. 181.

690. *THE BLACK FAMILY AND THE BLACK WOMAN, A BIBLIO-
        GRAPHY*. Bloomington, Indiana, Indiana University,
        1972, 107p.
This bibliography is divided into two sections. Part
One, The Black Family, includes 19th century slave
narratives and related works, background on the Black
family and 20th century material on Black groups (book

length studies, sections from books, journal articles, and government publications). Part Two, The Black Woman, covers general background/history, identity and liberation, autobiography/biography, the professionals, general labor force, sports, records and tapes, and government publications.

691. *THE BLACK WOMAN IN AMERICAN SOCIETY: A SELECTED, ANNOTATED BIBLIOGRAPHY.* By Lenwood G. Davis. Foreword by Dorothy Porter. Boston, G. K. Hall, 1975, 159p.
This bibliography focuses on the changing role of Black women in American society as revealed in books, chapters of books, articles, reports, pamphlets, speeches, government documents and autobiographical works. Each of the 700 items is annotated. The citations are arranged by format and indexed by subject and author/compiler/ editor. One third of the publication contains directory and statistical information: a directory of national organizations of Black women, statistics on Black women in rural areas, listings of libraries with major Black history collections, a directory of Black women newspaper publishers and editors, and a list of Black women elected officials. An author-subject index completes the work.

692. *THE CASE FOR WOMAN SUFFRAGE: A BIBLIOGRAPHY.* By Margaret Ladd Franklin. New York, National College Equal Suffrage League, 1913, 315p.
This is an annotated bibliography of several hundred citations dealing with women suffrage published before the passage of the 19th amendment. An author index is provided.

693. *CATALOG OF THE SOCIAL AND BEHAVIORAL SCIENCES MONOGRAPH SECTION OF THE LIBRARY OF THE INSTITUTE FOR SEX RESEARCH, INDIANA UNIVERSITY.* Boston, G. K. Hall, 1974, 4v.
The library of the Institute for Sex Research, founded by Dr. Alfred C. Kinsey, contains over 30,000 volumes and approximately 63 journals, primarily in the fields

of psychiatry, psychology and sociology. The Social
and Behavioral Sciences Monograph Section includes
books covering the historical aspects of human sex
behavior, the history of marriage, early sex education,
sex ethics and religion, women's rights, abortion,
contraception, and venereal disease. The four volume
catalog consists only of books cataloged prior to
October, 1973. A classified arrangement has been
developed, along with special subject headings. A
catalog of journal articles is planned for the future.

694. *CHICAGO WOMEN'S DIRECTORY: ARTICLES AND LISTINGS.*
       Chicago, Inforwomen, 1974, 225p.
For annotation, see Entry No. 311.

695. *CONTEMPORARY WOMEN.* Detroit, Biography Publish-
       ing Center, 1975, 4v.
Bibliographies accompany each of the 2,000 biographical
sketches. For a complete annotation, see Entry No. 183.

696. *DIVORCE: A SELECTED ANNOTATED BILBIOGRAPHY.* By
       Mary McKenney. Metuchen, New Jersey, Scarecrow
       Press, 1975, 157p.
Over 600 items, written on divorce in English through
1972, are arranged by subject in this annotated bibliography. Subdivisions are general and cover historical
works, legal aspects, financial situations, statistics,
divorced men, divorced women, children of divorce, psychological and sociological aspects, religious and
moral values, and miscellaneous entries. Literary
efforts, films, statistical sources, and legal works
are cited. There are appendices which list divorce
laws in various states, resource people and organizations, and women's divorce reform movements. Author
and subject indexes complete the publication.

697. *DOCUMENT AND REFERENCE TEXT (DART): AN INDEX TO
       MINORITY GROUP EMPLOYMENT.* Ann Arbor, Institute
       of Labor and Industrial Relations, University of
       Michigan-Wayne State University, 1967, 602p.

291

SUPPLEMENT, 1971.
Women are one of the groups covered in this bibliography. For a complete annotation, see Entry No. 419.

698. *EMPLOYMENT OF OLDER WOMEN, AN ANNOTATED BIBLIO-GRAPHY.* By Jean Wells. Washington, D.C., U.S. Women's Bureau, 1957, 83p.
Arranged by author, this bibliography lists books, articles, reports, etc. on the hiring practices, attitudes toward, and work performance of older women. Annotations (generally one-half page in length) are provided for each item. A subject index is included. This compilation supercedes an earlier publication by the Bureau entitled *BIBLIOGRAPHY ON EMPLOYMENT PROBLEMS OF OLDER WOMEN.*

699. *ENCYCLOPEDIA OF WOMEN.* Detroit, Encyclopedia Publishing Center, 1974- . To be published in 18v.
An entire volume of the set will be devoted to bibliographic references (21,500 citations to books, articles, and audio-visual materials) for further reading. For a complete annotation, see Entry No. 115.

700. *FAMOUS AMERICAN WOMEN.* By Hope Stoddard. New York, Crowell, 1970, 461p.
Short bibliographies are provided for each biographical sketch. For a complete annotation, see Entry No. 185.

701. *FEMALE STUDIES, 1970-* . Pittsburgh, Know, Inc., 1970- . Irregular.
This collection of course outlines and reading lists for women's studies in American colleges and universities is compiled by the Commission on the Status of Women of the Modern Language Association. Some volumes cover other aspects; Volume IV, for example, provides essays and bibliographies on "Teaching about Women." Volume VI "Closer to the Ground-Women's Classes" has 22 essays about the practice of women's studies on campuses in 1972. Approximately two issues appear each year.

702. *A GAY BIBLIOGRAPHY: EIGHT BIBLIOGRAPHIES ON LES-
BIANISM AND MALE HOMOSEXUALITY.* New York, Arno
Press, 1975, 410p. in various pagings.
This publication reproduces eight previously published
bibliographies on female lesbianism and male homosexuality. Marion Zimmer Bradley's two volume briefly
annotated bibliography on lesbianism, *ASTRA'S TOWER*
(1958, 1959) is included. So are Bradley and Gene
Damon's *CHECKLIST* and *CHECKLIST SUPPLEMENTS* (1960-
1962), previously mimeographed and privately distributed annotated bibliographies, and Stuart's *THE LESBIAN
IN LITERATURE* (1967)--an alphabetical listing of English language novels, short stories, poetry, drama,
fictional biography and miscellany coded to indicate
the extent of lesbian content in each item. The other
reprinted bibliographies deal primarily with male homosexuality.

703. *A GAY NEWS CHRONOLOGY, 1969 - MAY 1975: INDEX
AND ABSTRACTS OF ARTICLES FROM THE NEW YORK
TIMES.* New York, Arno Press, 1975, 150p.
All material on homosexuality published in the *NEW
YORK TIMES* from January 1, 1969 to May 1975 is abstracted in this publication. The entries are arranged in
chronological order and the source "thus gives a detailed chronological overview of how this subject has
been reported in America's foremost newspaper--from
the emergence of the 'gay liberation' movement to
legislation mandating equal opportunity for homosexuals and to more widespread acceptance of homosexuals
as 'normal' and more widespread recognition of their
demands for equal rights." The abstracts for each item
vary in length according to the amount of factual
material contained in the source articles, and frequen-
ly contain sufficient information so that there is no
need to consult the original articles. The abstracts
were obtained by tapping the New York Times Information
Bank, "a pioneering computerized system in which abstracts of all material published in *THE TIMES* and of
selected material published in some sixty other newspapers and magazines are stored 'on-line' and may be
retrieved by entering inquiries on a computer terminal."

704. *GOING STRONG/NEW COURSES, NEW PROGRAMS*. Edited
by Deborah Silverton Rosenfelt. Old Westbury,
New York, Feminist Press, 1973, 256p. (Female
Studies VII).
Bibliographies on the subject of the women's movement
are included. For an annotation, see Entry No. 313.

705. *HOMOSEXUALITY: A SELECTIVE BIBLIOGRAPHY OF OVER
THREE THOUSAND ITEMS*. By William Parker. Metuchen, New Jersey, Scarecrow Press, 1971, 323p.
Parker's 3,188 item bibliography lists all major works
on homosexuality published in English through 1969.
The bibliography cites books, articles, pamphlets,
popular magazines, newspapers, and legal journals.
One section lists over 100 court cases involving con-
sensual acts between adults. Another section lists
literary works, movies, television programs, and phono-
graph records dealing with homosexuality. An appendix
summarizes state and Federal laws on homosexuality.
Subject and author indexes are provided.

706. *HOMOSEXUALITY; AN ANNOTATED BIBLIOGRAPHY*. By
Martin S. Weinberg and Alan P. Bell. New York,
Harper and Row, 1972, 550p.
This annotated bibliography lists over 1,200 books,
articles, and pamphlets in the English language published between 1940 and 1968 on the subject of homosexuality. The areas of homosexuality, lesbianism,
sexual perversion, and sodomy are covered. The material is classified under three categories: physiology,
psychology, and sociology. A useful cross-referencing
system is included, plus author and subject indexes.

707. *INDEX TO WOMEN OF THE WORLD FROM ANCIENT TO
MODERN TIMES*. By Norma Ireland. Westwood,
Massachusetts, Faxon, 1970, 573p. (Useful Ref-
erence Series of Library Books, Vol. 97).
This index provides references to 13,000 women, whose
profiles and portraits appear in 945 collective bio-
graphies and serials (e.g., *CURRENT BIOGRAPHY, NEW
YORKER, TIME, BULLETIN OF BIBLIOGRAPHY*, etc.). The

women included in this source span all countries and
all time periods. The volume is arranged alphabetically, with birthday, nationality and vocation also
indicated. Since biographical information is provided
for each of the women listed, the *INDEX* serves not only
as a guide to further information but also as a source
of brief identification. A lengthy introduction traces
women's contributions to history, politics, religion,
fine arts, science, etc. The publication complements
the entries found in the more general *BIOGRAPHY INDEX*
(New York, Wilson, 1947- . Quarterly).

708. *INTERNATIONAL BIBLIOGRAPHY OF RESEARCH IN MARRIAGE*
      AND THE FAMILY. Minneapolis, University of Minn-
      esota Press, 1967- . Irregular, Annual.
The purpose of this publication is to provide "a comprehensive and systematic listing of current literature
which can be of value to all types of family professionals." Volume I (*INTERNATIONAL BIBLIOGRAPHY OF RESEARCH
IN MARRIAGE AND THE FAMILY, 1900-1964*, by Joan Aldous
and Reuben Hill, 1967, 508p.) lists 12,850 books, journals and pamphlets issued in English between 1900 and
1964 and indexes them by keyword, subject, author and
title. The second volume in the set (*INTERNATIONAL
BIBLIOGRAPHY OF RESEARCH IN MARRIAGE AND THE FAMILY,
1965-1972*, by Joan Aldous and Nancy Dahl, 1974, 1519p.)
covers the period 1965-1972. The third volume (*INTER-
NATIONAL BIBLIOGRAPHY OF RESEARCH IN MARRIAGE AND THE
FAMILY, 1973 & 1974 INVENTORY*, 1975) is an update and
modification of the earlier volumes in the set. While
it follows the same organizational and indexing patterns,
it differs from the first two volumes in that it is
restricted only to articles (2,000) and it no longer
concentrates solely on research materials. Beginning
in 1976, the *INVENTORY* will be published yearly and list
the English language journal literature dealing with
marriage and the family issued during that year.

709. *THE MANUSCRIPT, SUBJECT AND AUTHOR CATALOGS OF
      THE SOPHIA SMITH COLLECTION (WOMEN'S HISTORY
      ARCHIVE)*. Boston, G. K. Hall, 1973, 7v.
An internationally known research facility for women's

studies, the Sophia Smith collection contains thousands
of retrospective and contemporary manuscripts, pamphlets, books, periodicals and photographs. Major
holdings date from 1795. The published materials and
photographs are listed by author (two volumes) and
subject (three volumes). There is a separate listing
(two volumes) of manuscripts. The primary and secondary
sources of the Sophia Smith collection illuminate
women's roles in the movements for birth control, civil
rights and equal education, access to careers in the
humanities, fine and applied arts as well as the professions of medicine, settlement work and law, and in
the crusades for suffrage, women's rights and women's
liberation.

710. *MEDIA REPORT TO WOMEN INDEX/DIRECTORY.* Edited
      by Martha Leslie Allen. Washington, D.C., Media
      Report to Women, 1975, 225p.
For annotation, see Entry No. 119.

711. *THE NEW WOMAN'S SURVIVAL SOURCEBOOK.* Edited by
      Kirsten Grimstad and Susan Rennie. New York,
      Knopf, 1975, 245p.
For annotation, see Entry No. 120.

712. *NORTH AMERICAN REFERENCE ENCYCLOPEDIA OF WOMEN'S
      LIBERATION.* Edited by William White, Jr. Phila-
      delphia, North American, 1972, 194p. (North
      American Reference Library).
The purpose of this encyclopedia is "to present thousands of citations and cross references" as well as to
define all the terms relating to the women's movement.
For a complete annotation, see Entry No. 121.

713. *NOTABLE AMERICAN WOMEN, 1607-1950: A BIOGRAPHI-
      CAL DICTIONARY.* Edited by Edward T. James and
      Janet W. James. Cambridge, Harvard University
      Press, 1971, 3v.
Bibliographies accompany all of the biographical sketches. For a complete annotation, see Entry No. 191.

714. *ON THE PSYCHOLOGY OF WOMEN; A SURVEY OF EMPIRICAL
      STUDIES.* By Julia A. Sherman. Springfield,
      Illinois, Charles C. Thomas, 1971, 304p.
Nearly 900 empirical studies on the psychology of women
are summarized and ordered in this bibliographic essay.
Chapters deal with psychological sex differences, the
Freudian theory of feminine development, moral and sex-
role development, adolescence, female sexuality, preg-
nancy, motherhood, etc. The citations are indexed.

715. *THE ONE-PARENT FAMILY: PERSPECTIVES AND ANNOTATED
      BIBLIOGRAPHY.* By Benjamin Schlesinger. 3rd ed.
      Toronto, University of Toronto Press, 1975, 132p.
This book is intended as an aid for social work students,
researchers, and practitioners interested in the one-
parent family. The family situation that occurs through
desertion, separation, death, divorce, or unmarried
motherhood is classified as a one-parent family. The
first part of the book consists of three essays which
provide an overview of the subject: the status of
the one-parent family, methods of research in the field,
and a sociological analysis of widowhood. The second
section of the source is an annotated bibliography of
280 books, pamphlets, and journal articles published
through 1974. Statistical data are presented in the
appendix and an author index is included. The bibliography was originally published in 1969 and has been
revised three times.

716. *THE PSYCHOLOGY OF WOMEN: A PARTIALLY ANNOTATED
      BIBLIOGRAPHY.* By Joyce Jennings Walstedt.
      Pittsburgh, Know, Inc., 1972, 76p.
Books and articles dealing with various facets of the
psychology of women (adolescence, middle and old age,
primate studies, minority group status, sexuality, etc.)
are listed and critically annotated in this bibliography.
The source is not designed to be exhaustive; publications
issued after 1970 are emphasized. There is no index.

717. *RESEARCH GUIDE IN WOMEN'S STUDIES.* By Naomi B.
      Lynn, Ann B. Matasar, and Marie Barovic Rosenberg.

Morristown, New Jersey, General Learning Press,
1974, 194p.
While much of the book deals with general topics and
materials (selecting a research topic, footnotes and
bibliographies, general reference publications, etc.),
several chapters focus on sources useful in women's
studies research. In addition to appropriate reference materials, the publication identifies information
and research centers dealing with the women's movement
and women's studies course offerings. Short annotations accompany most entries. There is a brief general
index.

718. *THE ROLE OF WOMEN IN AMERICAN HISTORY*. Santa
Barbara, California, ABC-Clio, to be published
in 1977 (Clio Bibliography).
Abstracts of scholarly articles which focus on the role
of women in American history will be included in this
bibliography scheduled for publication in 1977. It is
issued as part of the *CLIO BIBLIOGRAPHY* series; other
titles include: *AFRO-AMERICAN HISTORY* (see Entry No.
553) and *INDIANS OF THE UNITED STATES AND CANADA* (see
Entry No. 503).

719. *THE SEXUAL BARRIER; LEGAL AND ECONOMIC ASPECTS
OF EMPLOYMENT*. By Marija Matich Hughes. San
Francisco, The Author, 1970, 43p. *SUPPLEMENT* 1,
1971, 79p. *SUPPLEMENT* 2, 1972, 85p.
The emphasis of this bibliography and its supplements
is on employment trends, discrimination, and legislation affecting women in the work force. Hundreds of
books, articles and documents are organized by subject.
The entries go back to the 1930s, but most were issued
after 1959. Foreign publications are included, but
American sources predominate. Up-dates are planned.

720. *SHE SAID/HE SAID: AN ANNOTATED BIBLIOGRAPHY OF
SEX DIFFERENCES IN LANGUAGE, SPEECH AND NONVERBAL
COMMUNICATION*. Compiled by Nancy Henley, et. al.
Pittsburgh, Know, Inc., 1975, 115p.
Several hundred books, chapters, and journal articles

dealing with sex differences in language, speech, and nonverbal communication are cited in this bibliography. Each entry is annotated. The citations are indexed by author.

721. *STATUS OF WOMEN IN HIGHER EDUCATION: 1963-1972; A SELECTIVE BIBLIOGRAPHY.* Compiled by Linda Harman. Ames, Iowa State University Library, 1972, 124p. (Series in Bibliography, no. 2).
Books, articles, documents, dissertations, ERIC materials, theses and ephemera published on women faculty, students, administrators, and librarians since 1963 are listed in this annotated bibliography. Women in non-academic positions are excluded. The citations are listed by author. There is no subject access. An appendix lists relevant U.S. legislation and identifies universities and colleges charged with sex discrimination.

722. *WOMAN AND MENTAL HEALTH; SELECTED ANNOTATED REFERENCES, 1970-73.* Washington, D.C., G.P.O., 1974, 247p.
The purpose of the bibliography is "to provide information on the social, economic, and psychological pressures on women and to show the diversity of, or lack of, expert opinion on female psychological and sociocultural processes." The 810 citations (to books, articles, and dissertations) are annotated and classified into such topics as abortion, contraception, divorce, education, family, lesbianism, marriage, prostitution, rape, sexuality, unwed mothers and widowhood. There is an author index.

723. *WOMANHOOD MEDIA: CURRENT RESOURCES ABOUT WOMEN.* By Helen Wheeler. Metuchen, New Jersey, Scarecrow Press, 1972, 335p.
This guide contains a variety of information on the women's movement. Part One, "A Women's Liberation Awareness Inventory," is a 200 question quiz which is designed to "evaluate attitudes and openmindedness." Part Two, "Documentation for Human Equality," is an

annotated bibliography of basic reference sources describing their treatment of women. Part Three, "A
Basic Book Collection," arranged by Dewey numbers, is
an annotated list of over 300 core books on women's
studies. Part Four, "Non-book Resources," lists pamphlets, movement periodicals, and audio-visual resources. The last part, "Directory of Sources,"
provides information and addresses on organizations,
foundations, philanthropies, women liberation groups,
women's studies centers, publishers, library programs
and subject collections. There is an author and title
index to the basic book collection. A supplement was
issued by Scarecrow Press in 1975 (see Entry No. 724).

724. *WOMANHOOD MEDIA SUPPLEMENT: ADDITIONAL CURRENT
RESOURCES ABOUT WOMEN*. By Helen Wheeler. Metuchen, New Jersey, Scarecrow Press, 1975, 482p.
Each of the main resource sections of Wheeler's *WOMAN-
HOOD MEDIA* (see Entry No. 723) are expanded in this
supplement. The supplement contains three sections:
a continuation of Wheeler's "Basic Book Collection"
arranged in Dewey order (bringing the annotated collection of available books to 826 titles); a subject
classified listing of pamphlets, movement periodicals
and audiovisual resources (including filmstrips, realia,
slides, films, recordings, transparencies, tapes,
microforms, posters, prints, pictures, etc.); and a
directory of 1,500 additional speakers, women's
commissions, liberation groups, and women's centers.
Most of the entries are annotated (although some with
only phrase descriptions) and cover such topics as
affirmative action, consciousness-raising, lesbiana,
sexism in education, self-defense, etc. These items
are indexed. The purpose of the supplement is to provide continuing coverage of source material and information relating to the contemporary women's movement,
along with practical information about these materials
and the movement itself.

725. *THE WOMAN'S GUIDE TO BOOKS, 1974-* . Edited by
Ruth Gordon Randall. New York, MSS Information
Corp., 1974- . 3 times/yr.

Issued three times a year, this serial descriptively
annotates the "best" new books written by, for and
about women. The emphasis is on American publications.
About 400 titles are covered in each issue. Included
are books on marriage and divorce, aging, day care,
women at work, parenting, the women's movement, etc.
The source is illustrated and indexed. All books
listed here can be obtained through the serial's
publisher (MSS Information Corp.), who has promised
to stock the cited items.

726. *WOMEN: A BIBLIOGRAPHY ON THEIR EDUCATION AND
     CAREERS.* By Helen S. Austin, Nancy Suniewick,
     and Susan Deveck. Washington, D.C., Human
     Services Press, 1971, 243p.
This is an annotated bibliography of 352 research
studies (most empirical, some historical) which in-
vestigate women's education and career development.
Most of the studies were done during the 1960s.
Entries include research reports, journal articles,
dissertations, unpublished papers, and some monographs
classified under seven broad headings (e.g., deter-
minants of career choice, marital and family status
of working women, continuing education of women. The
abstracts provided for each entry summarize sampling
techniques, methodology, findings and conclusions.
Two introductory chapters precede the abstracts themselves, and summarize content, criticize methodology and
conclusions, and identify areas needing further research. The first is an "Overview of the Findings"
by Austin. The second, "Beyond the Findings: Some
Interpretations and Implications for the Future,"
was prepared by Nancy Suniewick. The index provides
author and subject access to the citations. The
bibliography was also published in 1974, without
change, by Behavioral Publications.

727. *WOMEN AND SOCIETY: A CRITICAL REVIEW OF THE
     LITERATURE WITH A SELECTED ANNOTATED BIBLIOGRA-
     PHY.* Compiled by Marie Barovic Rosenberg and
     Len V. Bergstrom. Beverly Hills, California,
     Sage, 1975, 354p.

WOMEN AND SOCIETY is an annotated bibliography of over 3,500 items covering such topics as politics, economics, military science, society, morality, religion, education, science, medicine, philosophy, literature, and the law. Books, periodical articles, government documents, and unpublished materials are arranged by broad subject headings. The cited materials were published between the seventeenth century and 1974 and are generally in English (only one percent of the items are in French, German or Spanish). A critical review of the literature of women is given in 20 pages. A useful addenda includes a list of over 300 biographies and autobiographies of women; a list of addresses of women's organizations; a list of periodicals devoted to women; and a list of women's collections and libraries. An author, name, and subject index completes the source.

728. *WOMEN AT WORK: AN ANNOTATED BIBLIOGRAPHY.* By Mei Ling Bickner. Los Angeles, Manpower Research Center, Institute of Industrial Relations, University of California, 1974, unpaged.
In this computer produced bibliography, approximately 600 books, articles, and government documents published after 1960 are annotated and classified by topic: historical development, education and training, working women, occupation, special groups of women, bibliographies, etc. The cited works deal with all aspects of the employment of women--social, economic and legal. The entries are indexed by author, title, keyword and category.

729. *WOMEN IN AMERICAN LABOR HISTORY, 1825-1935; AN ANNOTATED BIBLIOGRAPHY.* Edited by Martha Soltow, Carolyn Forche, and Murray Massre. East Lansing, Michigan, School of Labor and Industrial Relations, Michigan State University, 1972, 150p.
Citations to nearly 500 books, articles, monographs, pamphlets, and U.S. government publications are arranged in eight sections (ranging from employment, to strikes and lockouts, to labor leaders) in this guide to the place of women in the American labor movement

prior to the 1930s. Each entry includes a brief
content summary. Two appendices cover 1) archival
collections in the United States relating to women
or labor and 2) a list of publications issued by
the U.S. Women's Bureau between 1918 and 1935.
Author, subject and cross-reference indexes complete
the source.

730. *WOMEN IN ANTIQUITY: AN ANNOTATED BIBLIOGRAPHY.*
     By Leanna Goodwater. Metuchen, New Jersey,
     Scarecrow Press, 1975, 171p.
Materials dealing with women in antiquity living
among the ancient Greeks, the Minoans, Etruscans,
Romans, etc. from the earliest times to 476 A.D.
are listed and described in this bibliography.
Biographies of individual women are stressed; materials on Cleopatra and the Greek poet Sappho, however,
are excluded because other bibliographies focus on
these figures (e.g., Besterman's *BIBLIOGRAPHY OF
CLEOPATRA* issued in 1926). Ancient works are included,
listed both in the original language and in transla-
tion. Modern works are also cited. For those published in English since 1872, the bibliography strives
to be complete. Selective coverage is provided for
books and articles written in foreign languages
(Greek, Latin, French, German and Italian). Ancient
sources are listed first, followed by modern sources,
in a simple subject arrangement. Over 500 sources
are included. They are indexed by author, editor and
translator. There is also an index to many of the
important women of antiquity, giving their dates, a
brief description, and references to numbered entries
in the bibliography which deal with them.

731. *WOMEN IN FOCUS*. By Jeanne Betancourt. Dayton,
     Ohio, Pflaum, 1974, 186p.
This is a bibliography of films which deal with the
qualities of life that affect women, the exploitation
of women, or the problems of women unique to their own
sex. These films are produced by feminists or male
allies. Each entry includes identifying information
(length, color or black/white, silent or sound, rental

or purchase price, etc.) and a description of the film.
Biographical sketches of the film writers and suggested
parallel feminist readings for the film are also included. There is a title and theme index. An annotated
bibliography of feminist books, prepared by Madeline
Warren, completes the work.

732. *WOMEN IN GOVERNMENT AND POLITICS: A BIBLIOGRAPHY
OF AMERICAN AND FOREIGN SOURCES.* By Rosaline
Levenson. Monticello, Illinois, Council of Planning Librarians, 1973, 80p. (Exchange Bibliographies no. 491).
The purpose of this bibliography is "to present some of
the leading works from earlier eras and most of the
recent publications" on women in government and politics.
Both American and foreign sources (books and articles)
are cited, although the major emphasis is on American
works. The bibliography is restricted primarily to
publications issued since 1940. It is divided into
four main sections: bibliographies and indexes, women
in politics, women in government, women in politics and
government in foreign countries. Each of these sections
is further subdivided by subject.

733. *WOMEN IN PERSPECTIVE: A GUIDE FOR CROSS-CULTURAL
STUDIES.* Compiled by Sue-Ellen Jacobs. Urbana,
Illinois, University of Illinois Press, 1974,
299p.
This "sourcebook does not pretend to be all encompas-
sing; rather it represents research into special areas
by [the author], colleagues, and students who are
seeking answers to specific questions about women."
Materials in all languages are included. The 4,000
sources (monographs and articles published during the
1900s) have been divided into two main sections. Part
I, "Geographical Topics," has sources arranged by culture areas and countries; in Part II, "Subject Topics,"
sources are arranged by major theme (e.g., primate
studies, anatomy and physiology, sex and sexuality,
homosexuality, prostitution, education, women in history).
The entries are indexed by author.

734. *WOMEN IN THE UNITED STATES CONGRESS, 1917-1972;*
THEIR ACCOMPLISHMENTS: WITH BIBLIOGRAPHIES.
Littleton, Colorado, Libraries Unlimited, 1974,
184p.
For annotation, see Entry No. 202.

735. *WOMEN STUDIES ABSTRACTS, V. 1- 1972-* . Edited
by Sara Stauffer Whaley. Rush, New York, Women
Studies Abstracts, 1972- . Annual.
Documents, books and articles written about women are
included in this quarterly issued annotated guide.
The abstracts are arranged alphabetically by author in
the following groups: education, sex characteristics
and differences, employment, society and government,
family, women in history and literature, family planning, abortion, etc. In addition to the abstract
section, each issue contains one or more interpretative
bibliographic essays, lists of biographical articles,
citations for recent book reviews, and classified lists
of unannotated procedural citations. There are cumulative yearly indexes to authors, books reviewed, book
reviewers, and subjects.

736. *WOMEN'S HIGHER AND CONTINUING EDUCATION: AN*
ANNOTATED BIBLIOGRAPHY WITH SELECTED REFERENCES
ON RELATED ASPECTS OF WOMEN'S LIVES. By E. M.
Westervelt and Deborah A. Fixter, with assistance from Margaret Cornstock. New York, College
Entrance Examination Board, 1971, 67p.
"Material directly pertaining to women's higher and
continuing education" is emphasized in this briefly
annotated bibliography of monographs, government documents, articles, anthologies and proceedings published
recently. Citations to materials on women's status,
social and cultural roles, psychology and employment
are also included. The entries are arranged alphabetically by author within nine subject groupings.
There is no index. A brief bibliography of bibliographies on related topics is appended.

737. *THE WOMEN'S RIGHTS MOVEMENT IN THE UNITED STATES,*

1848-1970; A BIBLIOGRAPHY AND SOURCEBOOK. By
Albert Krichmar, assisted by Barbara Case,
Barbara Silver and Ann E. Wiederrecht. Metuchen
New Jersey, Scarecrow Press, 1972, 445p.
This partially annotated bibliography lists over 5,000
books, articles, dissertations, pamphlets and government publications describing the women's rights movement in the United States. Topics covered include the
political, religious, educational, professional, economic and legal status of women since 1848. In addition,
listings of source materials for biographies, manuscript
collections, and women's movement serials are included.
Separate indexes are provided for authors, subjects,
serials and manuscript collections.

738. *WOMEN'S WORK AND WOMEN'S STUDIES.* Compiled by
Kirsten Drake, Dorothy Marks, and Mary Wexford.
New York, The Women's Center, Barnard College,
1971- . Annual.
Compiled at the Women's Center at Barnard College, this
annually abstracted bibliography of dissertations, articles, books and periodicals on women and feminism is
arranged in several subject sections: bodies, sex
roles, induction and stereotyping, socio-psychological
consequences of sex-role induction, its socio-economic
consequences, changing the status quo, history, and
literature - arts - media (images of women in literature,
theater, film, feminist presses, and bookstores).
Scholarly research is integrated with research in
progress and, where appropriate, information on women's
counseling services, legal services, etc. An author
index is provided.

INDEXES

AUTHOR INDEX

(Authors, Editors, Compilers, Translators, Illustrators, etc.)

*Numbers refer to entry numbers, *not* page numbers.

* Numbers refer to entry numbers, *not* page numbers.

310

Gridley, Marion E., 30, 138, 144, 177
Griffin, A.P., 664
Grime, William Ed, 89
Grimstad, Kirsten, 120, 317–8, 711
Gugman, Jessie P., 621
Guzman, Ralph, 668

Hale, Sarah, 198
Haley, James T., 60
Hall, Charles E., 374
Hall, James, 140
Halliburton, Warren J., 1, 412
Halliday, Thelma Y., 613
Hansen, Gladys C., 534
Harding, Anne D., 457
Hargrett, Lester, 219, 462, 484
Harman, Linda, 721
Harper, I. H., 265
Harris, Middleton, 241
Harrison, Cynthia Ellen, 325
Hayes, R. Jay, 48
Haywood, Charles, 415, 461, 569
Heathman, James E., 446, 654, 659
Heintz, William F., 534
Heizer, Robert F., 23, 44, 458, 469
Heller, Murray, 70
Henley, Nancy, 720
Henry, Jeannette, 496
Herman, Masako, 57, 236, 541
Hewlett, Leroy, 502
Hill, Edward E., 294
Hill, Reuben, 708
Hillson, Mauri, 425
Hirschfelder, Arlene B., 444
Hoard, Walter B., 64
Hodge, Frederick Webb, 34, 142, 491
Hodge, William H., 459
Hogg, Peter C., 552
Horn, Joan, 158
Hornsby, Alton, Jr., 65, 572
Horvitz, Diana Frank, 116
Howe, Mentar A., 595
Howes, Durward, 180
Hudson, Gossie Harold, 157
Hughes, Langston, 63, 95–6, 244
Hughes, Marija Matich, 719
Hughes, Thomas, 141
Hutchinson, E.P., 337

Ichioka, Yuji, 532
Icolari, Dan, 50, 146, 295, 514

Institute of Indian Service and Research, 460
Institute for Rural America, 439
Ireland, Norma, 188, 707
Irvine, Keith, 26, 30, 143, 189, 478
Irwin, Leonard B., 583
Israel, Stanley, 687

Jablonsky, Adelaide, 656
Jackson, Clara O., 562
Jackson, Miles M., Jr., 566
Jacobs, Sue-Ellen, 733
James, Edward T., 713
James, Janet W., 191, 713
Janeway, Elizabeth, 129
Janeway, William Ralph, 414
Jenkins, Betty, 582
Johnson, Guy B., 85, 602
Johnson, Harry Alleyn, 432, 607
Johnson, Steven L., 229, 486
Johnson, Willis L., 278
Jones, LeRoi, 63
Jones, Robert C., 653
Jordon, Lois B., 658
Juris, Gail, 305

Kaiser, Ernest, 62, 90, 98
Kappler, Charles J., 231–2
Katz, William Loren, 1, 101, 250, 412, 625
Kay, Ernest, 193, 207
Keesing's Contemporary Archives, 12, 97
Kelsey, C. E., 351
Kennedy, John F., 16
Kennedy, Louise Venable, 568
Kerri, James N., 452, 563
Kim, Hyung-Chan, 58, 237, 544
Kinton, Jack F., 411
Kiser, Clyde B., 395
Kitano, Harry H. L., 526, 530
Klein, Barry T., 50, 146, 295, 514
Kluckhohn, Clyde, 465
Knapp, Rue, 83, 249
Knor, Russell L., 449
Kolm, Richard, 416
Kopachevsky, Joseph P., 660
Kort, Blanche L., 148
Kraditor, Aileen S., 194, 268
Krichmar, Albert, 737
Kroeber, A. L., 23, 36
Kubiak, William J., 31

LaFarge, Oliver, 49
Layng, Anthony, 563

* Numbers refer to entry numbers, *not* page numbers.

Leffal, Dolores C., 561
Leitch, Barbara A., 25
Lemus, Frank, 174
Leonard, Eugenie A., 178, 681
Leonard, John William, 199
Lerner, Gerda, 182, 242, 262
Levenson, Rosaline, 732
Levitt, Morris, 241
Lewis, Roscoe, E., 595
Ligtze-Chung, 546
Lincoln, C. Eric, 95, 251
Lindenmeyer, Otto J., 98
Link, Albert D., 654
Liu, Kwang-Ching, 523
Livermore, Mary, 197
Lópes, Jóse A., 103
Lopez, Charles U., 378
Love, Barbara J., 187
Lowe, Chuan-hua, 535
Lowie, Robert H., 41
Ludewig, Hermann E., 508
Lum, William Wong, 527–8, 549
Lynn, Naomi B., 717

McCarroll, Jean, 611, 612
McClellan, Grant S., 5, 77
MacCulloch, John A., 45
McDowell, William Jr., 226
McGee, Harold Franklin, 520
McKenney, Mary, 696
McKenney, Thomas L., 140
McLean, Linda, 302
McLemore, S. Dale, 386
McNary, Laura Kelly, 24
McPheeters, Annie, 618
McPherson, James M., 587
Major, Clarence, 71, 79
Mangi, Jean, 195, 322
Manhart, Rev. Paul, 29
Mares, Renée, 173
Marken, Jack W., 500
Marks, Dorothy, 738
Marlow, H. Carleton, 686
Marquis, Arnold, 32, 293
Martinez, Arthur D., 176
Martinez, Cecilia J., 446, 654
Marx, Herbert L. Jr., 17
Massre, Murray, 729
Matasar, Ann B., 717
Matsuda, Mitsugu, 542–3
Meacham, Paul E., 155
Meier, August, 239

Meier, Matt S., 633
Meltzer, Milton, 95–6, 253
Messner, Stephen D., 437
Mexican American Study Project, 668
Mickey, Barbara H., 634
Miller, Elizabeth W., 609
Millstein, Beth, 269
Moquin, Wayne, 4, 215, 228, 259
Morais, Herbert M., 88
Morgan, Jean, 429
Morgan, Robin, 267
Murdock, George Peter, 433, 480, 494
Murray, Florence, 91, 369

NICEM. *See* National Information Center
    for Educational Media
Natella, Arthur A., Jr., 111, 261, 673
National Council of Women of the United
    States, 315
National Information Center for Educational
    Media, 605
National Minority Business Campaign, 286
Navarro, Eliseo, 629, 638
Neuman, Robert W., 467
New Jersey Library Association. *See* Bib-
    liography Committee of the New Jersey
    Library Association
Ng, Pearl, 550
Nicolas, Suzanne, 688
Nissen, Karen M., 469
Niswander, Jerry D., 492
Nogales, Luis G., 652
Norell, Irene P., 547
Norwitch, Susan, 431

Oaks, Pricilla, 438
Obudho, Constance E., 584
Ogawa, Dennis M., 542
O'Leary, Timothy J., 480
Ong, Paul M., 549
Ortego, Philip D., 670

Padilla, Amado M., 649
Palacios, Arthur, 172
Parker, William, 705
Patterson, Lindsey, 88
Patterson, Wayne, 58, 237, 544
Penn, I. Garland, 149, 297
Perkins, David, 510
Peterson, Deena, 321
Phillis, Susan, 582
Pilling, James, 455–6

*Numbers refer to entry numbers, *not* page numbers.

Pino, Frank, 655
Ploski, Harry A., 62, 90, 98
Porter, Dorothy B., 615–6, 691
Potter, Helen Rose, 518, 671
Powers, Anne, 589
Price, Daniel O., 73, 363
Prucha, Francis Paul, 225, 459
Puckett, Newbell Niles, 70
Putnam, Howard, 650, 653

Quarles, Benjamin, 256

Rael, Juan B., 630
Randall, Ruth Gordon, 725
Raphael, Ralph B., 22
Rather, Ernest R., 74, 364
Ray, Roger B., 501
Reams, Bernard D., 13, 100
Reische, Diana, 126
Rennie, Susan, 120, 317–8, 711
Rivera, Feliciano, 106–7, 259, 633, 643
Robins, Joan, 117
Robinson, Jackie, 88
Robinson, Lora H., 322
Robinson, Wilhelmena S., 88, 160
Rogers, J. S., 171
Rollins, Charlemae, 626
Romero, Patricia W., 88
Roseland, Samuel E., 147
Rosenberg, Marie Barovic, 717, 727
Rosenfelt, Deborah Silverton, 313, 322, 704
Rosmussen, Wayne D., 466
Ross, Frank Alexander, 568
Ross, Norman A., 497–8
Ross, Susan D., 124
Rouse, Irving, 454
Rubano, Judith, 537
Rudwick, Elliott, 239
Ruiz, Rene A., 649
Runes, Richard N., 80
Rutgers University. Center for American Women and Politics. *See* Eagleton Institute of Politics
Rywell, Mertin, 59

Saldaña, Nancy, 657
Sánchez, George I., 650, 653
Sánchez, Nellie Van de Grift, 52
Sanders, Charles L., 302
Santa Barbara (California) County Board of Education, 135, 422

Saunders, Doris E., 81, 365
Saunders, Lyle, 490, 630, 645, 653
Schatz, Walter, 301
Scherer, Joanna C., 43
Schlesinger, Benjamin, 715
Schmidt, Fred H., 385
Schneir, Miriam, 264
Schwartz, Bernard, 216
Senoir, C., 664
Sherman, Julia A., 714
Sikes, Melvin P., 155
Silver, Barbara, 737
Simmen, Edward, 640
Simmons, Lanier A., 467
Sloan, Irving J., 72, 243, 588
Sloane, Bruce, 116
Smith, Dwight L., 503, 553
Smith, Ernest, 241
Smith, Joan Dickson, 324
Smith, Michael R., 19
Smith, Murphy D., 489
Smythe, Mabel M., 66
Snodgrass, Jeanne, 137
Snodgrass, Marjorie P., 476
Sobel, Lester A., 8, 78
Soltow, Martha, 729
Soule, William S., 48
Spalding, Henry D., 83, 249
Spangler, Earl, 567
Spencer, Katharine, 465
Spradling, Mary Mace, 161, 604
Sprecher, Daniel, 603
Stanton, Elizabeth Cady, 265
Stegner, John F., 660
Stensland, Anna Lee, 507
Stewart, Omer C., 481
Stimpson, Catharine R., 114, 263
Stoddard, Hope, 185, 700
Stoutenburgh, John L., 28
Strugnell, Cecile, 679
Suniewick, Nancy, 726
Sutton, Imre, 499
Swanton, John R., 38, 42
Swift, Michiyo Yamaguchi, 529

Taft, Michael, 520
Talbert, Robert Harris, 384
Talbot, Jane, 640
Tambs, Lewis A., 551
Tanis, Norman, 510
Terrell, John Upton, 18
Teschner, Richard V., 675

* Numbers refer to entry numbers, *not* page numbers.

313

*Numbers refer to entry numbers, *not* page numbers.

* Numbers refer to entry numbers, *not* page numbers.

TITLE INDEX

* Numbers refer to entry numbers, *not* page numbers.

* Numbers refer to entry numbers, *not* page numbers.

* Numbers refer to entry numbers, *not* page numbers.

*Numbers refer to entry numbers, *not* page numbers.

319

* Numbers refer to entry numbers, *not* page numbers.

* Numbers refer to entry numbers, *not* page numbers.

*Numbers refer to entry numbers, *not* page numbers.

* Numbers refer to entry numbers, *not* page numbers.

* Numbers refer to entry numbers, *not* page numbers.

* Numbers refer to entry numbers, *not* page numbers.

* Numbers refer to entry numbers, *not* page numbers.

* Numbers refer to entry numbers, *not* page numbers.

A Mexican American Source Book, 107

Mexican-Americans: A Handbook for Educators, 47, 61

Mexican Americans: A Research Bibliography, 655

Mexican Americans: An Annotated Bibliography of Doctoral Dissertations, 656

Mexican-Americans in the Midwest: An Annotated Bibliography, 657

Mexican Americans; Resources to Build Cultural Understanding, 658

The Mexican Immigrant: An Annotated Bibliography, 653

Mexicans in the United States: A Bibliography, 653

Microfilm Abstracts, 539

Migrant Education: A Selected Bibliography, 659

Minorities and Women in State and Local Government, 338–9, 401, 405

Minority Business Enterprise: A Bibliography, 436

Minority Business Opportunities: A Manual on Opportunities for Small and Minority Group Businessmen and Professionals in HUD Programs, 284

Minority Group Employment in the Federal Government, 339

Minority Groups and Housing: A Bibliography, 1950–1970, 437

Minority Groups and Housing, A Selected Bibliography, 1950–1967, 437

A Minority of Members: Women in the U.S. Congress, 1917–1972, 190

Minority-Owned Businesses: All Minorities, 340, 347

Minority-Owned Businesses: Black, 347, 367

Minority-Owned Businesses: Spanish Origin, 347, 380

Minority Studies: A Selective, Annotated Bibliography of Works on Native Americans, Spanish Americans, Afro-Americans, and Asian Americans, 438

Missions of California, 107

Mother Tongue of the Foreign Born: Census of Population. Subject Reports, 341

Mother Tongue of the Foreign White Stock: Census of Population. Subject Report, 341

Ms. Magazine, 113

Multimedia Materials for Afro-American Studies: A Curriculum Orientation and Annotated Bibliography of Resources, 607

Music of the Black Americans, 89

Mythology of All Races, 45

Narratives of Captivity among the Indians of North America: A List of Books and Manuscripts on This Subject in the Edward E. Ayer Collection of the Newberry Library, 509

Natick Dictionary, 46

Nation-Wide Roster of Professional Minority Consulting Firms, 288

National Black Business Directory, 286, 304

National Directory of Chicano Faculty and Research, 173

National Directory of Minority Manufactures, 285

National Minority Business Directory, 286

National Origin and Language: 1970 Census of Population, Subject Reports, 329, 335, 341, 345

National Roster of Black Elected Officials, 162

National Roster of Minority Professional Consulting Firms, 287

National Roster of Spanish-Surnamed Elected Officials, 174

Native Americans of California and Nevada: A Handbook, 47

Native Americans of North America: A Bibliography, 510

Nativity and Parentage: Census of Population, Subject Reports, 341

Nativity and Parentage of the White Population: Census of Population. Subject Reports, 341

Navajo Bibliography, 511

Navajo Bibliography with Subject Index, 511–2

Needs and Opportunities for Study Series, 445

The Negro Almanac, 90

The Negro American; A Documentary History, 256

Negro Americans in the Civil War: From Slavery to Citizenship, 88

*Numbers refer to entry numbers, *not* page numbers.

* Numbers refer to entry numbers, *not* page numbers.

*Numbers refer to entry numbers, *not* page numbers.

* Numbers refer to entry numbers, *not* page numbers.

333

* Numbers refer to entry numbers, *not* page numbers.

SUBJECT INDEX

AV. *See* Media

Abernathy, Ralph, 132

Abolition. *See* Slavery

Abortion, 116, 125, 131, 317, 321, 677–8, 693, 722, 735. *See also* Family planning

Abzug, Bella, 190

Accounting, 288. *See also* Business and finance; Business enterprises

Acculturation, 41, 414, 416, 426, 435, 439, 496, 512, 527, 638, 640, 657

Adams, Abigail, 269

Addams, Jane, 269

Addiction. *See* Alcoholism; Drugs

Administrators, 721. *See also* Occupations

Advertising, 187, 298. *See also* Communications; Business enterprises

Aesop, 83

Affirmative action, 10, 15, 78, 130, 133, 266, 274, 278, 334, 424, 688, 724. *See also* Discrimination

Afro-American history. *See* History—Black Americans

Afro-American studies. *See* Black studies

Age, 329, 350, 353–4, 358–9, 371–2, 377, 381, 386–8, 390, 394–5, 397–8, 403–4, 406–7. *See also* Demography

Aged and aging, 212–4, 321, 327, 424, 688, 698, 716, 725

Agricultural workers. *See* Farm workers

Agriculture, 355, 358, 466, 476, 502, 636. *See also* Sciences

Akers, Dolly Smith, 189

Alaska, 349

Albuquerque Journal, 105

Alcoholism, 496. *See also* Drugs; Medical science

Alexander's Magazine, 557

Algonquin Indians, 31, 51, 456. *See also* History—American Indians

Alienation, 425

America: History and Life, 553

American Doctoral Dissertations, 565

American Indian history. *See* History—American Indians

American Indian studies, 47, 50, 296

American Negro Historical Society, 554

American Philosophical Society. Library, 489

American studies, 682. *See also* Economics; History; Humanities

American Studies Association. Commission of Women, 682

Anasazi Indians, 39. *See also* History—American Indians

Anatomy, 733. *See also* Physiology; Medical science

Anderson, Marian, 158

Annals of the Congress of the United States, 611

Annulment. *See* Divorce

Anthony, Susan B., 185, 684

Anthropology, 50, 105, 115, 313, 411, 448, 454, 463, 465, 472, 475, 485, 493–4, 506, 520, 634, 652, 655, 660, 683, 733. *See also* American Indian studies; Archaeology; History; Sociology

Anti-slavery. *See* Slavery

Apache Indians, 488. *See also* History—American Indians

Appointed officials. *See* Government

Archaeology, 18, 23, 27, 34, 50, 105, 448, 454, 458, 463, 465, 470, 472, 475, 485, 500, 517, 520. *See also* History

Architecture, 590, 653. *See also* Fine arts

Arizona, 27, 39, 205, 349, 376–7, 382, 384–5

Arizona Republic, 105

Armed forces. *See* Military service

Art, 30, 41, 50, 63, 88, 137, 191, 296, 313, 444, 448, 457, 470, 476, 590, 655, 658, 662, 680. *See also* Fine arts

Arthur and Elizabeth Schlesinger Library on the History of Women, 684

Arthur B. Spingarn Collection of Negro Authors, Howard University, 596

Artists, 137, 680

Arts. *See* Fine arts

Arts and crafts. *See* Art

---

*Numbers refer to entry numbers, *not* page numbers.

*Numbers refer to entry numbers, *not* page numbers.

* Numbers refer to entry numbers, *not* page numbers.

Constitutions, 219, 221, 223, 462, 474. *See also* Laws and legislation

Consultants. *See* Consulting firms

Consulting firms, 287–8, 306. *See also* Business enterprises

Consumerism, 613

Continuing education. *See* Education, continuing

Contraceptives. *See* Family planning

Contractors, 289

Contributions to North American Ethnology, 495

Cooking, 83, 684. *See also* Food

CORE, 132

Cosby, Bill, 158

Costumes. *See* Clothing

Counseling, 116, 396, 738. *See also* Education; Mental health; Psychology; Social work

County government. *See* Government

Court cases (*See also* Law enforcement):
—Minorities, 13, 57, 211–4, 216
—American Indians, 35, 217, 224–5, 227, 231, 233–4, 471, 497–8
—Black Americans, 59, 75, 82, 99–100, 246–7, 252, 254
—Women, 119, 128, 266, 705

Crafts. *See* Art

Creek Indians, 42, 51, 223, 226. *See also* History—American Indians

Crime, 81, 91, 124, 361, 375, 403, 595, 583. *See also* Law enforcement

The Crisis, 557

Culturally disadvantaged. *See* Disadvantaged; Poverty

Curly Head, 28

Current Biography, 707

Current Index to Journals in Education, 446, 635, 654

Current Population Survey, 397

Curriculum, 135, 625. *See also* Teaching

Daguerreotypes. *See* Photographs

Dakota Indians, 141, 473. *See also* History—American Indians

Dances, 33, 207. *See also* Fine arts

Data processing, 288

Davis, Angela, 132, 258

Day care centers, 317, 319, 725. *See also* Children

De Oñate, Don Juan, 111

Deaths. *See* Mortality

The Debate and Proceedings in the Congress of the United States, 611

Delano, California, 636. *See also* California

Demography (*See also* Economic characteristics; Migration; Social characteristics):
—Minorities, 341, 346, 428
—American Indians, 18, 20, 32, 34, 38, 40, 349–51, 353–55, 501
—Asian Americans, 56–7, 357–9
—Black Americans, 60, 63, 70, 74, 81, 90–1, 94, 100, 361, 363, 368, 371–2, 374–5, 586
—Spanish Americans, 376–9, 381–6, 641
—Women, 131, 180, 201, 387–90, 392, 394–5, 397–400, 403–4, 406–7

Dentistry, 590. *See also* Medical science

Denver Post, 105

Department of Health, Education and Welfare. Library. *See* U.S. Department of Health, Education and Welfare. Library

Department of Housing and Urban Development. *See* U.S. Department of Housing and Urban Development

Department of the Interior. *See* U.S. Department of the Interior

Desegregation. *See* Segregation and desegregation

Diegueño Indians, 463. *See also* History—American Indians

Disadvantaged, 418, 425, 435. *See also* Poverty

Discrimination, 7, 54, 114, 439, 507, 534, 549–50, 703. *See also* Discrimination in Education; Discrimination in Employment; Racial discrimination; Segregation and desegregation; Sex discrimination

Discrimination, race. *See* Racial discrimination

Discrimination, sex. *See* Sex discrimination

Discrimination in education, 13, 15, 99–100, 114, 421, 425, 441, 621, 685, 709. *See also* Discrimination

Discrimination in employment (*See also* Discrimination):
—Minorities, 7, 10, 124, 211, 212–4, 334, 419, 424
—Spanish Americans, 385

—Women, 114, 124, 130, 266, 334, 419, 424, 682, 688, 698, 719, 728

Discrimination in housing. *See* Segregation and desegregation

Diseases, 492–3. *See also* Health and health care; Illness

Dissertation Abstracts International, 565, 656

Dissertations. *See* Theses and dissertations

Divorce, 124–5, 127, 397, 399, 687, 696, 715, 722, 725

Dix, Dorothea, 185, 269

Doctoral research. *See* Theses and dissertations

Douglass, Frederick, 239, 251–2

Drama, 88, 158, 186, 238, 291, 702. *See also* Fine arts

Dress. *See* Clothing

Drugs, 49, 79, 496. *See also* Medical science

Dubois, W.E.B., 239, 251, 558

Duke University, 620

Earnings. *See* Income

Ecology, 26, 496, 600

Economic characteristics (*See also* Demography; Economics; Social characteristics):
—Minorities, 335, 341–2, 346, 420, 437
—American Indians, 349–50, 353–55
—Asian Americans, 357–9, 527
—Black Americans, 353, 361, 363, 371–2, 374–5
—Spanish Americans, 376–7, 381–4, 386
—Women, 387, 390, 392, 394–5, 398, 403, 406–7

Economic conditions. *See* Economics

Economic development. *See* Economics

Economic disadvantaged. *See* Disadvantaged; Poverty

Economics (*See also* Business and finance; Economic characteristics; Labor movement; Poverty; Social science):
—Minorities, 335, 420
—American Indians, 292, 476, 513
—Asian Americans, 57, 526, 530, 547
—Black Americans, 63, 91, 559, 563, 565, 580, 609, 613, 615–6, 622

—Spanish Americans, 105, 384, 638, 640, 645–6, 653, 655, 662, 668, 671, 676
—Women, 719, 722, 727, 737

Economy. *See* Economics

Editors. *See* Printing and publishing

Education (*See also* Counseling; Education, continuing; Education, higher; Sex education; Teachers; Teaching):
—Minorities, 13, 15, 342, 346, 421, 425, 435, 441, 453
—American Indians, 39–40, 47, 50, 349–50, 352–6, 435, 446, 448, 459, 477, 513, 654
—Asian Americans, 147, 357–9, 532, 547
—Black Americans, 61, 63, 66, 78, 81, 99–100, 158–9, 162, 169, 262, 302, 361, 363, 371–2, 375, 559, 565, 570, 574, 580, 586, 590, 595, 609, 615–6, 619, 621, 654
—Spanish Americans, 47, 105, 108, 306, 376–7, 381, 386, 435, 632, 635, 638, 640–1, 645, 650, 652–5, 657–9, 662, 675–6
—Women, 115, 121, 124, 186, 192, 262, 311, 387, 390, 392, 394–6, 403, 406, 683, 709, 722, 726–8, 733, 735, 737

Education, continuing, 736. *See also* Education

Education, elementary. *See* Education

Education, graduate. *See* Education, higher

Education, higher, 155, 170, 175, 281–3, 312–3, 322, 402, 431, 613, 624, 685, 721, 736. *See also* College students; Colleges and universities; Education; Faculty; Theses and dissertations

Education, professional. *See* Education, higher

Education, secondary. *See* Education

Edward E. Ayer Collection of Americana and American Indians, Newberry Library, 455, 475, 509

Elected officials. *See* Government; Politics

Elections. *See* Government; Politics

The Elementary and Secondary School Civil Rights Survey, 332

Elementary education. *See* Education

Elementary schools. *See* Schools

Ellington, Duke, 158

* Numbers refer to entry numbers, *not* page numbers.

Emotional health. *See* Mental health

Employee relations. *See* Labor movement

Employment (*See also* Affirmative action; Discrimination in employment; Employment skills banks; Job training; Occupations):
—Minorities, 10, 15, 334, 342, 346, 401-2, 419, 424
—American Indians, 39-40, 349-50
—Asian Americans, 55, 357, 359, 524, 547
—Black Americans, 63, 90, 239, 248, 262, 361, 363, 272, 375, 586
—Spanish Americans, 376-7, 379, 381, 385-6, 642, 657
—Women, 120, 125-6, 129, 262, 311, 317, 319, 334, 390, 392, 396, 401-5, 419, 688, 698, 719, 725-6, 728-9, 735-6

Employment skills banks, 278. *See also* Employment; Job training

Engineering, 539. *See also* Sciences

Enrollment. *See* Students

Entertainment, 161, 192, 580, 586

Environment. *See* Ecology

Equal Employment Opportunities Act, 338. *See also* Laws and legislation

Equal opportunity. *See* Affirmative action; Discrimination

Equal pay. *See* Affirmative action; Discrimination in employment

Equal rights. *See* Affirmative action; Civil rights

Equal Rights Amendment, 311. *See also* Laws and legislation—Women

Ethnic history. *See* History—Minorities

Ethnic studies, 9, 11, 14, 135, 208, 215, 275-6, 280, 335, 341-2, 346, 411-3, 416, 426, 428-30, 432, 438. *See also* History—Minorities

Ethnology, 454, 463, 465, 470, 472, 475, 480, 489, 495, 500, 506, 512, 520. *See also* Anthropology; History; Race

Evacuation. *See* Relocation

Executive Order 11246, 124

Executive Order 11467, 124

Explorers, 160. *See also* Occupations

Faculty, 147, 152, 155, 157, 170, 173, 186, 192, 322, 685, 721. *See also* Education, higher; Teachers; Teaching

Fair employment practices. *See* Affirmative action; Discrimination in employment

Families (*See also* Children; Marriage; One parent family):
—Minorities, 321, 342, 345-6, 416, 439
—American Indians, 349-50
—Asian American Indians, 357, 359
—Black Americans, 90, 361, 372, 375, 439, 577, 620, 690
—Spanish Americans, 376-7, 381, 657
—Women, 392, 395, 403-4, 407, 678, 690, 708, 722, 735

Family planning, 693, 709, 722, 735

Farm workers, 331, 354, 358, 368, 435, 636, 640, 642, 657, 659. *See also* United Farm Workers

Farmers, 368. *See also* Farm workers

Federal government. *See* Government

Federal Register, 222

Fellowships. *See* Financial aid

Female studies. *See* Women's studies

Feminism. *See* Women's movement

Feminist press. *See* Printing and publishing

Fertility, 371, 386, 388-90, 394-5, 403, 406-7, 688. *See also* Family planning

Field, Thomas W., 479

Films, 119, 121, 589, 603, 666, 696, 731, 738. *See also* Communications; Media

Filmstrips. *See* Media

Finance. *See* Business and finance

Financial aid, 124, 127, 277-8, 281-4, 290, 366, 685

Fine arts, 32, 34, 36, 48, 50, 66, 91, 129, 147, 192, 559, 583, 614, 684, 707, 709, 738. *See also* Art; Humanities

Fisk University. Library, 598

Florida, 376

Folk medicine. *See* Folklore

Folk poetry. *See* Folklore

Folk songs. *See* Folklore

Folklore (*See also* Humor; Literature):
—Minorities, 415, 461, 493
—American Indians, 45, 461, 482, 488, 493, 500, 512, 520
—Black Americans, 83, 89, 240, 415, 461, 569
—Spanish Americans, 110, 488, 630, 645, 676

Folktales. *See* Folklore

*Numbers refer to entry numbers, *not* page numbers.

Hoover Institution Archives, 548
Hopi Indians, 40. *See also* History—American Indians
House of Representatives. *See* U.S. Congress
Housing, 31, 42, 48, 50, 91, 284, 289, 335-6, 350, 359, 361, 372, 375, 381-4, 406, 437, 493, 586, 614, 657. *See also* Segregation and desegregation
Howard University, 80
Howard University. Library, 596-7
Hughes, Langston, 239, 258
Humanities, 445, 539, 551, 565, 631, 675, 709. *See also* Names of specific subjects, such as Art; Language; Linguistics; Philosophy; etc.
Humor, 83, 244. *See also* Folklore
Hurston, Zora Neal, 244

Idaho, 205, 502, 592
Identity, 21, 53, 68, 104, 416, 690
Illinois, 376. *See also* Chicago, Illinois
Illiteracy, 353-4. *See also* Reading
Illness, 671. *See also* Diseases; Health and health care; Mental health
Immigrants and immigration
—Minorities, 3-4, 9, 329, 335, 337, 341, 345, 414, 416, 543
—Asian Americans, 54-8, 524, 526, 530-1, 534, 536, 538, 547, 549-50
—Spanish Americans, 633, 653, 665
—Women, 329, 337
Imperial County, California, 463. *See also* California
Income (*See also* Economic characteristics):
—Minorities, 338-9, 346, 401
—American Indians, 349-50, 476
—Black Americans, 361, 363, 372, 375
—Spanish Americans, 376-7, 379, 381, 386, 657
—Women, 317, 338, 387, 390, 395-6, 398, 401, 403, 405-6
Indian agents, 468
Indian Arts and Crafts Board. *See* U.S. Indian Arts and Crafts Board
Indian chiefs, 140-2, 468. *See also* Names of individual chiefs

Indian Claims Commission. *See* U.S. Indian Claims Commission
Indian Division. *See* U.S. Indian Division
Indian reservations. *See* Reservations
Indian studies. *See* American Indian studies
Indiana University. Library, 693
Industrial Relations. *See* Labor movement
Infant mortality. *See* Mortality
Inner-city. *See* Ghettos; Urban life
Institute for Sex Research, Indiana University. Library, 693
Insurance companies, 63. *See also* Business enterprises
Integrated education. *See* Education; Segregation and desegregation.
Integration. *See* Segregation and desegregation
Internal migration. *See* Migration
Internment. *See* Relocation
Iroquois Indians, 31, 456. *See also* History—American Indians
Irrigation, 476. *See also* Agriculture

Jackson, George, 258
Jesse E. Moorland Collection of Negro Life and History, 597
"Jim Crow" laws, 247. *See also* Laws and legislation—Blacks
Job training, 274, 379. *See also* Employment
Jobs. *See* Employment; Occupations
Jones, LeRoi, 251
Journalism, 297-8, 590. *See also* Communications; Newsletters; Newspapers; Printing and Publishing; Writers and writing
Journals. *See* Periodicals
Journals of the Continental Congress, 611-2
Judges, 203. *See also* Attorneys; Occupations
Judicial decisions. *See* Court cases
Junior colleges. *See* Colleges and universities; Education, higher
Juvenile delinquency, 124. *See also* Children; Crime

Kay, Ulysses, 159
Kee, Maude, 202
Kelly, Edna Flannery, 202
King, Martin Luther, Jr., 97, 258, 601
Komisar, Lucy, 714

---

* Numbers refer to entry numbers, *not* page numbers.

* Numbers refer to entry numbers, *not* page numbers.

Marriage, 105, 115, 125, 127, 350, 353–4, 358–9, 371–2, 381, 384, 387, 390, 392, 394, 397–400, 403–4, 406–7, 439, 512, 657, 678, 693, 708, 722, 725. *See also* Divorce; Families; Miscegenation

Marriott Library. University of Utah, 575, 637

Master's theses. *See* Theses and dissertations

Maternity. *See* Fertility

Mayors. *See* Government

McCarran-Walter Immigration Act, 57. *See also* Laws and legislation—Minorities

Mead, Margaret, 269

Media (*see also* Communications; Films):
—Minorities, 275, 429, 432, 435, 437
—American Indians, 20, 50, 233, 291, 296, 460
—Asian Americans, 540
—Black Americans, 61, 298, 559, 566, 589, 605, 607, 680, 690
—Spanish Americans, 107, 640, 646, 658, 661–2, 666, 674
—Women, 115, 117, 119–21, 321, 325, 680, 690, 705, 723–4, 738

Medical science, 88–9, 123, 191, 207, 319, 590, 683–4, 709, 727. *See also* Diseases; Health and health care; Illness

Mental health, 127, 649, 722. *See also* Psychology

Meredith, James, 601

Mexican American history. *See* History—Spanish Americans

Michigan, 657

Micmac Indians, 520. *See also* History—American Indians

Migrant workers. *See* Farm workers

Migrants, 306, 309, 330, 439. *See also* Farm workers; Migration

Migration, 18, 108, 252, 361, 371, 379, 403, 459, 524, 568, 662, 664

Military service, 152, 170, 370, 547, 683, 727

Minority history. *See* History—Minorities

Minority studies. *See* Ethnic studies

Minnesota, 141, 567

Minnesota Historical Society, 473

Miscegenation, 247, 371. *See also* Marriage

Missions, 107, 111, 501, 597

Missouri, 517

Mohammed, 171

Mongollon Indians, 39. *See also* History—American Indians

Montana, 205, 502, 592

Monuments, 50

Mortality, 386, 388, 403, 512

Motion pictures. *See* Films

Moton, Robert Russa, 601

Movies. *See* Films

Ms. Magazine, 113

Museums, 32, 50, 72, 233, 296, 429, 457, 625

Music (*see also* Fine arts)
—American Indians, 36, 291, 448, 459, 470
—Black Americans, 63, 79, 88–9, 158, 240–1, 596
—Spanish Americans, 640, 662
—Women, 119, 207

Muskogee Indians, 223, 456. *See also* History—American Indians

Myths. *See* Folklore

NAACP. *See* National Association for the Advancement of Colored People

Names, 70, 124

Names, place. *See* Place names

Narcotics. *See* Drugs

National Anthropological Archives. *See* U.S. National Anthropological Archives, Smithsonian Institution

National Archives and Records Service. *See* U.S. National Archives and Records Service

National Association for the Advancement of Colored People, 32, 274

National Clearinghouse for Mental Health, 417

National Government. *See* Government

National Indian Law Library, 741

National Urban League, 274, 278

Navaho Indians, 465, 511–2. *See also* History—American Indians

Negro Collection of the Fisk University. Library, 598

Nevada, 47, 205

New American State Papers, 230, 255

New Jersey, 376, 619

New Mexico, 27, 205, 349, 376-7, 382, 384-5, 630, 645-6
New York (State), 319, 376, 379, 385
New York City, New York, 357, 385
New York Public Library, 560, 599, 606
New York Times, 129, 623, 703
New Yorker, 707
Newberry Library, 455, 475, 509
Newsletters, 275, 321, 429. *See also* Journalism; Newspapers
Newspapers (*See also* Communications; Journalism; Newsletters; Printing and publishing):
—for Minorities, 275, 423, 428-9
—for American Indians, 50, 450, 459, 483
—for Asian Americans, 57, 529, 542
—for Black Americans, 60, 298, 563, 567, 590-2, 618
—for Spanish Americans, 107, 631-2, 640, 658
—for Women, 119, 321
Non-book materials. *See* Media
North American Ethnology, 506
North Carolina, 136
North Carolina College, 620
Nutrition, 653

Occupations (*See also* Employment):
—Minorities, 281-2, 334, 401-2
—American Indians, 350, 353-4
—Asian Americans, 358-9
—Black Americans, 81, 363, 372, 375, 574
—Spanish Americans, 378, 381, 385-6
—Women, 121, 387, 392, 394-5, 401-6, 707, 726, 728
Office of Indian Affairs. *See* U.S. Office of Indian Affairs
Officials. *See* Government
Ohio, 428
Oklahoma, 33, 349, 484
One-parent family, 715. *See also* Families
Opportunities Industrialization Centers, 278
Oratory. *See* Speeches
Oregon, 205, 502, 592-3
Oregon State Library, 502. *See also* Oregon

Osage Indians, 223. *See also* History—American Indians
Owens, Jesse, 158

Painters. *See* Artists
Painting. *See* Art
Paintings, 49, 51. *See also* Portraits
Paiute Indians, 40. *See also* History—American Indians
Parks, 50, 296
El Paso Times, 105
Pay. *See* Income
Peabody Museum of Archaeology and Ethnology, Harvard University, 472
Pennsylvania Abolition Society, 554
Periodicals
—Minorities, 275, 423, 429
—American Indians, 50, 444, 450, 496
—Asian Americans, 542
—Black Americans, 298, 421, 551, 557, 563
—Spanish Americans, 631, 638, 640, 652, 658, 674
—Women, 321, 727, 737
Perkins, Frances, 180
Personality, 526, 630. *See also* Social characteristics
Peyote, 496. *See also* Drugs; History—American Indians
Philosophy, 662, 727. *See also* Humanities
Phonodiscs. *See* Media
Photographs (*see also* Portraits):
—Minorities, 134, 208, 215
—American Indians, 43, 48-9
—Asian Americans, 55
—Black Americans, 60, 74, 82, 94-5, 102, 106, 115, 117, 152, 165, 170-1, 241, 257, 590, 598
—Women, 183, 185-6, 190, 192-3, 201, 204-5, 208, 267, 269, 317, 709
Physiology, 706, 733. *See also* Anatomy; Medical science; Sciences
Picotte, Susan La Flesche, 177
Place names, 18, 24, 37, 52
Pocahontas, 177
Poetry, 238, 241, 267, 479, 561, 626, 702. *See also* Literature

*Numbers refer to entry numbers, *not* page numbers.

345

* Numbers refer to entry numbers, *not* page numbers.

Rhetoric, 581. *See also* Communications

Robeson, Paul, 258

Rose, Ernestina, 269

Rudolph, Wilma, 158

Sacajawea, 177

Sainte-Marie, Buffy, 20

Salary. *See* Income

San Antonio Express, 105

San Diego County, California, 463. *See also* California

San Francisco, California, 357. *See also* California

San Francisco Chronicle, 105

San Francisco Public Library, 534

Sanger, Margaret, 269

Sanitation, 493

Santa Barbara, California, 458. *See also* California

Savannah Indians, 226. *See also* History—American Indians

Schlesinger Library. *See* Arthur and Elizabeth Schlesinger Library on the History of Women.

Scholarships. *See* Financial aids

Schomburg Collection of Negro Literature and History, 560, 599

School busing. *See* Busing

Schools, 50, 332–3, 356, 574. *See also* Education

Schuyer, Philippa Duke, 680

Sciences, 30, 57, 158–9, 186, 192, 207, 539, 580, 614, 626, 631, 675, 707, 727. *See also* Names of specific sciences

Scott, Emmet J., 601

Sculpture, 680. *See also* Fine arts; Humanities

Second World Black Festival of Arts and Culture, 302

Secondary education. *See* Education

Secondary schools. *See* Schools

Segregation and desegregation, 13, 65, 100, 247, 425, 437, 440–1, 563, 582, 621. *See also* Discrimination

Self concept, 418, 656

Seminole Indians, 51. *See also* History—American Indians

Senate. *See* U.S. Congress

Separatism. *See* Segregation and desegregation

Sequoyah, 140

Serra, Father Junipero, 111

Sex and sexuality, 117, 119, 512, 678, 693, 706, 716, 722, 733

Sex composition, 329–30, 334, 337, 350, 355, 358–9, 370–2, 377–8, 381, 386, 397–8. *See also* Demography; Social characteristics

Sex discrimination, 114, 128, 130, 685, 688, 697, 719, 721, 728. *See also* Discrimination; Discrimination in education; Discrimination in employment

Sex education, 693. *See also* Education

Shawnee Indians, 51. *See also* History—American Indians

Single parent families. *See* One parent families

Sioux Indians, 29, 31, 456. *See also* History—American Indians

Skills banks. *See* Employment skills banks

Slang, 110. *See also* Language; Linguistics

Slavery, 65, 87, 95, 238–9, 253–5, 257, 262, 371, 552–4, 559, 564, 587, 595–7, 611–2, 619, 622, 690. *See also* History—Black Americans

Slides. *See* Media

Smith, Margaret Chase, 185, 190

Smithsonian Contributions to Anthropology, 506

Smithsonian Institution, 43, 48, 470, 485, 495, 506

Social characteristics (*see also* Economic characteristics):

—Minorities, 335, 341–2, 346–7, 421, 437

—American Indians, 349–50, 353–5

—Asian Americans, 357–9, 527, 547

—Black Americans, 361, 363, 371–2, 374–5, 553, 576, 615–6, 622

—Spanish Americans, 376–7, 381–4, 386, 653, 668, 671, 676

—Women, 387, 390, 392, 394–5, 398, 390, 403, 406–7, 722

Social sciences, 445, 539, 551, 631, 675, 680, 683, 693. *See also* Names of specific disciplines in the Social Sciences

Social services, 278, 317–9, 321, 327. *See also* Counseling; Social work

Social work, 483, 526, 530, 638, 709, 715. *See also* Counseling; Social services; Social sciences

Sociology, 17, 21, 53, 68, 104, 123, 411, 448, 526, 530, 632, 646, 652-3, 660, 683, 687, 693, 696, 706. *See also* Social sciences; Social work

Soldiers. *See* Military service

Songs. *See* Music

Sophia Smith Collection, 709

Sororities, 274

South Dakota, 349

Spanish American history. *See* History—Spanish Americans

Speeches, 258, 265, 552, 581-2, 691

Spingarn Collection of Negro Authors, Howard University, 596

Sports, 63, 66, 88, 105, 158, 161, 192, 580, 586, 616, 626, 690

Stanford University, 548

State legislatures. *See* Government

Stillbirths. *See* Mortality

Strikes, 636, 642, 729. *See also* Labor movement

Students, 332-3, 344. *See also* Education

Suffrage, 115, 199, 265, 570, 692, 709. *See also* Voting

Supreme Court. *See* U.S. Supreme Court

The Supremes, 80

Surnames. *See* Names

Talent Search, 278

Tallchief, Maria, 20, 177, 189

Tallchief, Marjorie, 177

Tapes. *See* Media

Teachers, 332-3, 421, 431, 621. *See also* Education; Faculty; Teaching

Teaching, 14, 61, 135, 157, 313, 322, 412, 420-1, 431, 507, 607, 625, 701. *See also* Education; Faculty; Teachers

Telecommunications. *See* Radio; Television

Television, 119, 275-6, 291, 298, 317, 429, 646, 674. *See also* Communications

Texas, 110, 376-7, 382, 384-6, 657

Thayendanegea, 40

Theatre. *See* Drama

Theology. *See* Religion

Theses and dissertations:
    —Minorities, 413, 448, 453, 628
    —American Indians, 448, 453
    —Asian Americans, 526-30, 535-7, 539, 546, 549

    —Black Americans, 552, 565, 589, 594, 597, 619, 623
    —Spanish Americans, 453, 633-4, 636, 640, 646, 649-50, 652, 654-6, 664, 675
    —Women, 721-2, 726, 737-8

Time, 707

Training. *See* Job Training

Transparencies. *See* Media

Transportation, 292

Travel agencies, 429

Treaties, 26, 35, 57, 107, 111, 217, 223, 225, 231-3, 259, 464, 516

Treaty of Guadalupe Hidalgo, 107

Treaty of Peace (1898), 111

Treaty of Tordesillas, 111

Truth, Sojourner, 239, 258

Tubman, Harriet, 87, 185

Turner, Nat, 171, 239, 251

Tuskegee Institute, 601, 621

Typography. *See* Printing and publishing

Underground railroad, 619

Unemployment. *See* Employment and unemployment

Union of Black Episcopalians, 302

Unions. *See* Labor movement

United Farm Workers, 636, 640. *See also* Farm workers; Labor movement

United Nations, 165

U.S. Armed Forces. *See* Military service; Wars

U.S. Attorney General, 231

U.S. Bureau of American Ethnology, 485, 506

U.S. Bureau of American Ethnology *Bulletin*, 495, 506

U.S. Bureau of Indian Affairs, 139, 222, 225, 274, 356, 468, 476, 483, 516

U.S. Civil Service Commission. Library, 424

U.S. Commissioners of Indian Affairs, 217

U.S. Comptroller of the Currency, 231

U.S. Congress, 72, 131, 162, 165, 190, 201-2, 204, 217

U.S. Department of Health, Education and Welfare. Library, 513

U.S. Department of Housing and Urban Development, 284

U.S. Department of the Interior, 231, 516

U.S. Department of the Interior. Library, 474

* Numbers refer to entry numbers, *not* page numbers.

U.S. House of Representatives. *See* U.S. Congress

U.S. Indian Arts and Crafts Board, 222

U.S. Indian Claims Commission, 224, 227, 497–8

U.S. Indian Division, 516

U.S. Library of Congress, 615

U.S. National Anthropological Archives, Smithsonian Institution, 48, 470

U.S. National Archives and Records Service, 516

U.S. National Museum of History, Smithsonian Institution, 470

U.S. Office of Indian Affairs, 294

U.S. Senate. *See* U.S. Congress

U.S. Smithsonian Institution. *See* Smithsonian Institution

U.S. Supreme Court, 623

U.S. War Department, 516

U.S. Women's Bureau, 729

Universities. *See* Colleges and universities; Education, higher

University of California, Berkeley. Library, 540, 550, 672

University of California, Los Angeles. Research Library, 532

University of Hawaii. Library, 538

University of Mississippi, 601

University of North Carolina, 620

University of Texas, Library, 647

University of Utah. Library, 575, 637

Unwed mothers, 715, 722

Upward Bound, 278

Urban development. *See* Community development

Urban government. *See* Government

Urban life, 17, 39, 63, 239, 452, 459, 527, 591, 600, 620, 668

Urban planning, 288

Urban renewal, 437. *See also* Housing

Utah, 27, 205

Utah, University. Library. *See* University of Utah. Library

Ute Indians, 40, 481, 522. *See also* History—American Indians

Venereal disease, 693. *See also* Health and health care

Videotapes. *See* Media

Violence, 119. *See also* Lynching; Race riots

Virgin Islands, 206

The Voice of the Negro, 557

Voting, 248, 363, 375, 403. *See also* Suffrage

Voting Rights Act of 1965, 78

Wages. *See* Income

Wakash Indians, 456. *See also* History—American Indians

War Department. *See* U.S. War Department

Wars, 20, 22, 26, 57, 152, 192, 233, 355, 479, 483

Washington (State), 205, 349, 502, 592

Washington, Booker T. 239, 251, 258, 601

Welfare. *See* Poverty; Social work

Widowhood, 125, 397, 679, 715, 722

Winnebago Indians, 141. *See also* History—American Indians

Winnemaucca, Sarah, 189

Women's Bureau. *See* U.S. Women's Bureau

Women's history. *See* History—Women

Women's History Archive, 709

Women's liberation. *See* Women's movement

"A Women's Liberation Awareness Inventory," 723

Women's movement, 117, 120–1, 126, 131, 317, 321, 590, 593, 690, 709, 723–5, 737. *See also* History—Women

Women's studies, 313, 322, 682, 701, 717, 738

Woolman, John, 251

Words. *See* Language; Linguistics

Wounded Knee, 233. *See also* Wars

Wright, Richard, 244, 251

Writers and writing, 160–1, 186, 207, 244, 680. *See also* Literature

Wyoming, 205

Young, Whitney M., 258

Young Mahaskan, 140

Zuharias, "Babe" Dedrikson, 185

---

* Numbers refer to entry numbers, *not* page numbers.